PROTECTING YOUR BUSINESS FROM CYBER ATTACKS IN ONLY 10 MINUTES A DAY

SIMPLE STEPS TO HELP YOU CREATE BETTER SECURITY HABITS TO REDUCE THE RISK OF BECOMING A CYBER VICTIM

BOAZ FISCHER

A copy of this publication can be found in the National Library of Australia.

ISBN 978-0-9925809-0-2

9 780992 580902 >

ACKNOWLEDGMENTS

It has been an honour and a privilege to write this book. As with any major project, there are a number of very special people who contributed to making this book happen. So, I'd like to take this opportunity to say "Thank You".

First, I'd like to thank my team at CommsNet Group who were the stimulus and motivation behind this book. They are Dr. David Garrard, who was patient with my many ideas; Kyaw Kyaw Soe Haling, who helped me kickstart this project together; Marianne Lo, for developing the first set of graphics; Nunzio Grassia, Melissa Maher, Maurice Consen, and Shane Maher for being helpful and supportive.

A huge thanks goes to Mark Walker who was the first person to read and provide feedback to this book.

I would like to thank Mark Herman from AICC for the gracious support, ideas, and encouragement.

To my two supportive friends Andrew Smith and Cairo Marchant, thanks for your feedback.

Next, an important and heartfelt thanks to my brother Oren Fischer and his family, Caterina van Moort, Pascal, and Axel.

Next, a special thanks to my parents, Gad and Brigitte Fischer for their love and support.

To all of the many clients that I have dealt with for the past seventeen years. Thank you for believing and trusting in my company and myself.

I have also been privileged to be touched by people who have had influence in my thinking and behaviour over the years. To Richard Branson for his inspiration and motivation of what is possible. To Anthony Robbins who helped me take the first step in understanding about human neural linguistic and associated communications and inspiring the leader qualities within me. To Bob Norton who inspired my business thinking in different tangents.

A huge thanks to Lawrence Petroni for doing a great job in promoting the book. Also, many thanks for Sarah Van Heertum who did a fantastic job in editing the book and for Benjamin Elleboudt for helping with the development of www.pi10m.com website

And finally a huge and gracious thanks to my lovely and loving wife, Alexandra, who endured much patience with lots of smiles and to my beloved son, Ilan Fischer.

YOUR PLAIN ENGLISH GUIDE TO ONLINE PROTECTION

Business is dependant on the internet for communication, financial transactions, information, marketing and sales. People want to access the internet from anywhere at any time.

With rapid advances in mobile technology and cloud computing, businesses are now on-line 24x7.

Greater convenience means greater risks. **There is a massive increase in online threats** and ***Cyber Attacks*** on business.

Business is struggling to ensure they are adequately protected – securing their data and their clients' data. Up until now this has been confusing, time consuming and expensive.

Protecting Your Business from Cyber Attacks in 10 Minutes a Day is written **in plain English and is easy to follow** and will teach you better security habits for your business.

You will learn your 10 minute daily routine; best security practices for Windows and Apple systems, Web browser guidelines and the 7 fallacies of safe Web browsing, Safe banking guidelines, Buying and selling safely online…, And so much more.

This book is jam packed full of excellent information!

Boaz Fischer is the CEO and Managing Director of CommsNet Group – an IT Security Company. An accomplished business leader with 20 years of experience, successfully leading and growing CommsNet Group to be a recognised Australian Information Security practice.

Boaz, a small business owner himself, realised there is nothing to help small to medium businesses.

And is passionate about helping organisations effectively manage their risks and adopt best security practices.

> *Don't be complacent. Don't think you know it all.*
>
> *Even if you include one improvement to your current IT security practices as a result of reading this book - You may have saved yourself from a potential disaster."*

Andrew Smith - Managing Director Five Phase Group

Doing nothing is NO longer an option, the risk is too great – YOU CAN LOSE YOUR BUSINESS.

If you want your business to survive the constant barrage of ***CYBER ATTACKS***
then, this is a MUST READ.

PLUS take advantage of the bonus material, FREE tools and resources to keep you and your business protected. There are links throughout the book.

Read it NOW – don't wait – even if you ONLY read the **first 2 chapters…**

Implement these practices you and your business will be far better prepared to defend against ***cyber-attacks***.

It could well save your business.

REFERENCES

"Protecting Your Business From Cyber Attacks In Only 10 Minutes A Day! offers practical, step-by-step tips to assist small business owners in minimising the risks to their IT systems. As strong advocators of the SME sector the IPA recommends that all small business owners do everything they can to protect their data. This book is full of useful recommendations for the security conscious small business owner." - Dr Andrew Conway, CEO, Institute of Public Accountants

~

"This book will give you greater confidence to take part in the online world and reap the benefits it offers" – Tim Reed, CEO, MYOB

~

"Protecting Your Business From Cyber Attacks In Only 10 Minutes A Day" was a great introduction to a broad selection of security risks in desktops, mobile devices, cloud, social networking, and more. The guidelines were easy to follow and relevant to many situations. A great book for a beginner to the cyber attack world" - Matt Bullock, CEO / founder, eWAY

~

"This book provides the reader with insights into the safe use of the Internet by business and is applicable to the novice as it is to the expert. Boaz has managed to encapsulate many complex ideas into a simple easy to understand presentation. A good read for those who intend using the Internet to take their business to another level of service." – Peter Major IT Security Advisor ACT Government.

~

"This book is both a reference tool for the uninitiated and the whole story for people who really need to address cyber security and feel a little behind the times."

"I love how the book is laid out so you can read about each issue as you need it, or become totally familiar with best practices to protect yourself personally and your company. And unlike so many books with big promising titles the ability to protect yourself with 10 minutes a day of reading is true."

"Like many specialties computer security can become a black hole of effort. I like the step by step guides taking you through each security procedure so even with little knowledge you can execute these precautions."

"I could not help but check all my computer settings as I read the book and, although I have been using computers as a software engineer and super-techie since 1981 I certainly completed the pre-flight checklist to

make sure my computer was secure. No one except full-time computer people can keep up with the constant changes." - Bob Norton, CEO - AirTight Management

"If you run a small or medium business, or even if you are looking to better protect yourself and your family from Cyber related threats, then the "Protecting Your Business In Only 10 Minutes a Day" security best practice guide is a must read. But just don't read, it implement it!
What Boaz has accomplished in this guide is an easy to read and focused set of tasks and techniques that help increase resiliency to the "real" threats and risks of being connected to the internet.
More often than not with technology, it can be difficult to determine where to start developing a strategy to protect what's important. Every strategy should evolve and adapt, the only real way to stay secure and safe online as threats change.
This guide is a great foundation for your Cyber strategy if you don't already have one, and if you already have a strategy; Use the guide as a basis to update and validate it.
There really are no excuses why every small and medium business owner can't do better to protect and improve their resiliency to Cyber threats, this guide MUST be part of the process to make your business more resilient." - Scott Deacon, IT Security Professional - CISSP, MIS

~

"As a senior risk manager working across many government and private organisations implementing multi-million dollar programs of work, I have a strong sense of the level of maturity of risk management in the workplace... and, in broad terms, it is not strong. So the chances are that your organisation is NOT identifying, analysing, evaluating or mitigating risks appropriately - even though you may think you are. This is particularly so when it comes to IT security risk management and the minefield of risks existing in that space.
Most organisations implement IT security practices... and still get hacked! But are we doing the right things at the right time? Or have we become complacent thinking that it will never happen to us? Are we across the length and breadth of IT security risks existing across our organisations? There are some horror stories of people thinking it would never happen to them and, guess what... it did - with catastrophic consequences.
Thankfully, we can all now benefit from Boaz Fischer's considerable experience in IT security through is excellent book Protecting Your Business In Only 10 Minutes a Day! and implement robust and proven risk management practices. I strongly recommend you invest in the time to read Boaz' book - and act on his advice.
Don't be complacent. Don't think you know it all.
Even if you include one improvement to your current IT security practices as a result of reading Protecting Your Business In Only 10 Minutes a Day! you may have saved yourself from a potential disaster. Better still, undertake an IT security audit using Protecting Your Business In Only 10 Minutes a Day! as a best practice guide.
This book is long overdue and I congratulate Boaz on making a significant contribution to helping us manage IT security risks. The rest is up to us." - Andrew Smith, Managing Director, Five Phase Group

"The IT (security) world is complex and fascinating at the same time and this book can be a great window to understand it." - Paul Brady, Chief Executive Officer, ObserveIT

~

"A great and usable reference for effectively helping you protect your systems from the online threat" VP Asia Pacific – Scott Robertson - WatchGuard

~

You Can't Stop Stupid

The vast majority of intrusions and resultant breaches are not very sophisticated. Hackers have long known that businesses carelessly do not do the very basics in securing their systems. Look at every headline making breach of late and you will find could have easily been prevented by simply following "the basics" of IT security:

Target

The HVAC company that gave up the passwords to the Target network were relying on a "free" AV product that only use signatures – no heuristics, behavior or real-time protections.

Home Depot

The companies AV product had not been updated since 2007. They had purchased a complete endpoint suite of products but decided to run with their standard Windows firewall instead. They apparently did not check references or do criminal background checks on their security engineer Ricky Joe Mitchell. In April he began his four years in Federal Prison for hacking his former employer.

RSA

A spear phishing email with an attached malicious flash object embedded within a spreadsheet was opened and provided hackers their entry point. The backdoor malware loaded into their network was Poison Ivy – a well know piece of malware that is a common component in hacking tool kits. RSA called the attack an Advanced Persistent Threat while I agree the hackers may have been persistent there is nothing advanced about the script kiddie malware Poison Ivy.

There is no AV signature, firewall rule or IPS signature for foolish or perhaps stupid behavior. Simply put he majority of risk mitigation is not achieved from some new Next Generation $100,000 security product but instead by developing sound IT security habits with little if any cost. This book from Boaz Fischer "Protecting Your Business In Only 10 Minutes a Day" is a great aid in helping develop good IT security habits for any computer user. - Paul A. Henry

MCP+I, MCSE, CCSA, CCSE, CISSP-ISSAP, CISM, CISA, CIFI, CCE, ACE, GCFE, MCP+GCFA, GSEC, GICSP, GCED, VCP4/5, vExpert, Senior SANS Instructor

~

"Clarity in your business is critical in managing your business. That's why it is imperative that businesses demonstrate competency and capability to ensure their organisation financial resiliency. This book – "Protecting Your Business from Cyber Attacks With Only 10 Minutes A Day" is an excellent testament to this principle. Applying the appropriate security guidelines to drive protection, governance, reduce liability and therefore increase level of resiliency. This book is a tremendous tool for ensuring that your business successfully interacts and transacts with the Internet, safely" – Vlado Lauc, CEO of Clarity Accountants

CONTENTS

ACKNOWLEDGMENTS III

FOR YOUR OWN PROTECTION READ AND IMPLEMENT IV

REFERENCES V

FOREWORD—CEO OF MYOB XIII

INTRODUCTION 1
- Have you been hacked this week? 5
- Yes, it's your responsibility too! 8
- How much protection do you really need? 10
- Understanding risk 11
- Security versus convenience 15
- Security index calculator 17
- What you need to do! 20
- How this book is organised 21
- How to use this book 23

1 - INCREASING YOUR BUSINESS PROTECTION WITH JUST 10 MINUTES A DAY 25
- Your 10-minute daily routine 27

2 - PROTECTING YOUR WINDOWS SYSTEM GUIDELINES 29
- Introduction 30
- Patching your systems and ensuring they are up to date! 31
- Implementing strong password practices 34
- Developing realiable backup practices 39
- Laptop lockdown 51
- Antivirus protection 53
- Firewall protection 55
- Application control 58
- Windows 8 additional security features 60
- 7 steps to hardening your system 61
- 7 simple steps to protecting your windows from malware 69
- Summary of points 72

3 - PROTECTING YOUR APPLE SYSTEM GUIDELINES 73
Introduction 74
Patching your systems 75
Implementing strong password practices 76
Developing backup practices 81
Implementing firewall practices 83
Implementing laptop lockdown practices 85
Antivirus protection 88
Applying additional security practices 89
7 simple steps to securing your Apple Mac from malware 91
Summary of points 95

4 - WEB BROWSER PROTECTION GUIDELINES 97
Setting Web browser security 98
Internet Explorer 9 100
Internet Explorer 10 106
Internet Explorer 11 107
Mozilla Firefox 108
Google Chrome 113
Apple Safari 116
Disabling Java 120
Private browsing 122
Summary of points 126

5 - INTERNET USAGE PROTECTION GUIDELINES 127
The internet threat landscape 128
7 fallacies of safe Web browsing 129
Web tracking 132
Behaviour profile 137
The internet address (URL) 140
Web Email guidelines 143
Protecting your Websites and applications 145
7 steps to securing your website & applications 147
Summary of points 155

6 - INTERNET FRAUD PROTECTION GUIDELINES 157
Safe banking guidelines 166
Buying safely online 168
Selling safely online 169

Point of sales protection guidelines ... 170
Recognizing identity theft attacks ... 171
Summary of points ... 176

7 - SOCIAL NETWORKING PROTECTION GUIDELINES ... 179
7 essential points to take immediate control of your social network sites ... 186
Facebook ... 188
LinkedIn ... 192
Google+ ... 193
Twitter ... 196
7 things you must not reveal on the social web ... 201
7 steps to developing your online reputation ... 206
Summary of points ... 214

8 - MOBILITY PROTECTION GUIDELINES ... 215
Working remotely ... 217
Securing your wireless device ... 218
7 steps to securing your smart mobile devices ... 219
7 steps to securing portable storage devices ... 225
Summary of points ... 229

9 - CLOUD COMPUTING PROTECTION GUIDELINES ... 231
Introduction ... 232
7 principles of cloud security ... 236
Summary ... 241

10 - DEVELOPING SECURITY POLICIES GUIDELINES ... 243
Introduction ... 244
Implementing 7 essentila security policies ... 246
Summary ... 253

WHAT DO I DO…? ... 255
If my computer has malware infection? ... 256
If I suspect I have a bot infection on my computer? ... 257
If my Windows machine won't start? ... 258
If I suspect a file may be infected on my computer? ... 259
If I susptect that an Email attachment may contain malware? ... 260
If I get an Email asking me to reset my bank credentials? ... 261
If I don't know whether the Email is a hoax or not? ... 262
If my system is taken for hostage – ransomware? ... 263

If I get a "pop up" message that my computer is infected? ... 265
If I suspect the internet link is malicious? ... 266
If someone is offering me something for free? ... 267
If I get a phone call letting me know that my computer is infected? ... 268
If I suspect that I'm a victim of a scam? ... 269
If I have entered my personal or financial information into a phishing website? ... 270
If I discovered that I have been a victim of fraud? ... 271
If I want to report a cyber incident? ... 272
If I want to manage all my online passwords securely? ... 273
If I need to send a large and secure document via Email? ... 274
If I need to dispose of my computer safely ... 275
If I received a computer, but is it legitimate? ... 276

RESOURCES ... 279
Common myths about security and what the truth is behing them ... 280
Microsoft and security ... 282
Common acronyms ... 283
Common security technologies – explanation ... 285

SPONSORS ... 293
Imperva ... 294
Know Ur Risk ... 295
MYOB ... 296
ObserveIT ... 297
WatchGuard ... 298
CommsNet Group ... 299

Foreword – CEO of MYOB

MYOB CEO Tim Reed

In today's increasingly digital global economy, there has never been a better time for businesses of all sizes to become better connected and more competitive by using online technologies.

Secure, reliable Internet-based tools can play a vital role in your business success, providing benefits including increased efficiencies and productivity, and greater connectivity and mobility. Protecting your business online just as you would offline is critical to this.

IT security, particularly with the Internet and cloud computing, is a common concern among business operators. We have all heard the unfortunate stories about people just like you who lose everything when their IT system crashes, their backup fails, they choose an unreliable technology provider, or they are a victim of hacking. Losing business data can be disastrous, especially if it includes tax records or sensitive client details.

A strong commitment to making business life easier—something we do for more than 1.2 million businesses today—has been the cornerstone of MYOB's philosophy since 1991. In the past few years we have introduced cloud-based business management solutions, to the point where more than 50% of all our new clients are taking these up. That is one big reason why we think 'Protecting Your Business In Only 10 Minutes A Day!' is a must-read for every business operator. Few small and medium businesses have a team of information security personnel or sophisticated security tools to draw on. This book will give you greater confidence to take part in the online world and reap the benefits it offers.

Whether you are just getting online for the first time or are a tech-savvy business owner, we urge you to see prioritising IT security as an important part of business. And we wish you every success!

Tim Reed
MYOB CEO

INTRODUCTION

Computers are incredibly fast, accurate, and stupid.

Human beings are incredibly slow, inaccurate, and brilliant.

Together they are powerful beyond imagination.

– ALBERT EINSTEIN

If someone could wave the magic wand and suddenly the whole world would change and the level of trust between each and every person would be of reliance, faith, respect, and confidence, then the simple answer is that this booklet wouldn't have been written.

We wouldn't have to worry about security. We wouldn't have to worry about theft. We wouldn't have to worry about loss and exposure of our business, our lives, and our identity. Life would be simple. We would trust and respect each other. Unfortunately, this is not the case and quite the opposite.

We fight for our freedom and we fight for our identity. The Internet exposes us to vulnerabilities, to threats, to scams, to fraud, and various other nasties.

We are constantly bombarded with new intimidations, new pressures, new coercions, new fears, and new weaknesses. We must adapt to the ever-changing threat landscape.

Although the Internet is one aspect of technology, it is the biggest threat vector that we face today.

Most business users typically work behind a large organisation, and all the security related matter is left in the hands of the information security people within that organisation. Generally these organisations have sophisticated security tools, developed policies and processes to ensure that their organisation is secure, compliant, confident that achieves a high level of security and governance.

Having said that, users these days are highly mobile. More workers are spending time away from their office doing work. More workers are demanding greater flexibility and greater agility.

Workers want to have the ability to work from home. They want to work on the road, at the hotel, at the airport, at a business lounge. They may work from a remote office or a shared desk. They may want to work at the client's office or collaborate with a partner or supplier on a given project.

Workers realise that with the technology capability and accessibility offered these days, they can now engage and access corporate data from anywhere at any time from any location and from any device.

The potential downside as more mobile workers increasingly work from outside the secure boundaries of their organisation, is an increased level of risk of security compromise that few users comprehend.

In short, the risk presented by mobile workers is greatly due to the fewer security measures, fewer controls, and of course, users are not as security savvy.

However, the biggest threat that we face is ourselves! We are the Biggest Security Risk!

Did you click on a link that you shouldn't have?
Did you visit a website that you shouldn't have?
Did you open an email attachment because someone told you to?
Did you leave your password stuck on the monitor for all to see?
Did you send your confidential information unencrypted?
Did you use someone else's thumb drive and found out that your machine is infected by malware?
Did you lose all of your data because the computer crashed and you had no backup?
Did you leave your smart mobile device in the taxi or bus?

"The majority of the attacks do not exploit any weakness in the operating system but instead take advantage of the bug in people's brains."

– GRAHAM CLULEY

We regularly do make silly mistakes. We inadvertently send emails to the wrong and unintended person. We can make important decisions that are guided by misunderstanding and confusions. We can be naïve too. However, being complacent borne out of believing that it "will never happen to me" and that "we are immune to cybercrime," is extremely foolish.

This book is therefore written for the simple purpose of helping you. Helping you navigate the myriad of threat exposures on the Internet. Helping you become aware of the possible weaknesses in your systems. Helping you find a way so that you can confidentially work, interact, transact, and share information with your colleagues, partners, clients, and whomever you want from where ever you are.

This book is therefore written for the specific purpose to help you easily take simple steps to mitigate the threats and find ways to overcome them in only 10 minutes a day!

> *We have to start addressing the human element of information security, not just the technical. It's only then, we will stop being the punching bag!*
>
> – CENTRE FOR STRATEGIC STUDIES IN THE CROSSFIRE: CRITICAL INFRASTRUCTURE IN THE AGE OF CYBER WAR, 2009

- Surely, you have 10 minutes in your day that you can put aside!
- Surely, your critical assets deserve your attention and protection at a minimum of 10 minutes.
- Surely, spending 10 minutes a day is going to be one of the most important investments that you will ever make!
- Surely, increasing security awareness every 10 minutes a day will help you minimise your business risk but increase your business resiliency

Question: Could you do it in 7 minutes a day? What about 5 minutes a day or even less? Off course you can! So long as you habitually condition yourself to implementing simple daily tasks that ensures your ongoing viability and sustainability of your key security practices.

HAVE YOU BEEN HACKED THIS WEEK?

> *The Internet has spawned a new way of doing business both legitimate and unlawful. And this story is just the start.*
>
> – BOAZ FISCHER

It was only a few years ago—or should I say early 2000—that hacking was still amateurish. When you got hacked, you had no doubt that you knew about it. Your website was defaced.

Hackers would gloat to one another and proclaim how wonderful they were and what websites they managed to deface. Ego played a competitive drive.

Although web defacement still takes place today (*According to SophosLabs, more than 30,000 websites are infected every day and 80% of those that are infected are legitimate websites—Sophos Security Threat Report 2012)*, hacking these days has by far taken a more sinister motive. It is no longer just common cyber hackers trying to deface your website, but cybercriminals who are primarily motivated by fleecing your money, your identity, and cyber espionage stealing your intellectual property.

Today attacks are ferocious, targeting the highest value opportunities. The sophistication of attacks is increasing using a combination of vulnerabilities and social engineering. The landscape has evolved quickly into a borderless mesh of connectivity. According to Sophos, 95,000 is the number of malware pieces they were analysing every day in 2010 (Security Sophos Threat Report 2011). In addition, SophosLabs were detecting around 4,900 pieces of OSX malware on Mac Computers on a weekly basis (Sophos Threat Report 2013). Websense 2013 Threat Report revealed that only 1 in 5 emails were legitimate and spam increased to 76% of email traffic.

One of the most persistent and successful threats has been the fake anti-virus. In short, the user receives a warning that their system is infected with nasty malware and is coerced to pay for a full version of software to remove the threat. Of course, paying money didn't provide any protection. Quite the contrary, users who have fallen prey have not only lost money but had their machine infected with malware to freely steal additional personal information.

In light of these, it is reasonable to assume that we are not immune to such threats and risks of being compromised. On the contrary, every digital Internet device is a target. In one instance, SophosLabs have revealed that over 9 million PCs are infected with the "ZeroAccess botnet" that was published on NakedSecurity, 19th of September 2012. In another example, Kaspersky Lab Confirms Flashfake/Flashback Botnet infected more than 600,000 Mac OS X Computers—9th of April 2012.

Questions most people and businesses are asking today are:
"Why would it happen to me?"

"I don't bank online. I don't store sensitive information on my machine. I only use it for emails. What would hackers possibly want from my computer?"

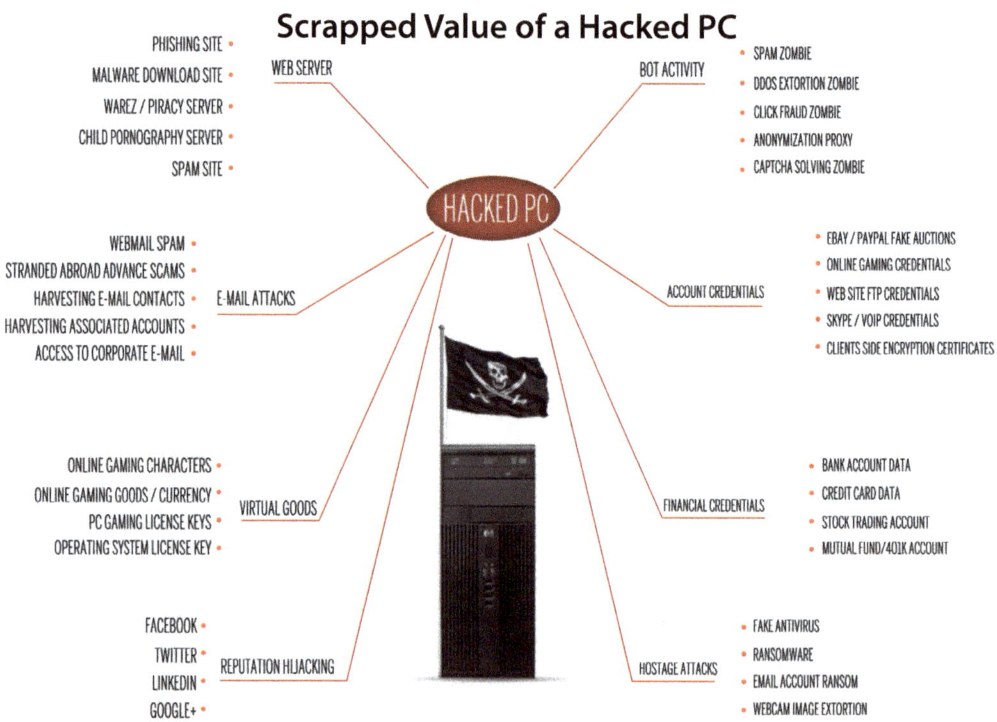

It is without a doubt that if you leave your machine on the Internet, unpatched and unprotected, then within a couple of minutes, your machine will be breached by malware.

Symantec Internet Security Threat Report 2013, reported that any business no matter its size was a potential target for attackers. In 2012, the largest growth area for targeted attacks in 2012 was businesses with fewer than 250 employees: 31% of all attacks targeted them.

This is especially bad news, because small businesses believe they are immune to attacks targeted at them. And while small businesses may assume that they have nothing an attacker would want to steal, they forget that they retain customer information, create intellectual property, and keep money in the bank.

Let's look at the value of your machine, for example. "The Scrap Value of a Hacked PC" as mentioned in a blog post krebsonsecurity.com

The blog went on to say that every aspect of a hacked computer and a user's online life can be, and has been commoditised. "If it has value and can be resold, you can be sure there is a service or product offered in the cybercriminal underground to monetise it."

The message is simple. If you are going to use the Internet, then be clever about it. Approach it like you are about to drive a car. Ensure your vehicle is road-worthy, registered, you have the appropriate insurance, and your driver's license is up to date. Make sure that the tires are inflated to the correct pressure. Ensure the oil level is at the correct level settings. Always secure the seat belts for all people within the car. When parking your car, lock it. Don't leave valuables for all to see. This just makes sense. This approach should be embraced in similar fashion on the Internet. It may not be your life that is threatened but your identity.

We all need to balance caution and precautions with usability. Security is all about people. Computers and smart mobile devices are simply tools to enable and simplify things people want to do. Social Engineering attacks are no more than attempts to trick people or their computers into doing things the bad guys want them to do. Understanding the threats, the methods, and their thinking is an important step to minimise danger.

> *An ounce of prevention is worth a pound of cure.*
>
> – BEN FRANKLIN

YES, IT'S YOUR RESPONSIBILITY TOO!

So you work in an office and your boss has told you to be careful and attentive about security. He has also reminded you to observe carefully to the guidelines published by the company's Security and Privacy Policy document.

But what's the big deal? Isn't security the responsibility of the guys in the IT department down on the third floor? Shouldn't the firewall block all viruses? After all, you are not responsible for securing your organisation's network.

To a certain extent, your thinking is correct. Ensuring the security of an organisation's network, computers, and other connected devices such as smart phones is, in fact, one of the key roles of the IT department.

Having said that, you alone are responsible for all your actions!

- Clicking on links that should not have been clicked on may have inadvertently downloaded some malware.
- Visiting websites that should not have been visited may have inadvertently downloaded some malware.
- Downloading games, music, and other applications may inadvertently lead to malware being downloaded.
- Trying to work around the controls IT has put in place by bringing your own personal laptop to work, and copying certain company documents to your laptop so that you can work from home or on the road. Unfortunately, your laptop doesn't have the same security controls and protection your organisation does. And then when you finish with your work, you copy the documents back to your network introducing other potential threats.

Here's an analogy that might make this clearer. Saying that network and data security is solely the responsibility of your IT department is like saying that the maintenance of your car is solely the responsibility of your mechanic. But if you're driving along the highway and your oil light is flashing and you ignore it, you're going to have a problem, and it's clearly not your mechanic's fault (unless he forgot to put in the oil when you last had your car serviced).

Security is your business. Yes, it's your responsibility! Do your best to not just comply with company security policies, but also understand and adopt security practices for yourself. Be aware of the dangers lurking on the Internet and be vigilant!

Never assume that anyone is providing you protection on your behalf. Take time to consider and understand the effectiveness and use the fullness of your security environment. Other people's interest may not necessarily coincide with yours.

Yes, your security is my security

Having taken the responsibility to adopt good security practices, your next step is to help other people be secure. That is a good thing in itself.

A compromised computer that is connected to the network, even if there is no data worth stealing on that computer, gets used for other criminal activity. The computer can be used for sending spam or attacking other systems.

A compromised computer joins the arsenal of the bad guys even if they don't do damage to its legitimate owner. This means that the cost of letting your computer be compromised is not borne by you, but is distributed over the rest of the net.

Helping a fellow user adopt appropriate and suitable security practices helps us all by minimising the risk to all.

In an article that I wrote, "Embedding Security Culture Within Organisation" for the Security Solutions magazine in 2007, I discussed that security is not just a technological issue but that security is everyone's responsibility, requiring participation from all.

Developing a culture of security creates greater awareness by all, better and wider visibility to see dangers, enhanced preparation and readiness to defend against threats, and therefore the ability to mitigate risks becomes much more efficient and cost effective.

In short, it's a win-win.

HOW MUCH PROTECTION DO YOU REALLY NEED?

With the complex and ever-changing threat landscape, it's difficult for any person and organisation to find the right balance. Too much investment can possibly suck your time, capital, and human manpower just managing it. Not enough can possibly jeopardise your business.

If you look around your business, there is a great deal of information assets that require protection: propriety customer data; your intellectual property information; your financial records; your customers' data; your employee data; your supplier data. Such data needs to be protected from disruptions and theft.

Your reputation as a smart and business-focused organisation needs to be safeguarded. Protecting your business means enabling your business to thrive, grow, and act on opportunities.

But the question still remains, how much protection do you really require?

Protecting your business means ensuring your business processes and data are fortified so that operations can withstand deliberate and accidental disruptions. It means being able to recover easily and seamlessly from unanticipated events. It means proving you are worthy of the trust your customers, suppliers, and partners have placed in your business.

How much protection is enough?

In making any investment, your determination will be based on a single key factor. What is your ability to withstand business loss?

The next few pages describe in more detail your Risk Appetite.

UNDERSTANDING RISK

In striving to achieve our corporate objectives, we relish the challenges that provide us the opportunity to inspire our staff, build our profits, and grow our business. We develop our strategy, seek the evidence to support our decisions, and then make decisions that ideally lead to the best outcomes. In essence, we manage the risks that could detract from us achieving our desired outcomes—including managing uncertainty.

We live in a world of uncertainty—a world that is changing at an ever-accelerating pace. Our lives are becoming more multi-layered, complex and intricate, particularly as we increasingly rely on more sophisticated IT systems, technologies, and processes to underpin our success. Having certainty in how we run our business makes it easier to manage the risks that may otherwise cause us problems.

Let's get a better feel for risk.

The Australian Risk Management Standard (AS/NZS ISO 31000:2009) describes risk as the "effect of uncertainty on objectives." More simply put, whenever we try to achieve an objective, there's always the chance that things will not go according to plan. If you like, there is always a degree of uncertainty that needs to be managed. Mind you, it is difficult, if not impossible, to do away with all risks to our business.

Whether you realise it or not, you perform the duties of a risk manager everyday by managing the risk associated with driving your car to work, crossing the road, investing in the stock market, travelling on a plane, or delivering a solution or project on time.
Perhaps a simple way to understand risk is to ask the question, "If something were to happen, what would be the impact to my business?"

If you like, Risk can be identified as an EVENT leading to an OUTCOME.
Risk can be thought of an equation. A risk rating (e.g. Low, Medium, High, or Extreme) can be determined by assessing:

- Risk = the likelihood of the event occurring **x** the consequence of that event should it occur.

LIKELIHOOD	CONSEQUENCE			
	MINOR	MODERATE	MAJOR	CATASTROPHIC
HIGHLY LIKELY	Medium	Medium	High	Extreme
LIKELY	Low	Medium	High	High
POSSIBLE	Low	Low	Medium	Medium
UNLIKELY	Low	Low	Low	Medium

This is usually determined using a "risk matrix" that matches risk ratings to the likelihood and consequence. A simple example is the figure from the previous page. Risks, including their risk rating, are usually recorded in a risk register.

How does this relate to Information Technology?

The increasing dependencies of our society on information and computer networks have intrinsic IT risks that need careful management. IT risks can take on many forms and, without doubt, can destroy your business in a "nanosecond" if you do not understand them and manage them effectively. Some of the potential risks include:

- Downtime - leading to loss of income and disgruntled customers
- Security breaches - leading to reputation damage and loss of information or the public release of sensitive information
- Power failure - leading to data loss, unhappy customers, and expensive repairs
- Loss, corruption, or theft of valuable data - leading to project delays or failure to achieve your corporate objectives
- Loss of the critical intellectual capital that makes your business stand out from others - leading to competitors gaining a market edge over you and taking your customers
- Denial of service attack - leading to potential business shutdown or blackmail.

And this is just the start of it.

Having said that, IT risk has a broader meaning. It encompasses not only the "negative" association of being impacted, but it also has the "positive" benefit and value, enabling risk associated to missing opportunities. For example, businesses can use a risk framework as a business tool to enhance business objectives or augment IT project management decisions for aspects such as overspending, lack of visibility, lack of delivery, and cost blow out.

As such, risk management can support management, achieve effective outcomes, and improved overall governance. In fact, let's get this clear—risk management is a PILLAR supporting how you do your business.

So how does this relate to Internet Risk?

The Internet is an exciting world, full of fresh and exciting opportunities. It creates the opportunity to do business across a global market place 24/7. However, the Internet is also fraught with new threats, obstacles, and dangers that the average business person and home user haven't even begun to understand. We just need a cursory glance at some of the horrific stories of the many cyber attacks that occur to high profile organisations such as

- eBay data breach, urges 145 million of its online users to change their passwords (May 2014)
- Target, the giant US retailer, suffers a massive security breach exposing credit card and personal data up to 110 million users (between 27th of November and 15th of December, 2013)
- Adobe suffers data security breach exposing 2.9 million users names and credit card details (3rd of October, 2013)
- Twitter—250,000 accounts compromised (3 February,2013)
- Gold Coast medical center patient database in Australia seized, encrypted and held for ransom (12 December 2012)
- LinkedIn—six million passwords were stolen (6 June 2012)
- Visa and MasterCard—1.5 million accounts were hacked (30 March, 2012)
- Facebook—worm steals 45,000 Facebook passwords (5 January, 2012)—did you change your password recently? Take my advice and do it TODAY!
- Sony—the personal information of around 100 million users compromised (April 2011)
- RSA—250 million ID's were compromised (17 March 2011)
- Sony Pictures Entertainment Hack is the biggest data breach, exfiltrating gigabytes and gigabytes of documents, emails and even entire movies (December 2014)

These cyber risks are real and not even scratching the surface of what is going on. What's more, because cyber risks are constantly evolving, many businesses are not adequately prepared and lack sufficient appreciation of the problem at large.

Your Risk Appetite

Your risk will be defined by the amount of risk your company or you are willing to accept in pursuit of your tasks and goals—we call this risk appetite. More simply put, what is your tolerance to risk?

Often organisations need guidance at a business and technical level to work this out in a way that will lead to success. Some of the questions we should ask are:

- What could stop or hinder me reaching my objectives?
- How am I going to identify risks so that I can rate them accurately?
- What will be the specific mitigations or treatments for each risk?
- How can I be sure that real and important risks are being addressed?
- What understanding, knowledge, and certainty do I require so that I can make the right decision about a certain risk?
- How do I use risk as a way to progress my business?
- What is a simple approach for undertaking risk management?
- How do I develop and implement a risk management framework?
- What are my budget, resources, timeframes, and accountabilities so that I can manage risk within an acceptable level and achieve my desired outcomes?

In essence, "you need to manage risk," not let "risk manage you."

Depending on the type of risk and its significance, the traditional approach to risk mitigation can include one of these choices:

1. **Mitigate** - implement measures and controls to minimise the risk to an acceptable level

2. **Transfer** - share the risk with partners or transfer to a third party

3. **Accept** - accept the risk and continue to monitor it.

> *I cannot imagine any condition which could cause the ship to founder. I cannot conceive of any vital disaster happening to this vessel.*
>
> – CAPTAIN OF THE TITANIC, 1912

What should I be thinking about right now?

In this book, our aim is to raise your awareness, understanding, and develop a risk appetite model so that you can make better decisions in order to generate better outcomes for your business and yourself.

Having a simple and effective approach to risk management would help you manage some immediate risks, for example:

Should you allow your employees full access to social networks sites?
Should you allow users to utilise their own mobile devices within your business?
Should you allow your business data to be pushed to the Cloud?
How do you ensure the protection of your intellectual property effectively?
How do you minimise the threat of malware attacks against your business?
How can you best protect your business against disruptions and downtime failures?

SECURITY VERSUS CONVENIENCE

In life, people choose as a general rule of thumb to follow the easiest outcome that involves the least amount of work or effort. This is some time referred as the **path of least resistance**.

Our lives are hectic. Our work is demanding. We lack time to accomplish our objectives. We are consistently put under stress in our work environments. It is no wonder that we seek the easiest way to reach our aims and solve problems within the shortest amount of time. Seeking for the path of least resistance is the mindset that we apply, to save time and make our lives easier.

In this world of high technology, we have come to expect that each new innovation will make our lives more convenient and easier than ever before. However, making things more convenient for ourselves isn't always the most secure thing that we can do. In fact, convenience is oftentimes inversely proportional to safety and security.

For the most part, we as users want an easy-to-use method to access our information anytime, from anywhere and from any device. We don't want to be riddled with complex and frustrating difficulties to access our information.

Is it true then the more secure the model is, the more inconvenient it is?

This paradigm holds true in real life as it does in the computer/network security world.

Let's consider your home, for example. It would be very convenient and time saving exercise to leave front and back doors unlocked, and your windows wide open all the time. Should you decide to go to work in the morning, upon your return in the evening it is possible you might find your valuables missing.

In Verizon Data Breach Report 2013, 75% of victims were targets of opportunity. Additionally, 76% of attacks were not highly difficult to undertake.

On the other hand, you could lock all the doors, lock all the dead-bolts, set the security alarm system, and have a number of guard dogs leashed to the front and back porch.

However, it's not very convenient when you're coming back from the store with two bags of groceries in one arm and a crying baby in the other arm.

This same simple model can be applied the world of computers. Should you leave your new computer "wide open" and not worry about any security (highly convenient) and then connect it to the Internet, your computer would be breached within a few minutes.

Strong password security causes almost as many problems as it solves. Everyone knows they're not supposed to use the word "password," or the name of their pet as their password. But, creating long passwords comprised of uppercase and lowercase letters, numbers, and special characters means they're also harder to remember.

More and more of your life is on the web, and each system is demanding your credentials. You bank is online, you socialise online, you buy goods online, and you work online.

It is not surprising, therefore, to find users using a single and simple to remember password that can also be easily guessed at and cracked by the bad guys.

In short, we store quite a bit of personal information on our PCs and business systems. Since this information tends to be quite valuable and sometimes even more valuable to people with less-than-honourable intentions, there should be adequate security measures in place to protect the data stored.

The Convenience versus Security model is a matter of balance. The balance ensures that our business is secure and meets the appropriate practices while our lives are reasonably convenient.

In this book, we have addressed both sides of the equation. I have provided you with a ten-minute daily routine to ensure that you adopt simple yet tested security protection practices, while at the same time ensuring that you can still have reasonable convenience for day-to-day business.

HOW SECURE ARE YOU RIGHT NOW?

Effective security practice requires understanding, accountability, commitment, and responsibilities of organizing the appropriate security practice measures in place.

The Security Index Calculator is a tool that we have developed. This tool will allow you to quickly assess your current security readiness environment called **Security Index**. The following assessment is nothing more than a careful examination. They are designed to help you to be better informed and assist you in the pursuit of enhancing and strengthening your own environment.

How it works:

- There are 28 questions.
- For each question, rank your answer from 0 to 5.
- Where 0 reflects a very negative dismal outcome and reputation difficulty;
  1: Failure and loss of control;
  2: On the border line and needs more focus;
  3: Pass but could be much better;
  4: Success with distinction;
  5: Outstanding.
- If the question doesn't relate to you, just put in a "3" in the answer box.
  If you don't know, then put "1."

1.	Can you identify where your most valuable data is located within your organisation? (0 = no idea; 3 = some of it; 5 = all of it)	
2.	Have you tested the ability to restore your data in the last 3 months to make sure that it works? (0 = never tested; 3 = once a year; 5 = 4 times a year)	
3.	Are you currently being protected by a firewall and antivirus whether it is just for your workstation or for the whole office? (0 = no idea; 3 = workstations are protected but not servers; 5 = all systems are protected)	
4.	Have you changed the default password on your Internet-facing devices such as your router, firewall and Wi-Fi devices? (0 = don't think so; 3 = only the router; 5 = all out Internet devices)	
5.	Have you ensured that your office workstations are regularly updated with the latest system updates and patches? (0 = not sure; 3 = some are; 5 = yes, all)	
6.	Have you setup a corporate email and Internet usage policy for your business? (0 = not all; 3 = no one follows it; 5 = yes, and enforced)	
7.	Do you enforce that all your Windows users have no administration rights to their workstation? (1 = no enforcement; 3 = some enforcement; 5 = total enforcement)	
8.	If your workstation or server/s were to fail, could you confidently be up and running within 24 hours? (0 = no idea; 3 = yes, but it would take longer than 24 hours; 5 = very confident)	

9.	If one of your employees' smart phone devices was accidently lost, would you confidently feel secure that your organisation has NOTHING to risk? (0 = very worried; 2 = no idea; 3 = we should be fine; 5 = all under control)	
10.	Would you know what users are doing online at any time? (1 = no idea; 3 = somewhat; 5 = have full visibility)	
11	Would you know whether users are downloading games or music during business hours? (1 = no idea; 3 = somewhat; 5 = have full visibility)	
12.	If you had a power failure or power surge in your office, would you confidently feel that your key assets are safe? (0 = no idea; 3 = somewhat comfortable; 5 = fully confident)	
13.	Have you experienced any downtime / system failure in the last month? (0 = major system failure for more than 1 week; 1 = few failures that lasted a few days; 2 = 1 failure that lasted less for 1 day; 3 = small failure that lasted less than 4 hours; 4 = minor availability issues or performance being slow; 5 = no failures	
14.	When disposing of sensitive information such as paper documents, do you shred them or just throw them in the bin? (1 = bin; 5 = all documents gets shredded)	
15.	Would you know whether users are posting comments about your business on social media without your authorization? (1 = no idea; 3 = somewhat; 5 = have full visibility)	
16.	Would you know whether users are actively engaged in social media for personal reasons during work hours? (1 = no idea; 3 = somewhat; 5 = have full visibility)	
17.	If the bank were to send an email to your staff asking them to verify their identity, how confident would you feel that your staff would NOT respond? (0 = most would respond; 3 = some would respond; 5 = no one would respond)	
18.	If someone sent you an email with an attachment of the latest exciting news that Michael Jackson was seen alive, how confident would you be that neither your staff nor yourself would open it? (0 = most would open it; 3 = some would open it; 5 = no one would be fooled)	
19.	Would you prevent your children from downloading games or applications on your work computer at home (0 = have no control and no visibility; 2 = have some visibility, but let them do it anyway; 4 = have total visibility and control; 5 = don't allow any access)	
20.	Are you fully and correctly licensed for all your software? (0= no idea of what licensing you have; 5 = regularly assess what's installed and compare it with software purchases)	
21.	If someone found a USB in the car park, would you or any of your staff be curious to see what is on it? (0 = most likely; 5 = no, not at all)	
22.	Would you know who has access to your corporate and sensitive files that are on your network? (1 = no idea; 3 = somewhat; 5 = have full visibility)	
23.	If you allow remote connectivity to your office, would you perform an assessment on a regular basis to see which people connect and what computers they used to connect with? (0 = don't care; 3 = we know who logs in, but we don't do any assessments; 5 = regularly assessed)	

24	Have you developed a business continuity plan in the event that either your business or your Cloud provider experiences major downtime?	
25.	Do you regularly provide user training about company security policies and good governance? (0 = never; 3 = once a year; 5 = at least twice or three times a year, and it is also part of staff induction when they are employed)	
26.	Have you documented and understood your corporate network and systems? (0 = no documentation; 3 = some documentation, but not reviewed for the past 12 months; 5 = fully documented and reviewed every 6 months)	
27.	Is critical, sensitive and any intellectual property information encrypted within your organisation? (0= no encryption; 3 = identified sensitive data, but no encryption; 5 = encryption on all sensitive information)	
28.	Do you control what applications are running on your workstations? (0=No visibility & no control on what users are doing; 3=Have visibility when manually checking on workstations; 5=Using Application Whitelisting to provide real time visibility & Control on all applications on workstations)	

Next Step—Tally up the scores and identify your Security Index

Result & Outcome

0 to 55—Fail!

At least you are being honest in evaluating your business security practices. However, you do have a serious mountain to climb. It would be advisable to hire a security consultant to help you plan the necessary protection for your business and carry out those activities as soon as possible. Return to this questionnaire six months after you have done this and re-evaluate your business security practices. Your Security Index score needs to be higher!

56 to 83—You have passed

But, you are by no means out of the woods. There are some serious "holes" in your security practice. You need to take some immediate action. Use this booklet to pinpoint areas where you are weak and then follow the process outlined to resolve the problem. Review this questionnaire in about six months' time and re-evaluate your business security practices. Hopefully, your Security Index score has matured to the next level.

84 to 112—Well done

You have achieved a credible security practice rating. Finer tuning may be required to achieve the necessary protection. You may want to view specific critical areas of your business to ensure ongoing protection. Use this booklet to pinpoint areas of improvement. Review this questionnaire in about six months' time and re-evaluate your Security Index.

113+—Excellent

Continue to regularly review your security business practices to ensure optimal protection.

WHAT YOU NEED TO DO!

News of computer fraud, data theft, and system breaches are regularly being published and distributed, if not daily then weekly. It seems there are a myriad of potential threats and vulnerabilities that require the user to increase the security and vigilance of their Internet-connected machine.

Yet without fail, most information available is written in a language that is more suited to a computer geek. Added to this, the sophistication of trying to handle the security problem can be overwhelming. What does it mean? What do I need to do? Is this a problem? How do I know that this site is safe? What happens if my computer is infected? It sounds like we all need a thesis in security protection.

Well not anymore, compiled by our team of experienced and expert people at CommsNet Group, these tips are written in a plain language. We have purposely addressed it, so that any user should be able to follow and appreciate the significance of the recommendations and importantly take the appropriate actions.

Treat this book as you would an a la carte menu. Look at the table of contents and decide where our tips can provide you with some help and implement them. Reread the table of contents on another day and dive into some new tips that may be of help to you.

Developing security habits develop resilient practices. This is one habit that you should undertake:

Increasing Your Business Protection in Just 10 Minutes a Day—Chapter 1

When these recommendations are implemented and you have run your systems for a while, then dive back into the table of contents and review some more guidelines that may be of help in securing your business computers.

This book is a living document. If you have any questions or concerns or even some feedback of your own, please do not hesitate to contact us here at CommsNet Group.

Be sure to check out our website to gather security protection tips that go beyond this book at www.pi10m.com. This website will encompass additional features such as

- Updates to this book on an ongoing basis
- Tools and resources
- URL links
- Additional educational material
- Technology tools
- Discount offerings
- Free alerts and news subscription

Assumption

We are assuming that you are reading this book because you need to understand and address a very serious challenge for either yourself or your business in regards to ensuring that your key information assets and data are protected.

This book therefore focuses on how to go about protecting your corporate data using available resources and recommended tools in a very simple manner.

HOW THIS BOOK IS ORGANISED

Each chapter in this book covers a different aspect of security challenge and the specific solution guideline for you to follow.

We begin with Chapter 1, the most important chapter which addresses your 10 minutes daily safe protection routine. We then follow with the remaining chapters, where each of these chapters maps out the challenges that we face: the What, Where, When, and Why. Each chapter will then provide you with the How—How to proceed with solving this challenge.

Chapter 1: Increasing Your Business Protection in Just 10 Minutes a Day—By following this 10 minute daily practice, you will ensure that your systems are soundly protected and therefore minimise your security exposure.

Chapter 2: Protecting Your Windows System Guidelines —In this chapter we help you develop security practices for your Windows system. We start from patching your system with the latest updates, to locking your laptop and to engendering a strong password culture.

Chapter 3: Protecting Your Apple System Guidelines —Like Chapter 2, this chapter is dedicated in helping you setup secure practices for your Apple system.

Chapter 4: Web Browser Protection Guidelines—This chapter provides you with a guideline of safe web browsing configuration protection.

Chapter 5: Internet Usage Protection Guidelines—This chapter provides you with a guideline of safe Internet usage practices; how to determine whether a website is malicious or not; what is considered a secure web email practice; how do you buy and sell online safely.

Chapter 6: Internet Fraud Protection Guidelines—This chapter helps you grasp the understanding of how Internet fraud takes place and ways to mitigate against them.

Chapter 7: Social Networking Protection Guidelines—This chapter provides you with a guideline of how to use social networking in a secure way.

Chapter 8: Mobility Protection Guidelines—This chapter provides you with a guideline for developing remote security work practices, including setting up security practices for smart mobile and tablet devices.

Chapter 9: Cloud Computing Guidelines—This chapter provides you with a guideline and key steps should you consider moving your business or portions of it to the Cloud.

Chapter 10: Developing Security Policy Guidelines—This chapter provides you with key security policy guidelines that you can implement within your business.

What Do I Do If—If you had a burning question and wanted it answered, then go to this chapter. It has most likely been answered.

Resource—This chapter is filled with useful insights, such as, Common myth about security; All about Microsoft security; Common Acronyms and understanding of the IT jargon; Description of common security technologies.

HOW TO USE THIS BOOK IN THE MOST EFFECTIVE WAY

We recommend starting with Chapter 1—Increasing Your Business Protection With Just 10 Minutes A Day. This will setup a strong baseline protection for your business.

Next, complete the assessment "How Secure Are You Right Now?" This will give you a snapshot of your security standing. We call it "Security Index." The higher the score, the more resilient you are. This should take you about 10 minutes to complete.

This will set the foundation for the rest of the book and establish areas that you can start working on. Proceed to the appropriate chapters to be able to quickly address a challenge that you may have.

Finally, subscribe to the www.pi10m.com website to get the latest security alerts, book updates and other useful information.

Run through this regularly throughout the year and see how you are progressing.

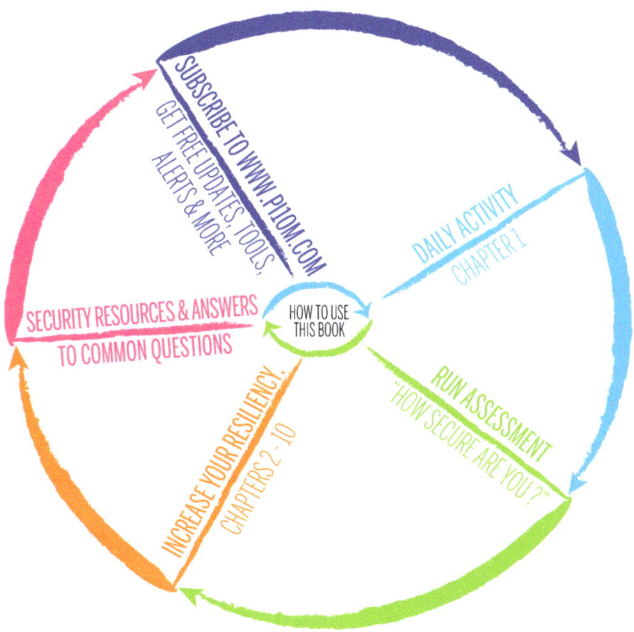

Remember, there is no such thing as 100% security!
The cornerstone of security is awareness and vigilance.

– BOAZ FISCHER

1

Increasing Your Business Protection With Just 10 Minutes A Day

Small and deliberate and consistent action speaks louder than words. It's the foundation of habits that grow to consistent results!

– BOAZ FISCHER

You and I both know that it is no secret that technology is changing rapidly and faster than it has ever before. It's become more sophisticated with additional layers of complexity. At the same time security threats and vulnerabilities are increasing with force and vigor. It is difficult enough just trying to ensure that your computers have the latest security updates and protection, but it is getting very difficult when threats are becoming targeted and our level of understanding is pretty small.

So what do we need to do? Spend 10 minutes a day following tested processes and activities to ensure key information assets are protected. This will invariably help you build resiliency to your own practice.

But before I continue, I just want to spell out one big myth. There is no security tool that will provide you with 100% protection.

Having said that, with what I'm about to tell you, you can put some simple processes into place that can minimise potential downturn.

Applying some simple steps to secure your key systems and data is just common sense. You wouldn't leave your front door to your home open when there is no one there. You wouldn't leave your car unlocked in a public car park. You wouldn't leave your credit cards lying around in a restaurant and just walk out.

Protecting your business is easy and it definitely doesn't have to be expensive. In fact all you need is to find the right balance between implementing the necessary security measures and the appropriate resources to accomplish the work.

YOUR 10-MINUTE DAILY ROUTINE

STEP 1 Ensure your workstation operating systems are up to date.

STEP 2 Ensure all your applications are up to date.

STEP 3 Ensure you have the latest antivirus protection enabled. I recommend that you scan your systems on a weekly basis.

STEP 4 Ensure your firewall is turned on.

STEP 5 Ensure that all your key information data is backed up daily. Test your recovery on regular basis.

STEP 6 Use strong passwords and different passwords for different uses. Also, consider using different and unique user names when authenticating to different online businesses. If you have many online systems to authenticate, consider using a password manager program.

STEP 7 Only download applications from reputable websites. And if you haven't asked to download the application, then don't download it!

STEP 8 When not in use, lock or close the workstations. Shut down your Wi-Fi. Disable Bluetooth. This minimises network breach, data theft, and unwarranted software installs.

STEP 9 When logging onto your system, log onto it without the administrator privilege rights. It is difficult for malware to infect your system if it is doesn't have administrator privilege rights.

STEP 10 When receiving an email, look for signs that this email may not be legitimate. Treat all emails suspiciously. Be careful clicking on a link. Treat all emails that request you to download a file from a website as mistrustful.

STEP 11 Do not respond to emails or phone requests asking you to provide them with personal information such as banking details, identity information, birthdates, or otherwise. If you are unsure, verify the validity of the person or organisation or seek advice.

STEP 12 Practice safe web browsing. Be careful on what you click. Be careful what you visit. Be careful what user you wish to link up as friends. They may not be who they say they are!

STEP 13 Never leave personal information lying around the desk such as passwords, pin numbers, or other identification.

STEP 14 Keep your identity safe! Never post key personal information on social networks and other social media sites. Regularly check your privacy settings on such sites.

For the more security conscious organisation

STEP 15 Use multi factor authentication to access key applications and systems.

STEP 16 Encrypt all of your sensitive data you may have and store your keys in a safe place.

STEP 17 Implement Application White listing and Application Control. Check that you have the visibility and the ability to identify and block what applications are running on your business systems.

STEP 18 Regularly assess security vulnerabilities on your environment. This will allow you to make quick and effective decisions of what mitigation steps are required to be in place.

STEP 19 Scan the social world to determine what is being said about you. Google your business and Google your name.

> *It is not necessary to do the extraordinary things to get extraordinary results.*
>
> – WARREN BUFFETT

2 Protecting Your Windows System Guidelines

*Truly,
nothing is to be expected
but the unexpected.*

– ALICE JAMES

INTRODUCTION

On the 15th of January, 2002, Bill Gates, then the co-founder and chairman of Microsoft, sent a companywide memo stating that Microsoft must make "Trustworthy Computing" the highest priority for the company and for the industry over the next decade.

With the ever increasing adoption of the Internet, Bill Gates recognised that Microsoft and the technology industry needed to prioritise security, privacy, and availability to instill trust in computing.

The security of users and business computers and networks is a key priority. Microsoft approach to security includes both technological and social aspects to strive and ensure that information and data are safe and confidential.

Drawing on industry best practices, Microsoft made huge investments to increase the security of their technologies and to provide guidance and training to help minimise the impact of malicious software.

This chapter therefore provides an overview of Microsoft Trustworthy Computing key security focus elements:

- Fundamentals of Security
- Threat and Vulnerability
- Identity and Access

Businesses today use the Internet more than ever to communicate with customers and suppliers and to conduct commerce. This chapter will therefore assist you in developing sound security practices while interacting on the Internet.

Safeguarding the confidentiality of your information and the integrity of your computers and business is going to be your responsibility to ensure Trustworthy Computing.

PATCHING YOUR SYSTEMS AND ENSURING THEY ARE UP TO DATE!

One of the keys to keeping your computer secure and clean is to ensure that the operating system and applications are kept up-to-date.

For a windows-based computer this is very easy to do: Turn on **Automatic Updates** also known as **Windows Update** from the control panel and set updates to occur daily at a convenient time.

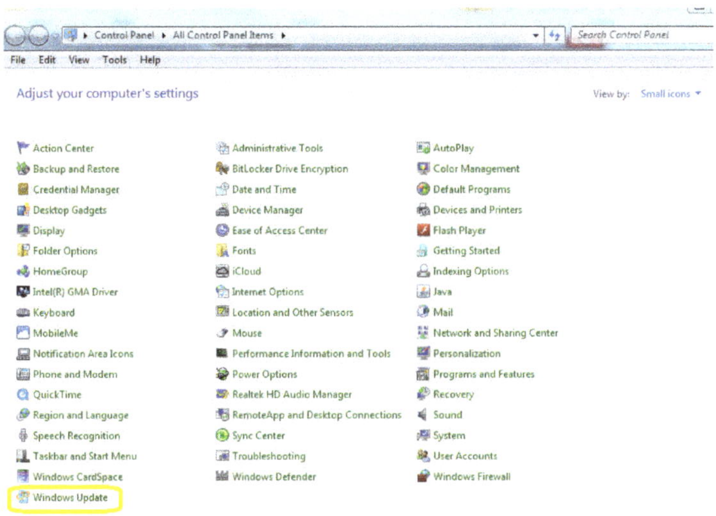

Alternatively visit www.pi10m.com/b1/60

Windows Update is a service provided by Microsoft that provides updates for the Microsoft Windows Operating System and its installed components, including Internet Explorer.

Updates are normally provided over an Internet connection, although there is provision for updates to be installed on computers without an Internet connection.

There are different kinds of updates. *Security updates* or *critical updates* protect against vulnerabilities to malware and security exploits. Other updates correct errors that aren't related to security, or enhance functionality.

Windows Vista, Windows Server 2003, Windows 7, Windows Server 2008, Windows 8, and Windows Server 8 provide a **Control Panel** to configure update settings and check for updates.

Security updates are routinely provided on the **second Tuesday of each month** called **Patch Tuesday**. It can also be provided whenever a new update is urgently required to prevent a newly discovered or prevalent exploit targeting Windows users. Windows Update can be configured to install critical updates automatically so long as the computer is connected to the Internet, without the user needing to install them manually, or even be aware that an update is required.

Critical Update Notification Tool / Utility

The Critical Notification Tool is important and should not be dismissed. By default, your computer is checked every 5 minutes and when Internet Explorer starts. The Critical Notification Tool then compares the list of critical updates with the list of your installed components and will then display a message informing you of any new critical update

Windows 8 Automatic Updates

In Windows 8, automatic updates should be on by default. To check this, right click on the desktop and choose **personalise**. This will present a screen similar the following:

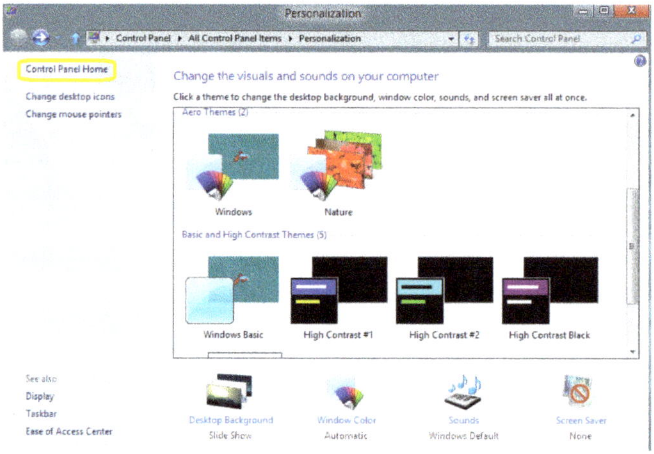

Click the **Control Panel Home** link and you will be presented with a screen similar to the following:

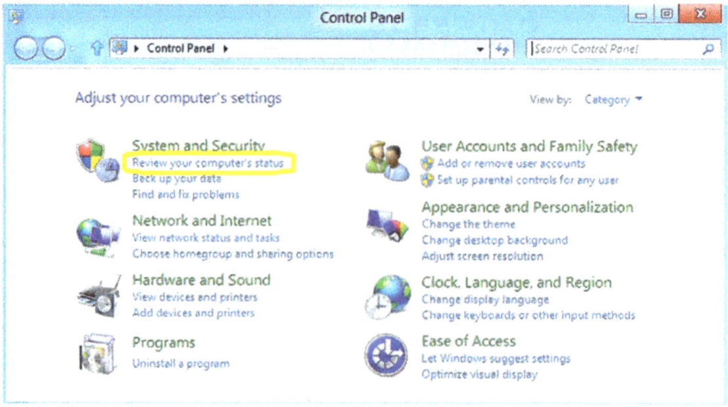

Click **Review your computer's status** under System and Security, and this will present a screen similar to the following:

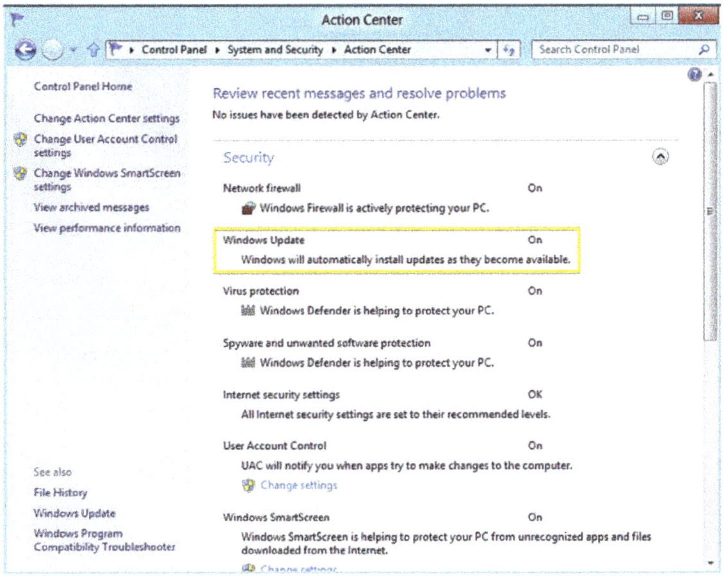

If Windows Update is turned off, go back to the previous screen and click the **System and Security** link in the Control Panel. Then click **Turn automatic updating on or off.**

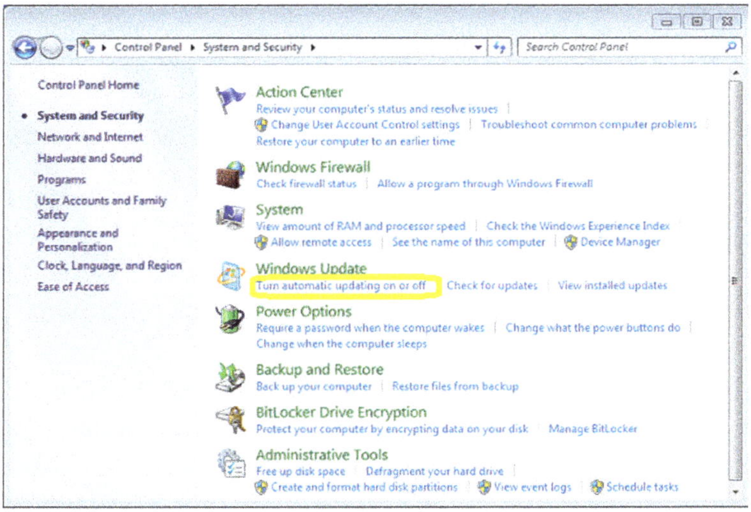

IMPLEMENTING STRONG PASSWORD PRACTICES

We all know that strong passwords are all that stands between us and a potential security breach. The number one most commonly used password is "123456," and the fourth most commonly used is "Password." Your own name is also a common choice. So any password attacker and cracker would try these three passwords immediately.

Other weaknesses are how users choose and manage them:

- Simple passwords—Short in length, that use words found in dictionaries
- Passwords others can find—On sticky notes on monitors, in a notepad by the computer, in a document in computer, whiteboard reminders, smart device storage in clear text, etc.
- Using the same password—Using the same password for multiple sites, never changing account passwords, etc.
- Shared passwords—Users posting password notes on their screens; sending unencrypted emails with password information; using same password for all their accounts.
- Allowing your browsers to save your logins and basic information for automatic form-filling. This is convenient, but definitely not a secure option.

When a system tries to guess your password, the only thing an attacker can know is whether a password guess was an exact match… or not.

The attacker doesn't know how long the password is, or anything about what it might look like. So after exhausting the entire standard password cracking lists, databases and dictionaries, the attacker has no option but to either to give up and move on to someone else or start guessing every possible password.

Choosing a good password is an important part of lowering the risk of becoming the victim. The following guidelines should help you when choosing passwords for your online accounts.

- Make your passwords memorable, so that you don't have to write them down or store them in a file on your computer
- Never use real words that a hacker or cybercriminal can find in a dictionary.
- Don't use obvious passwords that can be easily guessed, such as your spouse's name, your child's name, pet's name, car registration, postcode, etc.
- Use a mixture of uppercase and lowercase letters, numbers and non- alphanumeric characters such as punctuation marks.
- Don't recycle passwords, e.g. don't use 'password1', 'password2', 'password3', etc. for different accounts.

- If possible, use a passphrase, rather than a single word, e.g. "this is how it is done."
- Make the password long. Many sites enforce a minimum password length and often add additional requirements (such as a mixture of lower case, upper case, number, and punctuation).
- Don't use the same password for multiple accounts. If a cybercriminal finds the password to one account, they can use it to access other accounts.
- Don't share your passwords with others.
- Changing passwords on regular basis is a good idea, but it is troublesome to remember. Suggestion: you develop a strong password instead.

The following site will help assess the strength of your password:

- Password Meter— www.pi10m.com/b1/1
- Microsoft Password Checker—www.pi10m.com/b1/2

The Challenge with Multiple Accounts / Passwords

Remembering a single password is relatively easy. However, remembering twenty unique passwords because you have a number of web access logins to various accounts is a tough challenge.

How do you then go about managing all your authentications IDs?

That's why we would highly recommend you to use a **password manager**. A password manager is software that helps a user organise passwords and PIN codes. The software typically has a local database or a file that holds the encrypted password data for secure logon onto computers, networks, websites, and application data files.

Many password managers also work as a "form filler." They fill the user and password data automatically into forms.

Password managers can also be used as a defence against phishing and pharming. A password manager program can also incorporate an automated login script that first compares the current site's URL to the stored site's URL. If the two don't match, then the password manager does not automatically fill in the logon fields to safeguard against visual imitations and look-alike websites.

Password managers can protect against key loggers or keystroke logging malware. When using a multi-factor authentication password manager that automatically fills in logon fields, the user does not have to type any user names or passwords for the keylogger to pick up.

Suggested Password Managers

- LastPass is a terrific password manager which is easy to use and compatible with pretty much every device—Windows, Apple, Smartphones, Tablets—www.pi10m.com/b1/3
- KeePass is an Open Source solution that is suitable to the more security conscious users—www.pi10m.com/b1/4
- Dashlane is also a great password manager—www.pi10m.com/b1/5
- Some antivirus software providers have also bundled a password manager.

Additional Points

- Develop fictitious questions and answers when you're required to recover your password. Typical questions such as "what city were you born?" or "What was your name of your first pet?" or "what model was your first car?" These answers can be tracked down in time. To be more secure, create a fake persona or better still, use fake data. For example, "what city were you born?" You could answer "The Moon." "What model was your first car?" You could answer "Pink Giraffe." It's rather absurd, but at least you will remember it!
- Make sure that you change your entire Internet-facing administration passwords devices. That means, changing the "default" password on your firewall, router, and Wi-Fi devices. This is critical!

Securing Windows passwords

Your Windows password is the password you use to authenticate on to your computer. Using a strong password is among the most important steps you can take to protect your computer from hackers and other unwelcome users.

In Windows, a password can be made up of letters, numbers, symbols, and spaces. Windows passwords are also case sensitive.

To help keep the information on your computer secure, you should not give out your password or write it in a place where others can see it.
If you are logged on as an administrator, you can create a password for any account.
If you are connected to a domain, Group Policy settings might prevent you from completing these steps.

The steps that you should follow will vary, depending on whether your computer is on a domain or a workgroup.

Computers on a home network are usually part of a workgroup, and computers on a workplace network are usually part of a domain.

In a workgroup

- All computers are peers. No computer has control over another computer.
- Each computer has a set of user accounts. To use any computer in the workgroup, you must have an account on that computer.
- If you have a user account on any computer, you can change settings for that account.
- There are typically no more than ten to twenty computers.
- All computers must be on the same local network or subnet.

In a domain

- One or more computers are servers. Network administrators use servers to control the security and permissions for all the computers on the domain. This makes it easy to make changes because the changes are automatically made to the other computers.
- If you have a user account on the domain, you can log on to any computer on the domain without needing an account on that computer.
- If you use a computer on the domain, you probably can make only limited changes to settings. (That's because network administrators want to ensure consistency among computers and maintain configuration control as much as possible.)
- You can have an unlimited number of computers in the domain and they can be on different local networks.
- To check if your computer is on a workgroup or domain
- Go to the "Control Panel," clicking "System and Maintenance," and then clicking "System."
- Under computer name, domain, and workgroup settings, you will see either "Workgroup" or "Domain," followed by the name.

My Computer is on a Domain

1. Open User Accounts by clicking "User Accounts" in Control Panel.
2. Click "Manage User Accounts." If you are prompted for an administrator password or confirmation, type the password or provide confirmation.
3. On the User's tab, click the account you want to create a password for, and then click "Reset Password."
4. Type the password in the new password box, type the password again in the Confirm new password box, and then click "OK."

My Computer is on a Workgroup

1. Open User Accounts within Control Panel, clicking "User Accounts and Family Safety," and then clicking "User Accounts."
2. Click Create a password for your account.
   - Note—If your user account already has a password, you can change your password by clicking "Change your password."
3. Type the password in the new password box, and then type the password again in the Confirm new password box.
4. If you would like to use a password hint, type the hint in the Password hint box.
5. Click Create password.

Change your Windows password

You can help keep your computer more secure by changing your Windows password regularly, and by using a strong password.

- Press CTRL+ALT+DELETE, and then click Change a password.

Type your old password, type your new password, type your new password again to confirm it, and then press ENTER.

Create a password reset disk

If you forget your computer password, you can use a password reset disk to create a new one. We recommend that you create a password reset disk when you create your password, so you don't lose access to your files and information.

- Note, a password reset disk can only be created for local user accounts. If your computer is on a domain, a network administrator can reset your domain logon password.
- To complete these steps, you'll need removable media such as a USB flash drive or another portable drive.
- Go to the Control Panel, click on "User Accounts and Family Safety," and then click "User Accounts."
- In the left pane, click "Create a password reset disk," and then follow the instructions. Make sure you store the password reset disk in a safe place.

DEVELOPING RELIABLE BACKUP PRACTICES

Have you considered the financial impact of losing your data?
It is without a doubt critically important to protect the integrity of your data. Your data is your hard-earned "sweat and tears." It's your intellectual property. It's your lifeblood. Without it, there is no business!

Organisations typically have some form of regimented backup process. Having the understanding that should they require to recover their data, this could be effectively handled.

However, this is an area that most business pays little focus and then suffers loss of consequence when their Server/Desktop/Laptop/mobile device is:

- Stolen
- Damaged in a Fire, Flood, cyclones
- Server/Desktop/Laptop/mobile device is corrupted or system failure occurs
- Accidental deletion
- Virus infection

Why is that? Most businesses very rarely ever test their recovery. And when the time comes to restore their data, it's not available.

The following section will therefore discuss the various ways we can develop resilient backup methods.

There are many products and solutions in the market place to lessen the risk of system and data loss and we will break this into two distinct categories—Imaging and Backup.

Backup

Windows Vista and Windows 7 have their own built-in backup programs, which work quite well at backing up a computer from individual files through to total systems. The great advantage is that these are free applications included in the operating system.

For the more secure conscious organisations that require a more comprehensive set of backups that include virtual and physical environments, third party backup software solutions would be highly recommended.

Free backup tools

Microsoft provides native backup. It won't backup to a tape, but will back it up to another network device.

Window 8 has a file history backup capability that can backup files to any external media with full history and versioning control. Details on how to set this up can be found at the following website: www.pi10m.com/b1/6

Imaging

Imaging is a method where a total snapshot or imaging of the whole internal hard drive is then transferred to another disk drive. The great advantage of imaging is that:

- All data is captured, and it is very difficult to accidently omit a critical individual file from recovery.
- Should you have either a corruption on your drive or a hard drive failure, you can restore the image very quickly and be up and running within a few minutes.
- It is also a great recovery solution before working on a computer/server for quick rollback.
- Fantastic approach to migrate a system to similar or dissimilar hardware or virtual machines

Shadow Copy (Volume Snapshot Service or Volume Shadow Copy Service or VSS) is a technology included in Microsoft Windows that allows taking manual or automatic backup copies or snapshots of data, even if it has a lock, on a specific volume at a specific point in time over regular intervals. It is implemented as a Windows service called the *Volume Shadow Copy* service.

Windows 7 Imaging Backup

Windows 7 has a built-in imaging program called **Backup and Restore**. Go to the Control Panel, click the **Backup and Restore.**

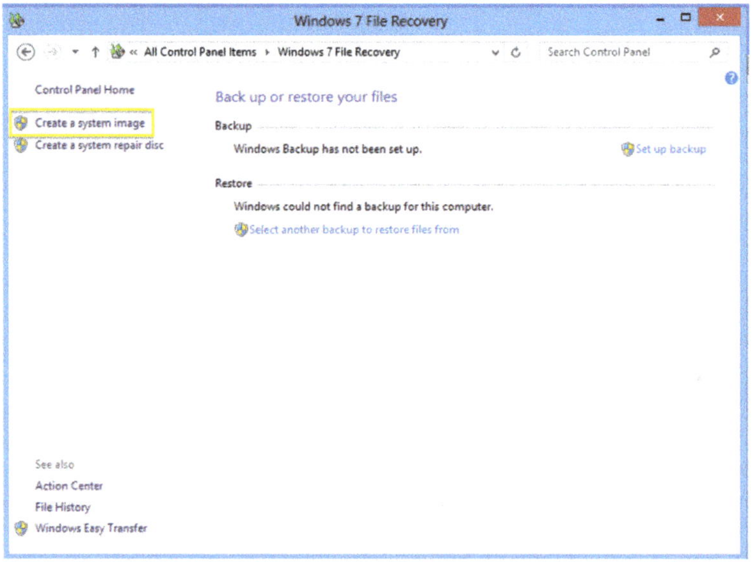

Click **Create a system image.**

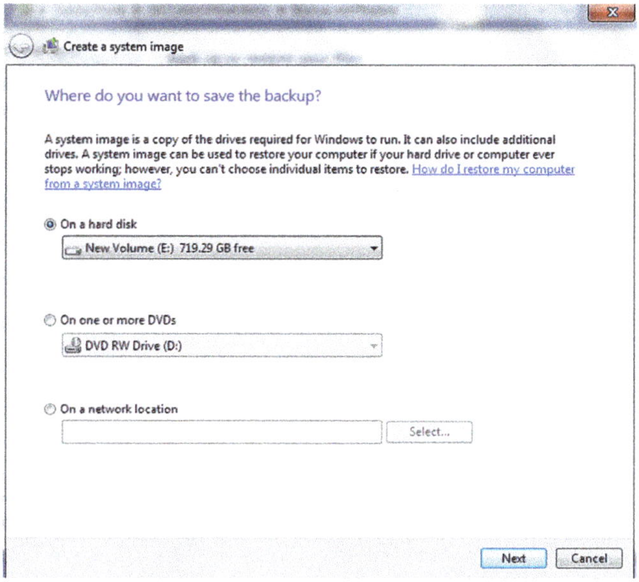

Select where you want the system image to be restored, in this case Drive E: Click the **Next.**

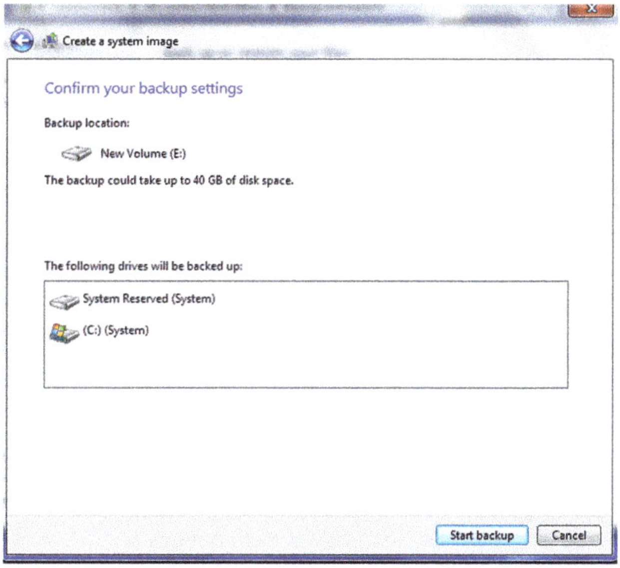

Click the **Start Backup.**

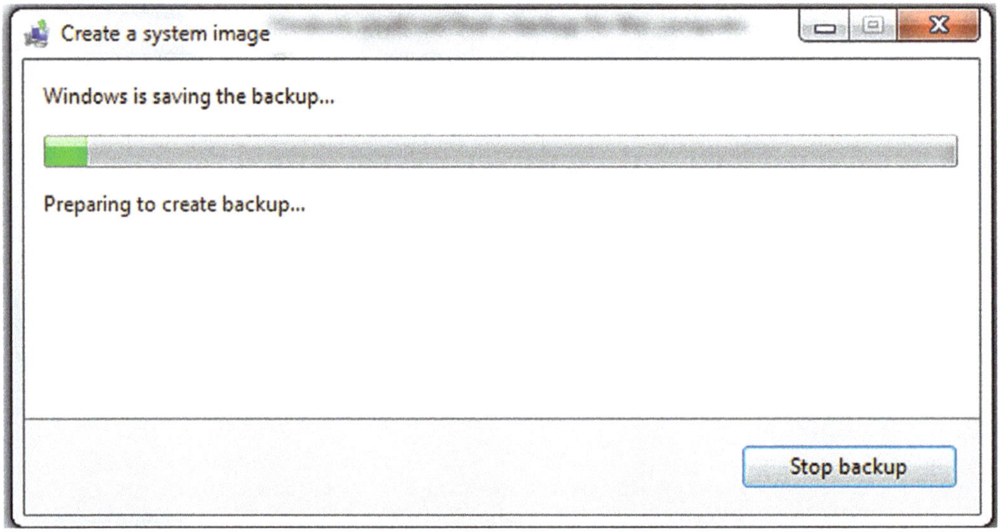

Windows 7 will start the backup. Once the backup is complete, you will be prompted to make a system restore disk. We strongly recommend you do so.

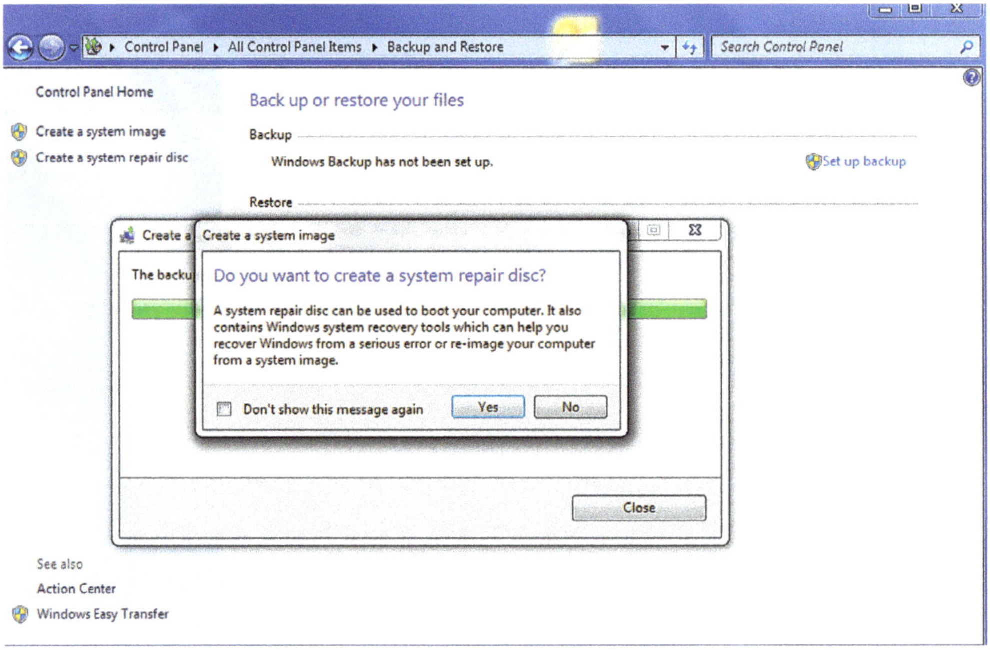

Restore from a Systems Backup

Open Control Panel and click the **Backup and restore** files.

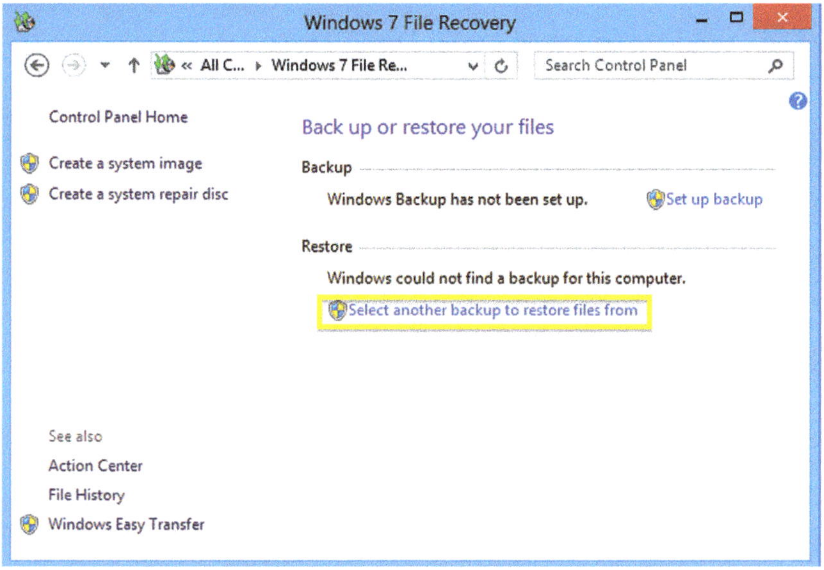

Click **Select another backup to restore your files from.**

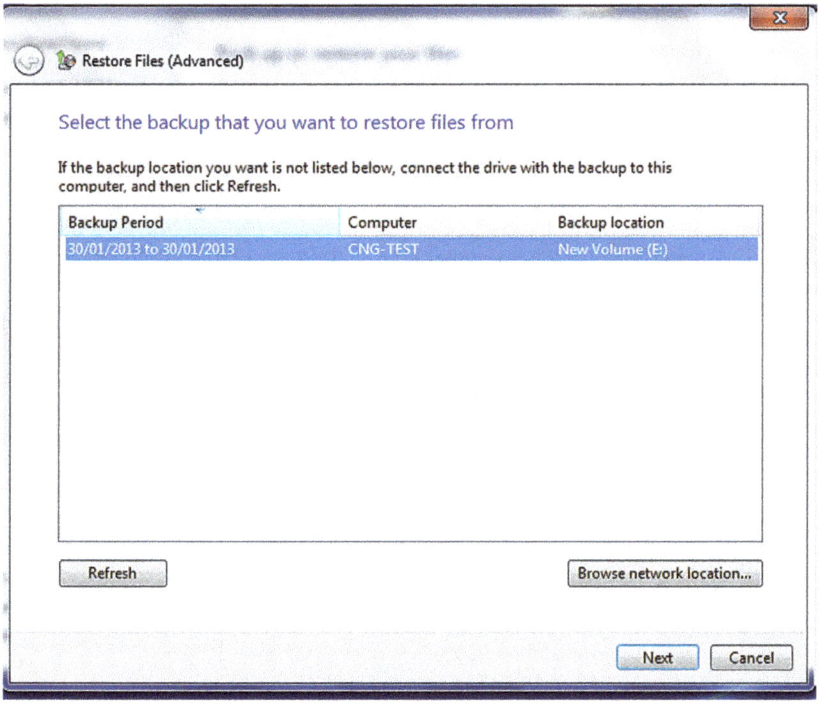

Click the **Next** button.
Ensure **Select all files from this backup** is restored and click the **Next** button.

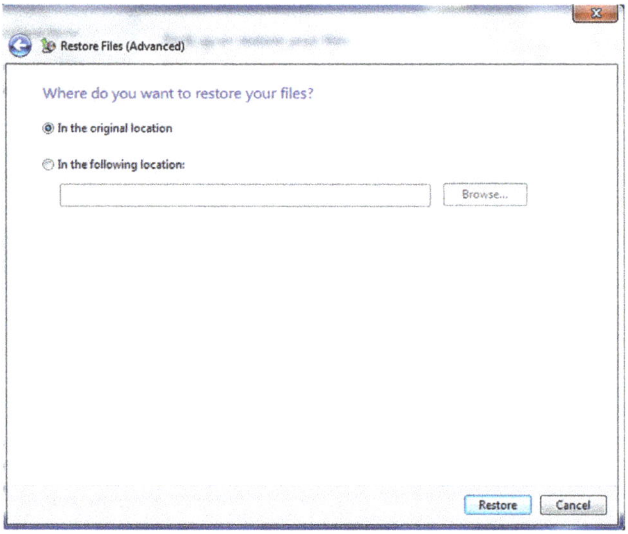

Choose in the original location and click the **Restore** button.

Windows 8 Imaging Backup

Like Windows 7, Windows 8 has a built-in imaging capability. Open up Control Panel, then click **File History**.

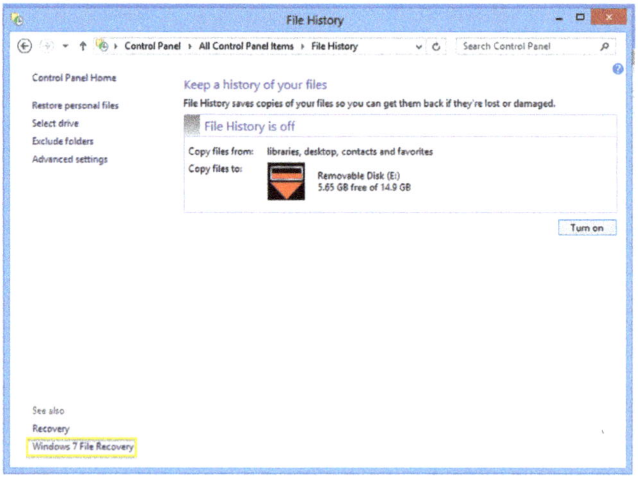

Next click on the button labeled **Windows 7 File Recovery.**

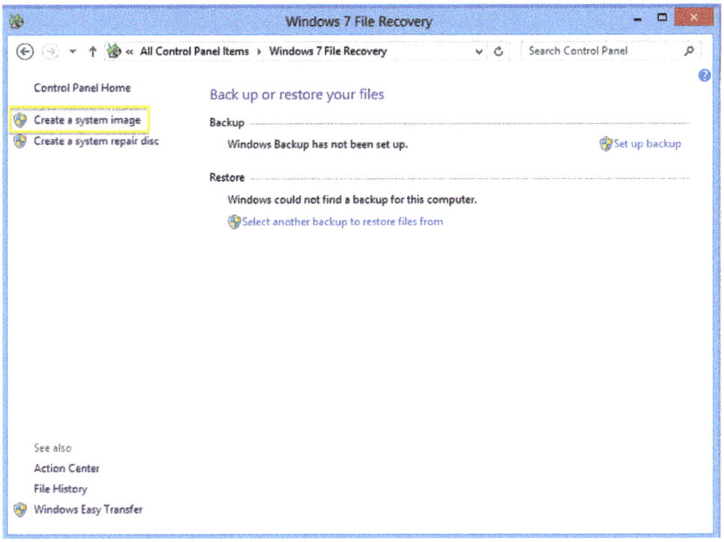

Click on the button marked **Create a systems image.**

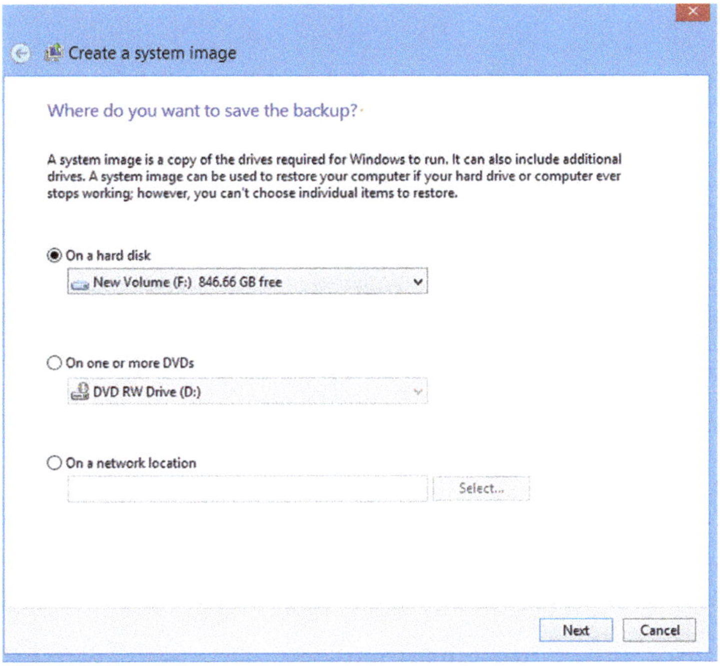

Choose the location you want the image to go to. In this example it is being saved to drive F: and click on the **Next** button.

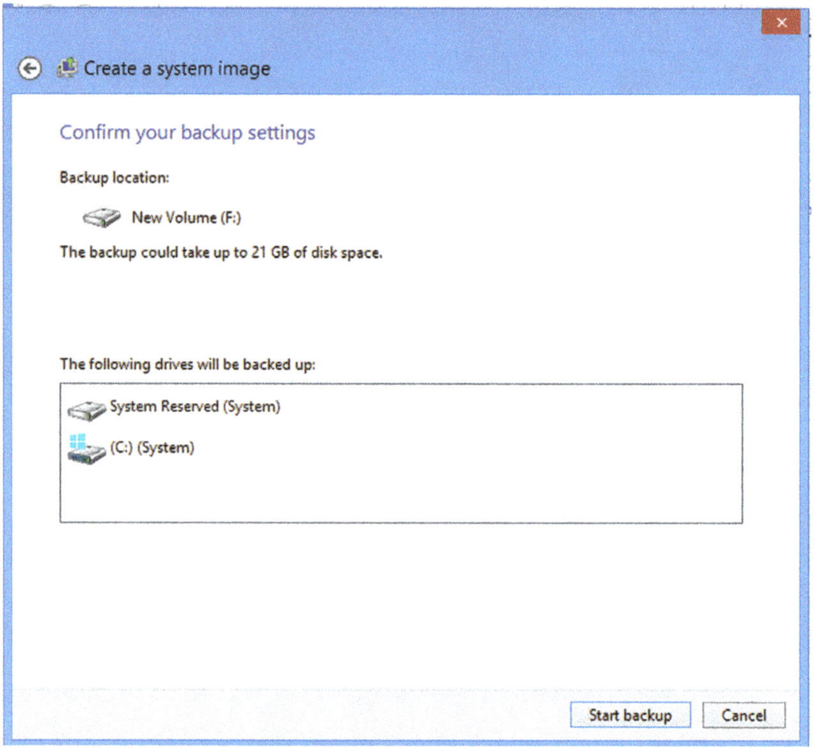

Click the **Start backup** button.

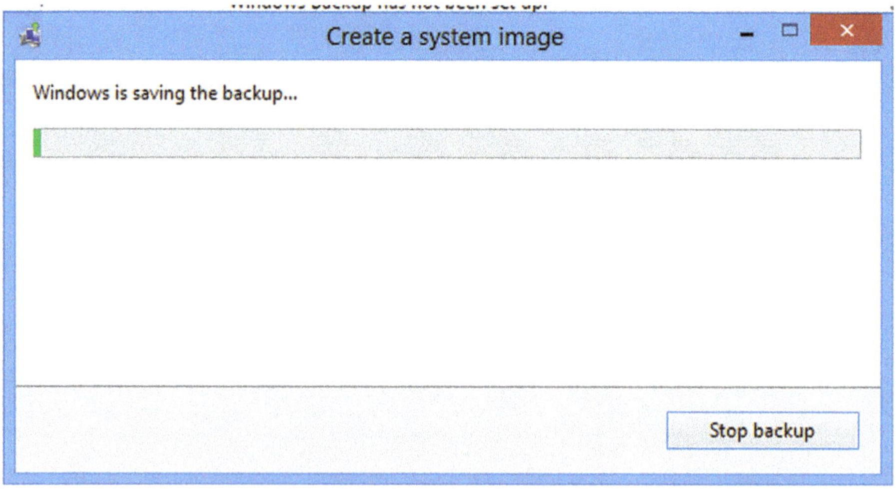

Once the imaging is complete, you will be prompted to create a repair disk which we highly recommend you do.

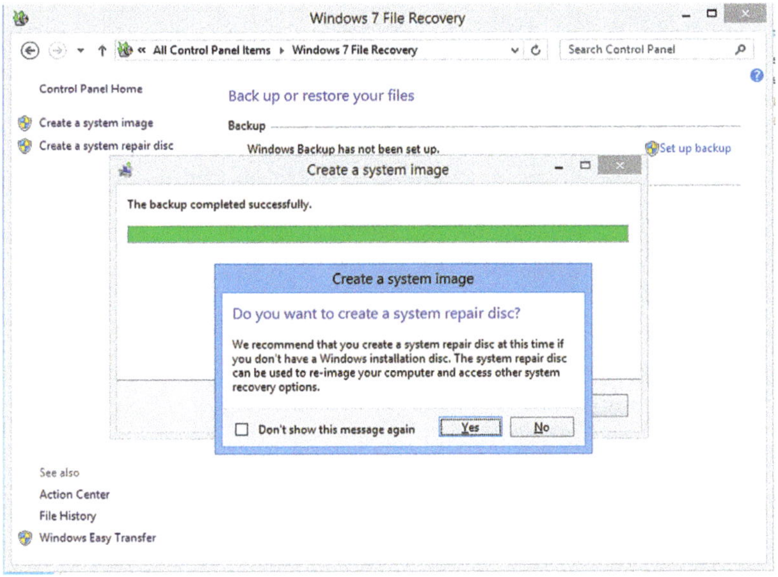

You have now created a system image that you can recover your Windows 8 system from.

Restoring from a Windows 8 backup image

Bring up the Control Panel and click the icon labeled **Windows 7 File Recovery.**

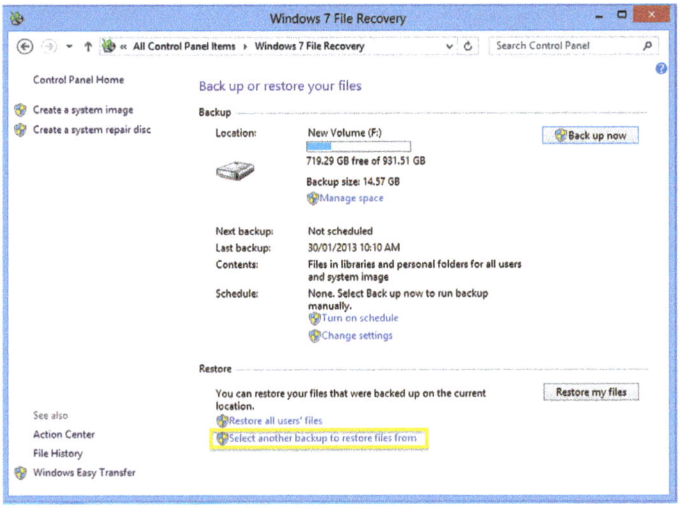

To choose a backup to restore from, click the icon labeled **Select another backup to restore from**.

This will scan all drives for backups and present them as a list to choose from. In the example shown here, there is only 1 backup image on drive F:

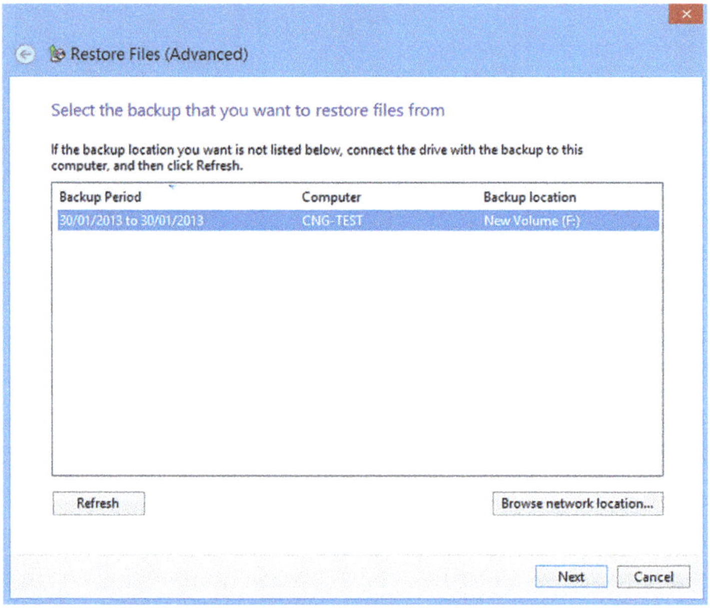

Choose the image you want to restore from and click **Next**.

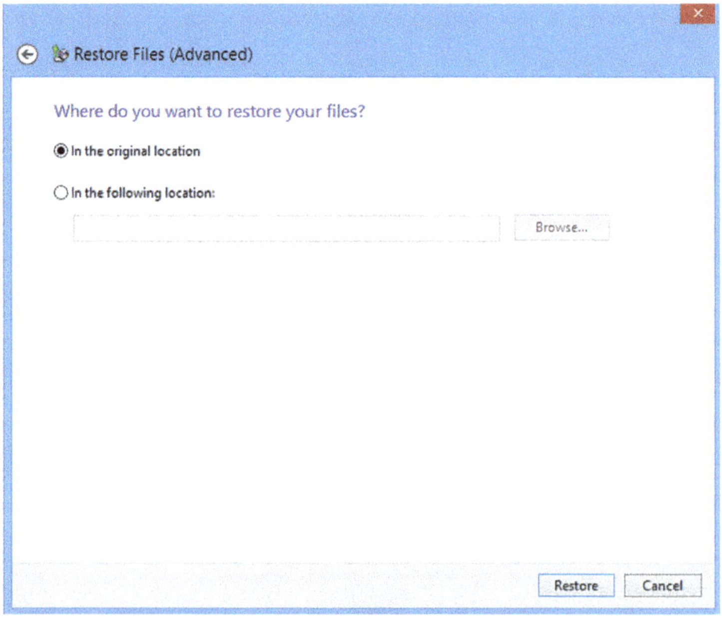

Choose where you would like the files restored from and then click the **Restore**. The file restoration process will then begin.

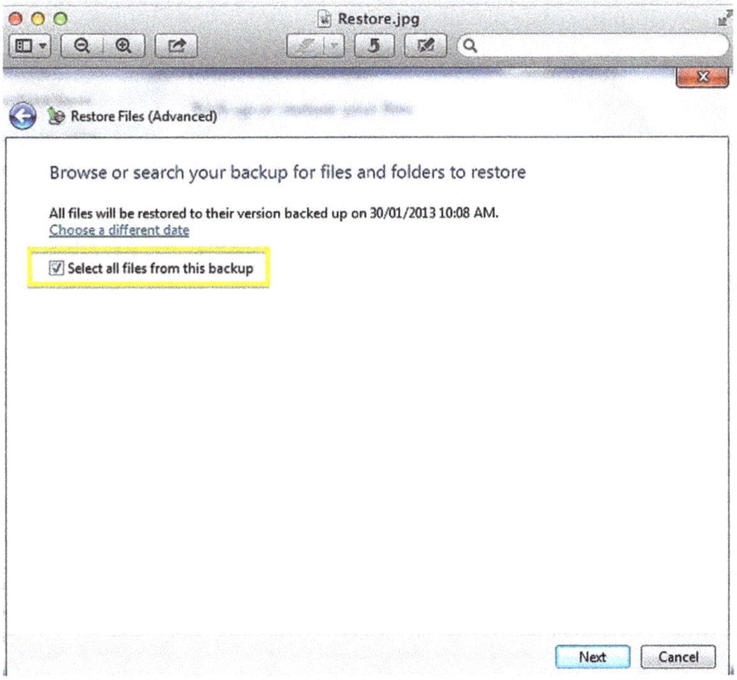

Click **Select all files from this backup** and click the **Next** button.

Offsite storage

If you are using media backup such as tapes, CDs, DVDs, it is highly recommended to store your backup media/device offsite (neighbour's/friend's house/safe house). If your backup is stolen or destroyed in a fire, flood, etc., then all data is lost in the typical scenario. Having offsite storage in another location provides you with a degree of business continuity.

Online/cloud—backup and storage

Online or Cloud backup service is a service that provides users with a system for the backup and storage of computer files.

Online backup systems are typically built around a client software program that runs on a schedule, typically once a day, and usually at night while computers aren't in use. This program typically collects, compresses, encrypts, and transfers the data to the remote backup service provider's infrastructure that can be located anywhere around the world.

Advantages

- Backups are stored in a different location from the original data.
- Backup does not require the end user intervention. No swapping out tapes or other manual operations.
- here is unlimited data retention.
- Client is not required to invest in expensive backup infrastructure hardware and software.
- Data restoration can be accessed at anytime from anywhere.

Disadvantages

- Depending on your bandwidth, data restoration can be slow.
- If the encryption password is lost, data recovery will be impossible.
- Your data can be located in various different countries which may be subjugated to their legal jurisdiction.
- Some service providers cannot guarantee that the stored data will be kept private.
- If the service provider goes out of business or is purchased, it may affect the accessibility of your data.

Testing

At the end of the day, it is all good to take your backup or image at a regular occurrence, but it is all worthless unless you test your recovery of your files/images on regular occasions. Do not take it for granted that your backups/images are working and have been backed up correctly. Always test! Test that your restoration works smoothly.

For the More Security Conscious User

Adopt the 3-2-1 Backup Methodology. For all of your important and sensitive data,

- Have 3 copies of each piece of data.
- Store these on two separate media such as tape and CD or something else.
- Have one of your backup media located offsite.

LAPTOP LOCKDOWN

With an increasingly mobile work force, there is an increasing use of laptops within an organisation and consequentially a rise in the amount of confidential data stored on these machines.
If a laptop is stolen, confidential data stored on the device is lost. There are numerous tools that can be used to minimise the loss of data when a laptop is lost or stolen.

Encryption

The use of full disk encryption on a laptop and a computer is the best way to protect confidential data. However before deploying a full disk encryption solution, please take care to store the encryption key safely. Modern full disk encryption cannot be broken so once the key is lost, so is the data stored on the laptop.

There are two very affordable disk encryption products we would recommend.

1. If your laptop is running Windows 7 Ultimate, then you have Microsoft Bitlocker available. Full details of how to use Bitlocker for full disk encryption can be found here—www.pi10m.com/b1/7

2. If you do not want to use Bitlocker, then chose either of the following:
   a) The open source program can be used to provide full disk encryption for your laptop. Details on how to set up full disk encryption can be found using Truecrypt—www.pi10m.com/b1/8
   b) Alternatively, some of the third party vendor's endpoint security solutions include encryption.

3. Windows 8 has Bitlocker built-in, and can be used as described above for Windows 7.

Tracking a stolen computer

You don't have to be overly careless to lose your laptop or for your computer to be stolen. The more you use your laptop, the more you have to lose.

Should it land in the hands of a stranger, they probably have access to your computer, and possibly have access to your email, as well as your Internet history, which probably contains details of where you shop and bank. The worst case scenario is that your computer will automatically log you on such sites, allowing them to fleece your money, or they could access Facebook—which is a treasure of valuable personal information.
You can protect your machine by ensuring that it is password protected—and even better, ensure that your data and system are encrypted.

Having said that, there are ways to track your stolen computer should the thief decide to connect your machine onto the Internet.

With the right software, your stolen laptop can seize the opportunity to phone home, delivering a wealth of information that could help you see it again. Alternatively, you can prime a service to destroy everything as soon as it checks into the Internet.

Many of the hardware vendors now include with their laptops a remote access service that allows you to login to your laptop remotely from the Internet and remotely delete confidential data.

An interesting software solution called **Prey** can keep an eye on the whereabouts of your computer and how the computer thieves are using your device, information that will be handy once you report the theft.

Prey can only track devices if you install it before it goes missing. For further information, visit the following Prey site: www.pi10m.com/b1/9

Guidelines

- Keep your laptop close to you at all times in public.
- Be aware of your surroundings.
- Don't leave your laptop in the car in full view of a passing walker. If you intend to leave your laptop in your car, then hide it and make sure your car is locked!
- If you are flying, do not leave your expensive laptop in a checked baggage device, and, be sure to pick it up when you are going through the X-ray scanner.
- Never leave security login details as part of your laptop bag.
- Keep track of your laptop serial number and model number.
- There are numerous tools that will allow you to remotely access your stolen or lost laptop when it is reconnected to the Internet.

ANTIVIRUS PROTECTION

Antivirus software protection is as important as ever in providing comprehensive security protection for your end point systems.

Antivirus technology typically are founded on signature-based and heuristic-based software. Signature-based antivirus software today is most common. The antivirus signature files are developed by security companies and look to detect and match a specific threat from infecting your system. Signature-based antivirus are effective somewhat, but largely reactive.

The problem with signature-based antivirus is that they are continuously losing ground to the thousands of new malware variants that are coming through.

And because signatures are developed from known threats, there is usually a lag when new threats appear, known as “zero-day” or “zero-hour” emerge. This lag can be several hours or several days and exists because when a new threat is released into the wild, it first must be captured, analyzed, then a solution developed, tested, and then distributed to your system.
In short, signature-based antivirus are becoming less and less effective in combating new threats.

Heuristic-based antivirus software uses a more proactive approach. Heuristic-based antivirus monitors normal operating system and applications behavior to determine whether unusual activity behavior may possibly be associated with a virus occurring; it then prevents its execution.

For example, launching Notepad in Windows should not normally open up in a stealth mode and start to transfer files on the Internet.

Many of the antivirus solutions today incorporate both signatures-based and heuristic-based strategies to protect against known and emerging virus threats.
In addition, a comprehensive end point security solution should protect against spyware, adware, trojans, and rootkits. These threats are often installed unknowingly on end points through unauthorised applications.

Microsoft Security Essential

Use Microsoft Security Essentials to guard against viruses, spyware, and other malevolent software. It provides real-time protection for your home or small business PCs.
Microsoft Security Essentials is a free software tool. It was designed to be simple to install and use. It runs quietly and efficiently in the background so you don’t have to worry about interruptions or making updates.

For more information visit the following site: www.pi10m.com/b1/10

Microsoft Endpoint Protection

Microsoft Security Essentials is available for small businesses with up to 10 PCs. If your business has more than 10 PCs, you can help protect them with Microsoft System Center 2012 Endpoint Protection deployed and managed—www.pi10m.com/b1/11

Common questions asked

Question: *What if I suspect that I have a virus or malware on my computer?*

➥ Use the Microsoft scanner which is a free downloadable security tool that provides an on demand scanning and helps remove viruses, spyware, and other malicious software—www.pi10m.com/b1/12

Question: *What if my computer has been successfully cleaned from malware, should I still trust it?*

➥ With malware, one never knows what back doors it has created and opened. It is highly recommended that you reinstall the operating system and associated applications from scratch.

Question: *What happens when I visit a website and I get a "pop up message" indicating that I have a virus on my computer from an unknown vendor, should I take it seriously?*

➥ Majority of such pop up messages are in fact fake virus hoax. And by clicking, you are thereby downloading malware onto your machine. If you are worried, scan your own machine with your installed antivirus.

Question: *Is my computer 100% protected from malware at all times?*

➥ No. New viruses and malware are constantly being introduced and security companies are extremely challenged to deliver a resolution to such threats in a timely manner. Take care what you do on the Internet; what email attachments you want to open; what USB thumb drives you use.

FIREWALL PROTECTION

Windows 7 Firewall Version

Windows 7 comes with Windows Firewall, a two-way firewall that is automatically turned on. It's as powerful as the firewall in previous versions of Windows (Windows Vista, Windows XP), but now it's more flexible and easier to use.

To configure Windows Firewall go to the **Control Panel** and click on **Windows Firewall** icon.

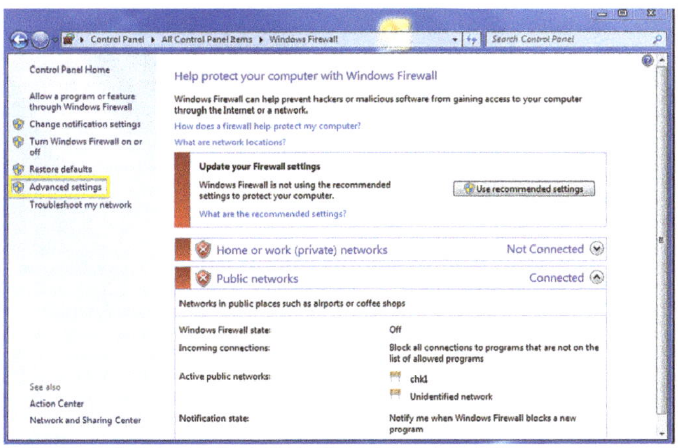

If the Windows Firewall state is Off, then click **Turn Windows Firewall on or off** and select **Use recommended settings.**

Click **Advanced settings** and from that page, you can configure the Windows 7 inbuilt firewall.

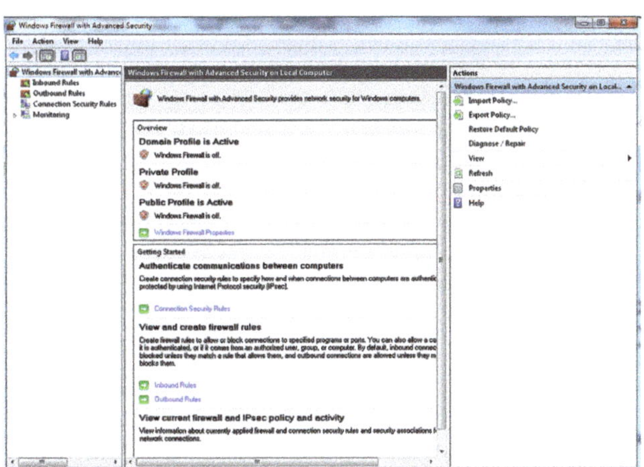

Note: You do not have to use Windows Firewall. You can install and run any firewall that you choose. Evaluate the features of other firewalls and then decide which firewall best meets your needs. If you choose to install and run another firewall, turn off Windows Firewall.

To turn Windows 8 Firewall on or off, proceed to the **Control Panel** as discussed earlier in this book and click the **System and Security link.**

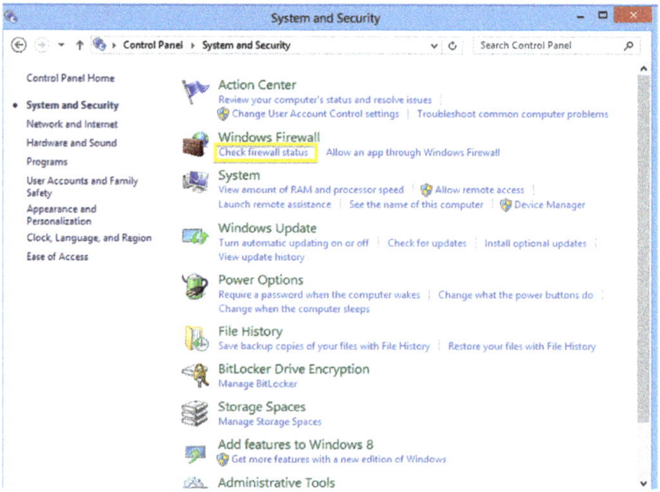

Click the **Check firewall status.**

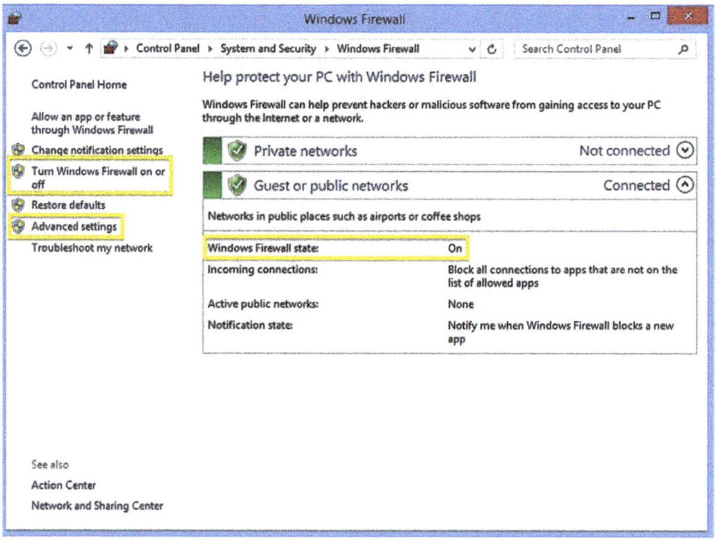

From this screen you can **Turn Windows Firewall on or off**. To configure the firewall click the **Advanced settings**.

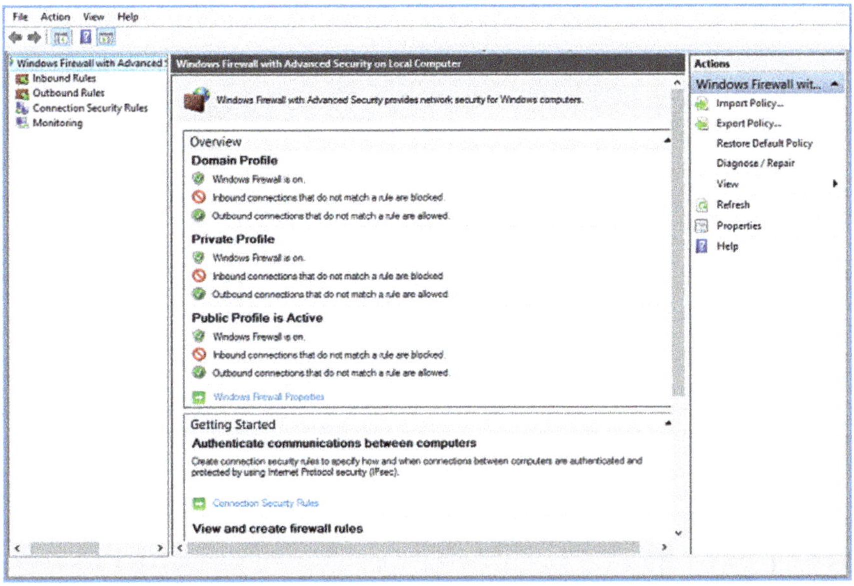

From this page, the Firewall rules can be customised.

APPLICATION CONTROL

Do you know what's running on your systems?

Most users have no way of knowing what exactly is executing on the computers. This lack of knowledge is a form of insecurity. If you don't know what's running, how do you know there isn't malware doing damage?
But then again, you would have thought that your current antivirus software should provide you with all the necessary protection? Right? Well, not really.

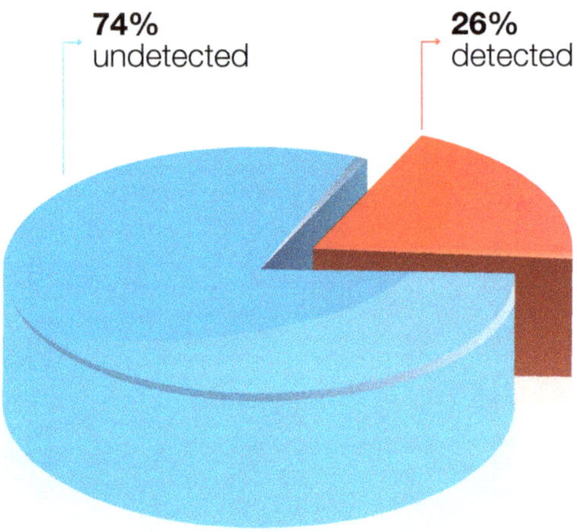

Advanced Malware Detection by Antivirus – Gartner—Burton It1 research. ID# G00208636—10 March 2011. "Application Control and Whitelisting for Endpoints."

In short, antivirus perimeter defences are struggling to keep up with the vast amount of new released malware.

Furthermore, antivirus signature-based libraries are growing at 50,000 a day, with current libraries anywhere from 6 to 20 million signatures. At this pace, basing endpoint security solely on antivirus libraries is unsustainable in terms of sheer volume and efficient endpoint scanning.

Yet, antivirus still plays an important protection practice.

Hence application control software is an additional control and measure to provide protection to your system and your business.

Application control blocks or restricts the use of unauthorised applications that may adversely impact your system or your network, such as instant messaging or file sharing.

These applications could also contain vulnerabilities that could be exploited to obtain entry into your business. Such applications could be a file, music, or movie sharing applications that could be unknown to you, but can be used to download gigabytes of data from the Internet, causing massive blowouts in data carriage costs.

Such applications can also be used to intentionally, accidentally leak confidential information out, or even steal personal financial information.

As such, Application Whitelisting is about identifying what application you want to run within your environment. Application Control builds on Application Whitelisting by providing you with the real time detection of unauthorised programs, visibility, and management of all your applications.

What can you do to implement Application Control on your machine?

Many of the security antivirus vendors have built application control into a suite of products, so you won't have to deploy or manage a separate product.

For the more security conscious organisation

Microsoft has developed an Application Control called AppLocker (not enabled within Windows XP or Windows 7 Home Edition). AppLocker helps administrators control which applications and files users can run. It is ideal for organisations that currently use Group Policy to manage their Windows-based computers. When would you use it?

- The potential that unwanted software can be introduced in your environment is high, so you need to reduce this threat.
- Organisation's security policy dictates the use of only licensed software, so you need to prevent users from running unlicensed software and also restrict the use of licensed software to authorised users.
- An application is no longer supported or revoked by your organisation, so you need to prevent it from being used by everyone.
- A new application or a new version of an application is deployed, and you need to prevent users from running the old version.
- Specific software tools are not allowed within the organisation, or only specific users have access to those tools.
- A single user or small group of users needs to use a specific application that is denied for all others.
- Some computers in your organisation are shared by people who have different software usage needs.
- You need to control the access to sensitive data through application usage.

Alternatively, there are some dedicated enterprise security organisations that focus on Application Whitelisting and Application Control.

WINDOWS 8 ADDITIONAL SECURITY FEATURES

Ever since Microsoft committed itself to its "Trustworthy Computing" program, each new version of Windows has introduced new security features and significantly improved its security posture. Windows 8 is no different, but this fact appears to be somehow lost in the coverage it has received, due mostly to its polarised view about its user interface.

So what makes Windows 8 more secure?

- Integrated anti-malware (Defender)—Windows Defender, which has been beefed up to incorporate the antivirus features from Microsoft Security Essentials, including an expanded set of malware signatures. Defender will only turn itself off if it detects an active third-party antivirus program that's receiving signature updates. While Windows Defender is fine for home users, most businesses will want to continue using their own more robust and more familiar antivirus solution.
- Windows 8 Secure Boot—Is intended to replace the traditional BIOS (Basic Input Output System) which provides protection during the system startup process to prevent low level malware such as rootkits from loading. As part of the Secure Boot process, an Early Launch Anti-Malware (ELAM) driver ensures that only known, digitally signed anti-malware programs can load, preventing fake antivirus programs from executing during the startup process.
- SmartScreen Protection—This has been a very effective tool for guarding against malicious downloads when using Internet Explorer. Now this extends to the entire operating system. SmartScreen will warn and protect you even if you're using an alternate browser, such as Firefox or Chrome, or just downloading a file across the network.
- Windows Store—The creation of the Windows Store enables Microsoft to better control the legitimacy of applications users can install. Much like Apple's App Store, all applications in the Windows Store are reviewed prior to approval.
- Modern Reader—Microsoft integrated document reader could replace Adobe Reader. This may unburden some organisations that need to deal with the Adobe standalone patching process.
- Dynamic Access Control—Lets IT admins restrict access to files and folders based on users and groups. The new Dynamic Access Control gives IT admins much more granular control, enabling access to be defined by virtually any Active Directory attribute.

Essentially, Windows 8 works on both touchscreen tablets and traditional desktops.
A business that wants to harness the new security features within Windows 8 properly, will improve their overall security posture.

7 STEPS TO HARDENING YOUR SYSTEM

We all have a challenge on our hands and that is to ensure that our computers are secure. One easy way is to harden our system.
Hardening your computer is an essential step for securing your personal information and data. However, many people do not know what simple steps can be taken to safeguard their systems

Hardening is usually the process of securing the operating system by reducing its possible vulnerabilities. Reducing available directions of attack typically includes the removal of unnecessary software, unnecessary usernames or logins, and the disabling or removal of unnecessary services.

Hardening a computer involves several steps, which are listed as follows:

1. Create a Non Administration User Account

Make sure that your Windows user account you use for day-to-day work, is not a member of the **Administrators Local Group**. This is because an administrative user account has full privilege access to your system. Should you be logged on as an Administrator, malware could easily install itself on your computer without you knowing. Therefore, you will need to create another user login that doesn't have administrative privileges.
In Windows 7, go to **the Control Panel** from the start menu, then click on the **User Accounts and Family Safety** icon, this will present a screen similar to the following:

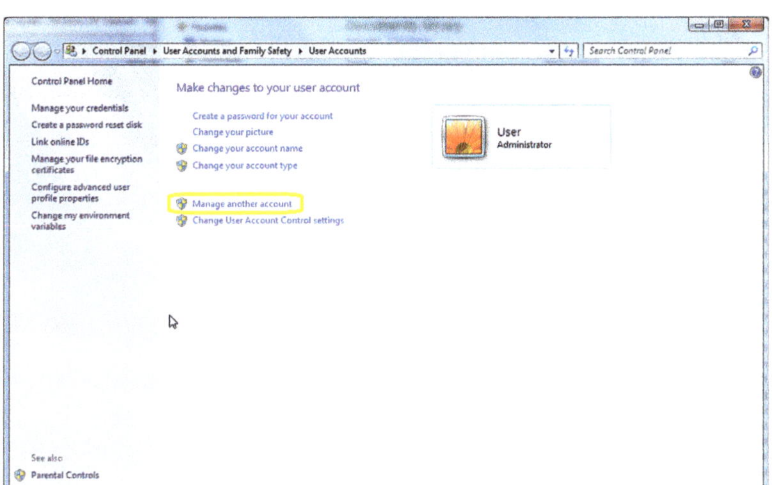

Click **Manage another account.**

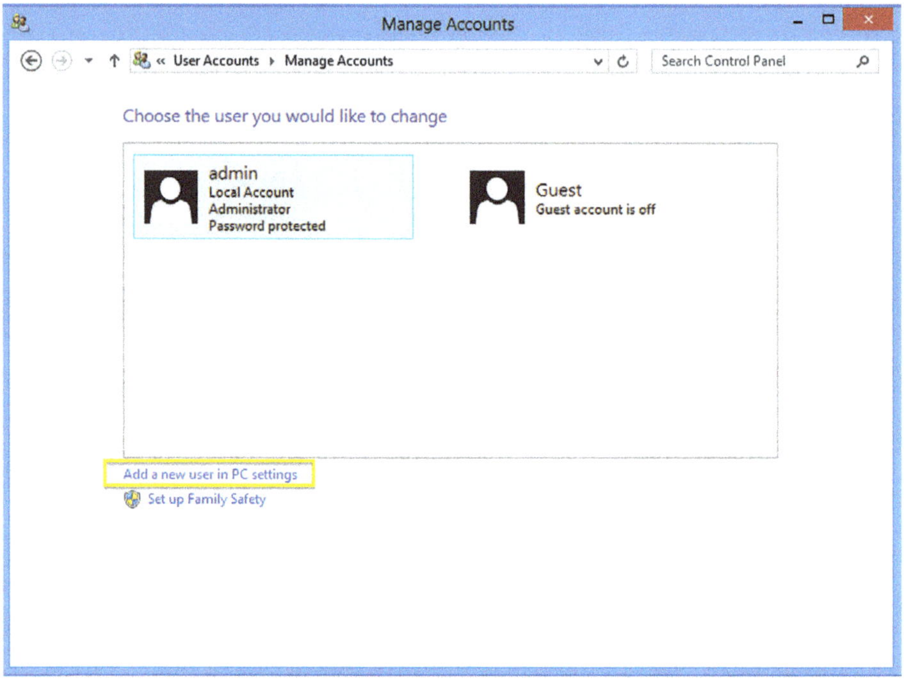

Click **Add a new user in PC setting** to create a new account.

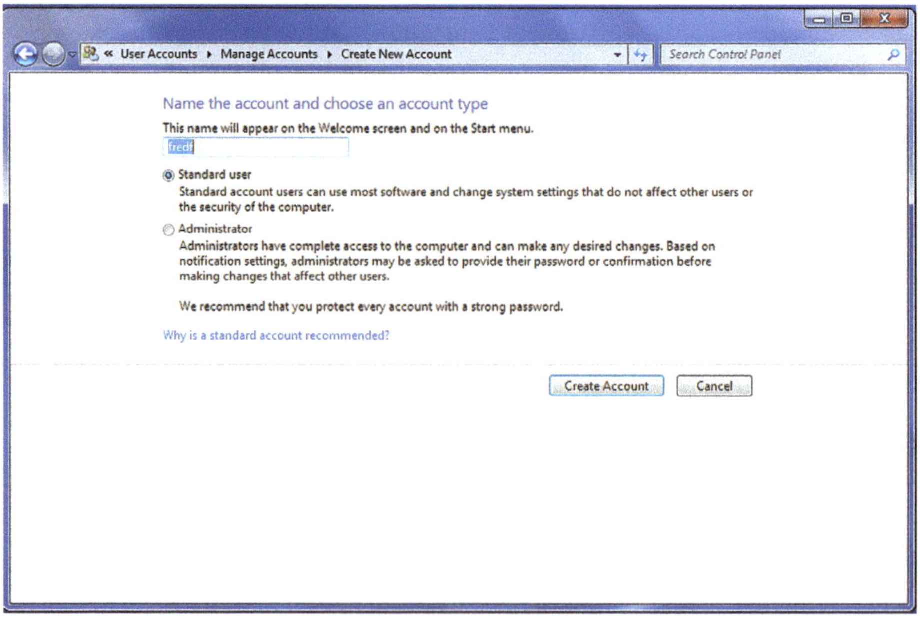

Enter the information asked for and click **Create Account.** This will result in the new user account being created.

Next you need to create a password for the new account. Once you have created the account, you will be taken back to the account management page.

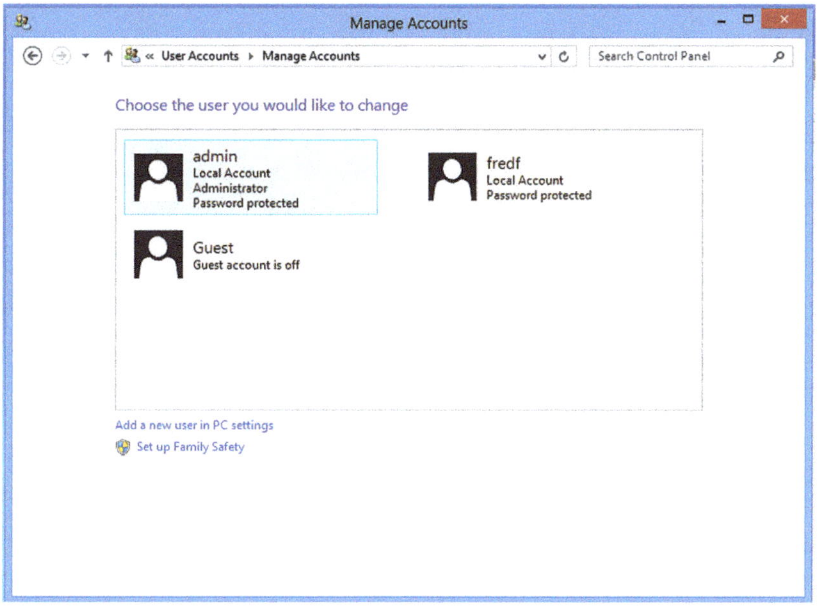

Windows 8 Account Creation

Open **Control Panel** and then click on **User account and Family Safety**.

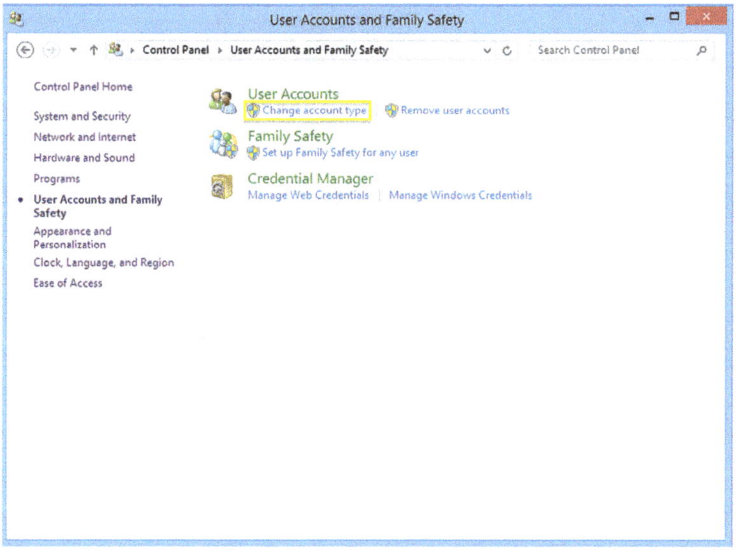

Click **Change Account type.**

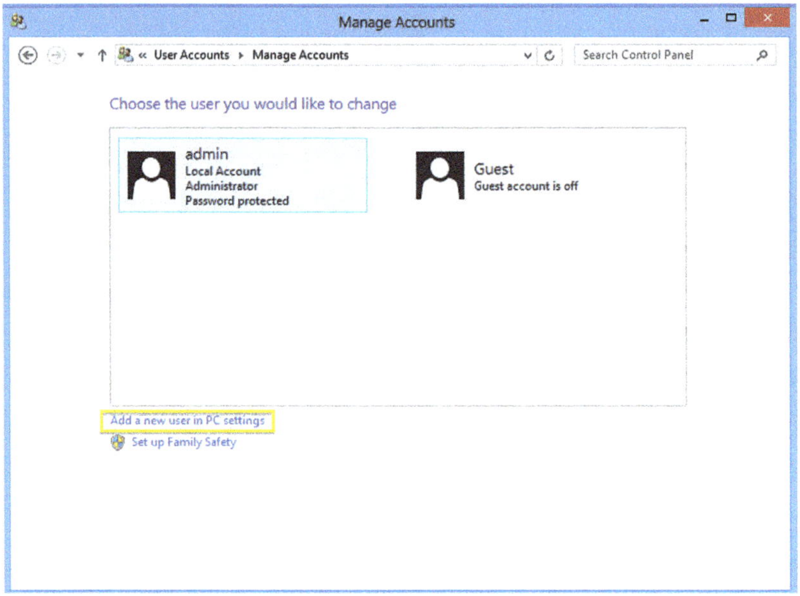

Click **Add a new user in PC setting.**

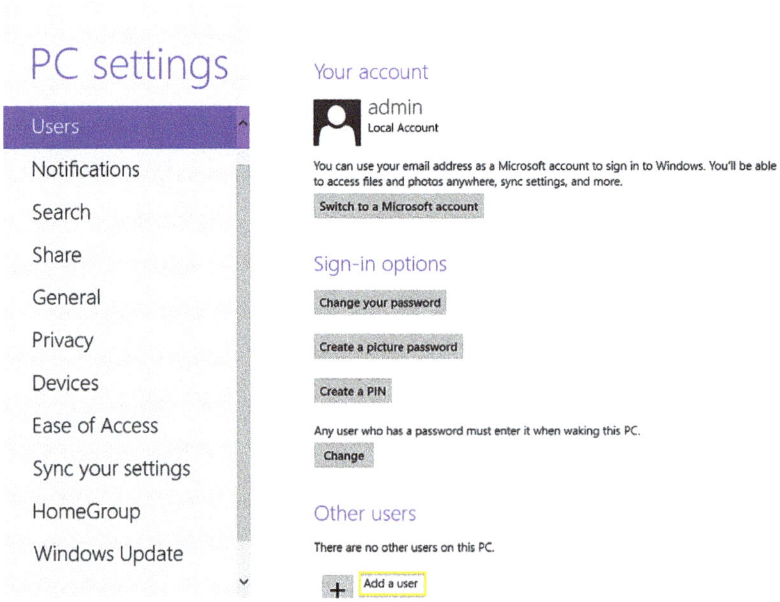

Click on **Add a user**.

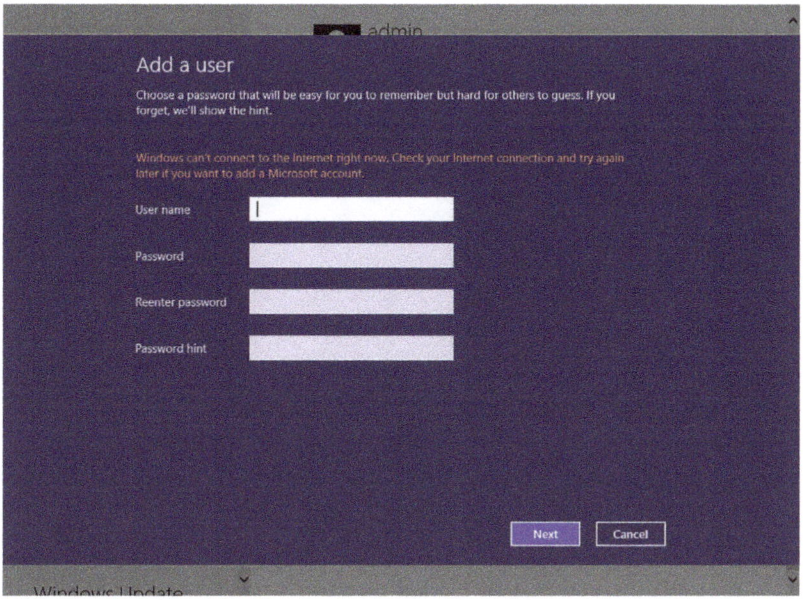

Fill in the details asked for.

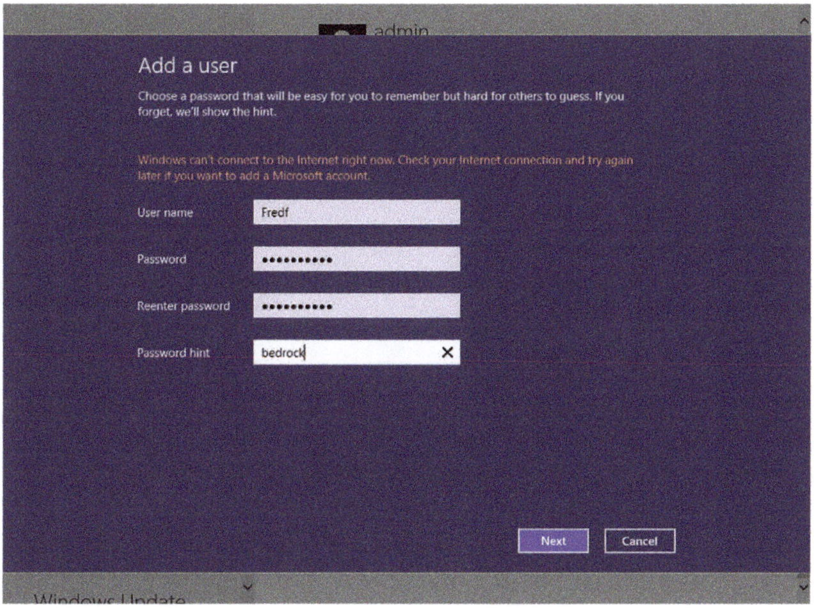

Press **Next** to create the user.

2. **Enable Windows and other third party applications updates.**
   Keeping up with the latest updates and patches for your system and applications can significantly help protect your machine.

3. **Enable Windows or third party firewall.**
   Enable a hardware firewall device or software that controls what traffic can travel from your computer to the Internet and from the Internet to your computer. It is one of the key elements in protecting your computer system.

If you do not need to share anything with other people and computers, you can safely choose to drop all inbound connections to make sure no one can access anything on your computer from the network.

4. **Disable remote assistance and remote desk-top connections.**
   If you do not want to allow people messing with your system remotely, that is, if you do not want to give other people the option to connecting to your Windows system and sharing your resources, you can specify that this will not be an option.

- Go to Control Panel
- Click on Systems. Then Click on Advanced System Settings as can be seen from the following diagram.
-

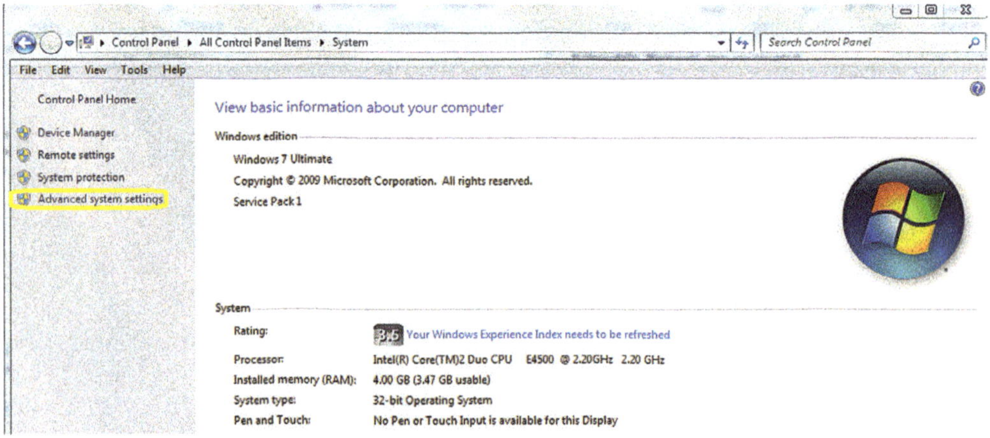

- Click Remote Tab and check Don't allow connection to this computer.

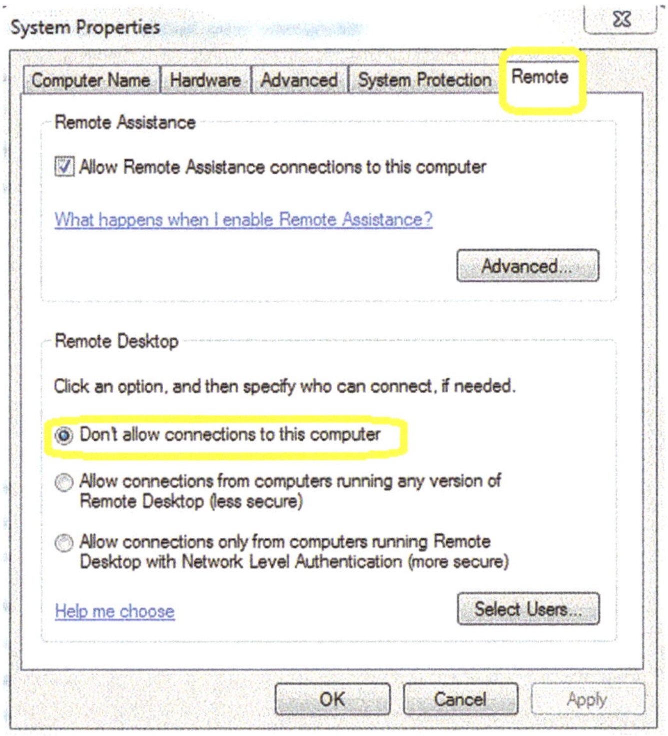

5. Change User Account Control Settings to highest level.

You might get prompted a bit more, but the overall security is raised as you will get prompts for more common administrative system tasks, enabling you to take a stand on whether you will actually allow the specific task to run.

- Go to Control Panel -> User Accounts and Family Safety -> User Accounts -> Change User Account Control Settings = Set to highest level

6. Disable sharing and the NetBios protocol.

If you are pretty sure you will not need to share your files over the network, you can remove the option to share files. Disable NetBios over TCP/IP on the network adapters on the computer. Remove check mark on Network and sharing, so that the machine is not using the 'File And Printer Sharing For Microsoft Networks' protocol.

- Go to Control Panel ->Network and Internet ->Network Connections
- Right click the adapter of your choice (if you have more than one) and choose Properties.

- Double click the Internet protocol version 4 (TCP/IPv4) Navigate to 'Advanced' and choose Wins.
- Check Disable NetBios over TCP/IP.

7. **Disable Bluetooth & Infrared.**

   By default, laptops and computers have Infrared and Bluetooth capability. This can be used to transfer files from one computer to another. All of these conveniences are enabled usually by default and an attacker could possibly take advantage without your knowledge if they happen to be in your vicinity. If you are not using these services, disable them.

Note of Reference:

What is NetBios? NetBIOS (Network Basic Input/Output System) is a program that allows applications on different computers to communicate within a local area network (LAN).

For the more security-conscious user

8. **Implement Application Control**

   Application Control blocks or restricts the use of unauthorised applications that may adversely impact your system or your network. This is about putting the appropriate policies of what applications are allowed to run on your system. It is sometime referred to as Application Whitelisting.

Application Control is software that typically is purchased as part of an Endpoint protection suite.

9. **Implement Device Control.**

   Consider using device control for all your machines. It will help you reduce the risk of data loss and malware infection by giving you control of removable devices like USB keys, drives, and wireless networking devices.

   Device Control is a software solution that typically is purchased with one of the security vendors that have integrated this as part of their endpoint protection.

10. **Implement Encryption.**

    If you have sensitive data on your machine, utilise encryption software to encrypt your machine from prying eyes.

7 SIMPLE STEPS TO PROTECTING YOUR WINDOWS FROM MALWARE

Interestingly Windows-based computers represent around 91 percent of the market at this point of time (Worldwide OS Market Share: December 2012—TNW). For this reason malware writers get more value in targeting Windows machines. Not only does a Windows virus spread farther and faster due to its numbers, but the people writing viruses are more likely to have Windows machines upon which to code—and the banks are running Windows as well, so Windows is where the money is.

Here are seven simple steps to secure your Windows from malware.

1. Ensure your Windows operating system has the latest updates

   Use the latest operating system version, which typically incorporates newer security technologies.

   As well, regularly update your system with the latest security patches to cover for possible high risk vulnerabilities.

2. Patch your applications.

   Like step 1, ensure your applications are regularly updated and patched, especially PDF viewer, Flash Player, Microsoft Office, Java, web browser, and web browser plugins such as ActiveX.

   Use the latest version of applications, which typically incorporate newer security features.

   I would highly recommend you keep an inventory of software installed on each of your computing devices. Any unrecognizable applications that are found should be a warning.

3. Update your antivirus software to the latest version

   Run antivirus software on your system and make sure:

   - It's up to date
   - Regularly scan your machine for malware on a weekly basis

4. Ensure you use a firewall

   Use a firewall to protect your machine and networks from unauthorised access while permitting legitimate communications to pass.

   Each Windows machine should have an enabled firewall.

5. Don't use administrative accounts for everyday use.

You should use a separate unprivileged account for everyday use. This will reduce the chance of your machine being compromised.
If you do intend to log in with administrative privileges, realise that if your machine is compromised at that time, it is easy for the malware to install its software.

6. Don't use guessable passwords.

Create a memorable password that is difficult to guess. This has been described in detail in section—Implementing Strong Password Practices.

7. Don't install random applications you didn't ask for!

Keep your wits about you and stay informed! If you keep clued-up about security threats, you are less likely to be tricked by a cybercriminal into making a poor decision.

Don't install random applications! If you come across a "pop up window" asking you to install a program on your machine that you didn't initially request, don't install it.

Exercise caution about the programs you install, the links you click on, and the attachments you open.

8. Beware of what you CLICK on

Beware of hype. Beware of amazing offers. Beware of astonishing or shocking news. Beware of requests. Simply clicking on links may inadvertently take you to a site that has malicious content.

Beware of what you click on! Have you heard of Click jacking? Click jacking is a malicious technique of tricking you into clicking on something different to what you perceive you are clicking on, with the potential of revealing confidential information or taking control of your computer while clicking on seemingly innocuous web pages.

For the more security-conscious user

9. Implement Application Control

Designed to protect your computer against unauthorised and malicious programs executing.

10. Utilise host-based intrusion detection / prevention systems

Utilise host-based Intrusion Protection Systems to identify anomalous behaviour such as process injection, keystroke logging, driver loading, and call hooking.

Some antivirus products are evolving to provide a full end point protection that includes Host-based Intrusion Protection Systems.

11. Don't use file sharing programs such as BitTorrent

BitTorrent is a peer-to-peer file sharing protocol used for distributing large amounts of data over the Internet. As of January 2012, BitTorrent has 150 million active users according to BitTorrent. BitTorrent has on average, more active users than YouTube and Facebook combined.

BitTorrent is widely used to transfer copyrighted music, movies, video games, books, and software which is unlawful. But importantly, it is a great portal of transferring malware between systems.

REMINDER! Don't forget to register at www.pi10m.com

By registering your details, we will be able to provide you with free updates to the book, critical security alerts, valuable security tools that you can start using right now for free, answer your questions and much much more.

SUMMARY OF POINTS

This chapter presents a number of considerations and attention steps for you to follow. They are not difficult. Some actions are automated. Some require manual intervention.

- Patch Your System — Ensure that your systems and applications are regularly updated with the latest patches and updates.
- Hardening Your Computer — Take steps to ensure that your computer is hardened, thereby minimising possible threats to your computer.
- Strong Password — Develop strong passwords. Longer passwords are better. Do not use the same password for all your access accounts.
- Make sure that you change the entire Internet-facing devices passwords. That means changing the "default" password on your firewall, router, and Wi-Fi devices.
- Regular and Consistent Backups — Backup your data regularly and on different devices. Get into the habit of doing that regularly. Test your backup to ensure that data can be recovered.
- Laptop Lockdown — Lock your PC with a password and consider encrypting your data in case you misplace your laptop or it gets stolen.
- Antivirus — Ensure that your antivirus software is up-to-date. Regularly run a scan against your system.
- Firewall — Make sure that you have a firewall in place.
- Application Control — Be aware and monitor the applications you are using on your computer.
- When not in use, close your machine down.

FOR THE MORE SECURITY-CONSCIOUS USER

If security is a great concern, here are some additional steps for your consideration:

- Adopt Hardening Recommendations as suggested in this chapter.
- Encrypt Your Data – Ensure that any data sensitive on your computer is encrypted. Any data leaving your computer is also encrypted. And if you are using a USB or any other mobile storage device, that is also encrypted.
- Image Your Machine. Develop strong backup practices which include daily backup of your data and imaging of your system.
- Daily, scan your machine for malware.
- Use a Hardware Firewall Device—Use a hardware firewall device unit rather than a software firewall. You want to separate your computer from the direct connection from the Internet and let the firewall provide you with the protection.
- Use Third Party Application Control System—Use third party software to manage and monitor what applications are being installed on your system.
- Cover up your webcam when not in use.

3

Protecting Your Apple System Guidelines

I want to put a ding in the universe.

– STEVE JOBS

INTRODUCTION

The mass appeal of Apple products is undeniable. Every product or software release is often anticipated and greeted with much fanfare. Whether it's a humble iPod Nano, or a state of the art Mac desktop, Apple gadgets reside in half of all households in the United States according to the CNBC survey published on the 28th of March 2012. As its desirability gathers momentum, it also became a target like Microsoft for cybercriminals due to its large amassed user base.

We can also expect other threats to jump ship and target Mac OS. Due to online banking's importance and prevalent use, online banking malware fraud will surely invade the Macs in greater numbers.

While the number of Mac malware isn't as high as those for Windows, this doesn't mean that Mac malware should be taken lightly. Like its Windows counterparts, Mac malware can do serious damage to an infected system.

This chapter therefore provides an overview of some the recommended features in hardening your Mac OS X. This chapter can assist you in securing your Apple computer. It does not provide information about securing Apple servers (OS X Server)

PATCHING YOUR SYSTEMS

Apple Mac OS X includes an automatic software update tool to patch the majority of Apple applications. Software updates often includes important security updates, which should be applied to your machine. The tool automatically checks what updates are available and, with major upgrades, can download patches rather than full installations, to minimise the amount downloaded.

It is best to configure Software Update to automatically check for updates on a frequent basis:

- Apple Menu -> System Preferences -> Software Updates
- Click Check for updates
- Choose Daily from drop-down menu

IMPLEMENTING STRONG PASSWORD PRACTICES

We all know that strong passwords are all that stands between us and a potential security breach. The number one most commonly used password is "123456," and the fourth most commonly used is "Password." Your own name is also a common choice. So any password attacker and cracker would try those three passwords immediately.

Other weaknesses are how users choose and manage them.

- Simple passwords—Short in length, that use words found in dictionaries
- Passwords others can find—On sticky notes on monitors, in a notepad by the computer, in a document in computer, whiteboard reminders, smart device storage in clear text, etc.
- Using the same password—Using the same password for multiple sites, never changing account passwords, etc.
- Shared passwords—Users telling others passwords, sending unencrypted emails with password information, contractors using same password for all their accounts, etc.
- Allowing your browsers to save your logins and basic information for automatic form-filling. This is convenient, but definitely not a secure option.

When a system tries to guess your password, the only thing an attacker can know is whether a password guess was an exact match… or not.

The attacker doesn't know how long the password is or anything about what it might look like. So after exhausting the entire standard password cracking lists, databases and dictionaries, the attacker has no option but to either to give up and move on to someone else or start guessing every possible password.

Choosing a good password is an important part of lowering the risk of becoming the victim. The following guidelines should help you when choosing passwords for your online accounts.

- Make your passwords memorable, so that you don't have to write them down or store them in a file on your computer
- Never use real words that a hacker or cybercriminal can find in a dictionary.
- Don't use obvious passwords that can be easily guessed, such as your spouse's name, your child's name, pet's name, car registration, postcode, etc.
- Use a mixture of uppercase and lowercase letters, numbers and non- alphanumeric characters such as punctuation marks.
- Don't recycle passwords, e.g. don't use 'password1', 'password2', 'password3', etc. for different accounts.
- If possible, use a passphrase, rather than a single word, e.g. "thisishowitisdone."

- Make the password long. Many sites enforce a minimum password length and often add additional requirements (such as a mixture of lower case, upper case, number and punctuation).
- Don't use the same password for multiple accounts. If a cybercriminal finds the password to one account, they can use it to access other accounts.
- Don't share your passwords with others.
- Changing passwords on regular basis is a good idea, but it is troublesome to remember. Suggestion: you develop a strong password manager instead.

The following site will help assess the strength of your password:

- Password Meter—www.pi10m.com/b1/1
- Microsoft Password Checker—www.pi10m.com/b1/2

The Challenge with Multiple Accounts / Passwords

Remembering a single password is relatively easy. However, remembering twenty unique passwords because you have a number of web access logins to various accounts is a tough challenge.

To make it somewhat harder, accessing your accounts using other devices such as a smartphone, notebook, and other workstations makes it even more frustrating. How do you go about managing all your authentications IDs?

That's why we would highly recommend you to use a password manager. A password manager is software that helps a user organise passwords and PIN codes. The software typically has a local database or a file that holds the encrypted password data for secure logon onto computers, networks, websites, and application data files.

Many password managers also work as a "form filler." They fill the user and password data automatically into forms.

Password Managers can also be used as a defence against phishing and pharming. A password manager program can also incorporate an automated login script that first compares the current site's URL to the stored site's URL. If the two don't match, then the password manager does not automatically fill in the logon fields to safeguard against visual imitations and look-alike websites.

Password managers can protect against keyloggers or keystroke logging malware. When using a multi-factor authentication password manager that automatically fills in logon fields, the user does not have to type any user names or passwords for the keyloggers to pick up.

Suggested Password Managers

- LastPass is a terrific password manager which is easy to use and compatible with pretty much every device—Windows, Apple, Smartphones, Tablets—www.pi10m.com/b1/3
- Dashlane is also a great password manager—www.pi10m.com/b1/5
- Some antivirus software providers have also bundled a password manager.

Additional Points

- Develop fictitious questions and answers when you are required to recover your password.
- Typical questions such as "what city were you born?" or "What was your name of your first pet?" or "what model was your first car?" These answers can be tracked down in time. To be more secure, create a fake persona or better still, use fake data. For example, to answer any of the above questions, you could say "The Pink Giraffe." It's rather absurd, but at least you will remember it!
- Make sure that you change your entire Internet facing administration passwords devices. That means, changing the "default" password of your firewall, router, and Wi-Fi devices. This is critical!

Securing Apple passwords

Whether you are using an Apple Mac OS X, Windows machine, or even a UNIX machine, having a strong password is critical.

Apple Mac OS X includes a Password Assistant, an application that analyses the complexity of a password or generates a complex password for you. You can specify the length you would like to generate.

- Apple Menu -> System Preferences -> Users & Groups

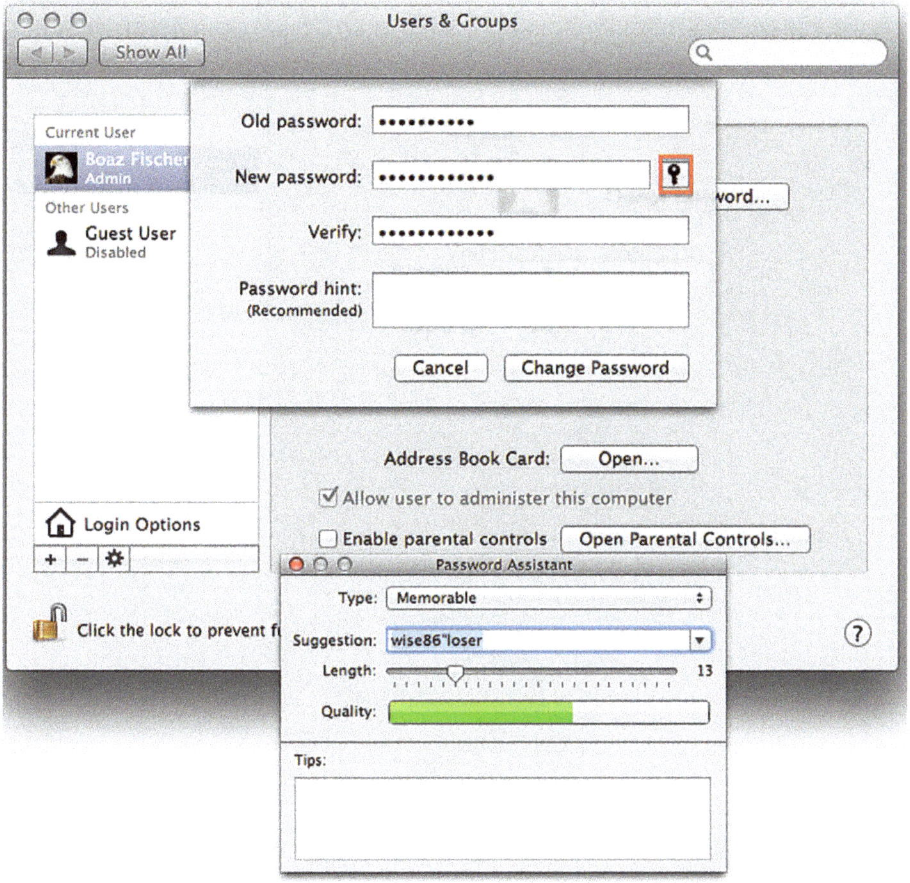

You should change the password of the first account that was created. If you are an administrator, you can reset other user account passwords by selecting the account and clicking Reset Password.

For the more security conscious user, consider the following login guidelines:

- Modify login options to provide as little information as possible to the user.
- Disable automatic login if enabled.
- Require that the user enter a name and a password and that the user authenticate without the use of a password hint.
- Disable Restart, Sleep, and ShutDown buttons. The user cannot restart the computer without pressing the power key or logging in.
- Lock your computer automatically after 15 minutes of inactivity.

As can be seen in the following diagram:

- Apple Menu -> System Preferences -> Security & Privacy -> General Tab
- Click on Advanced

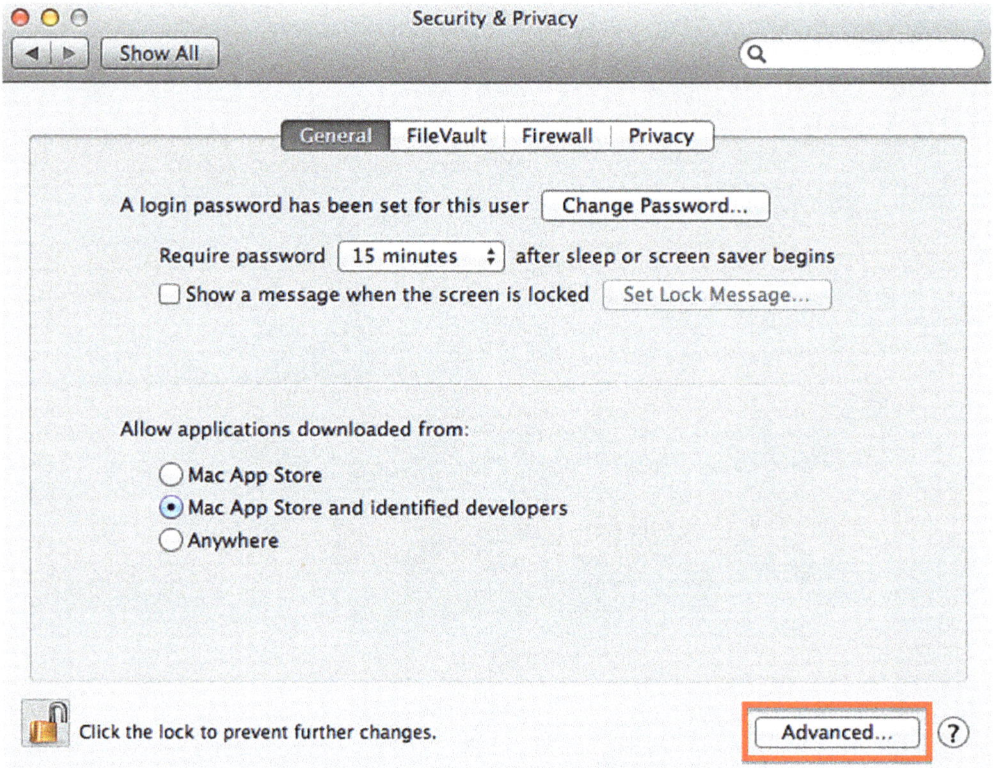

DEVELOPING BACKUP PRACTICES

Apple Mac OS X Time Machine makes an up-to-date copy of everything on your Mac and lets you easily recover the files should you need to.

Time Machine is off by default. After you enable Time Machine for the first time, no authentication is required and subsequent changes require authentication.

- Apple Menu -> System Preferences -> Time Machine

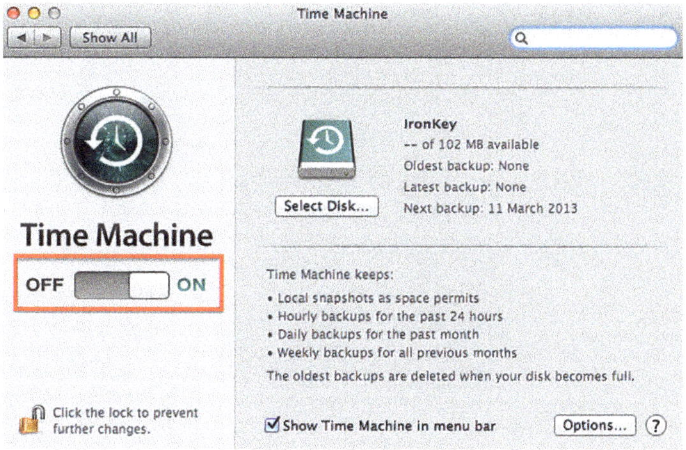

To enable Time Machine:

- Slide the switch to **ON**.
- **Select Disk** where backups will be stored, and click Use for Backup as can be seen in the following screen.
- Make sure you also select **Encrypt backups.**

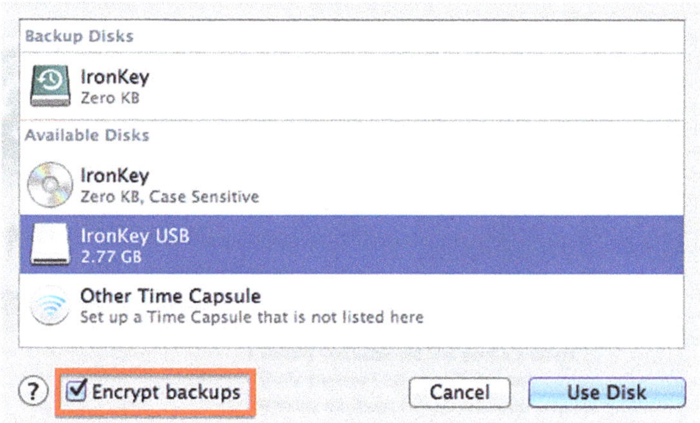

For the More Security-Conscious User

Adopt the 3-2-1 Backup Methodology. For all of your important and sensitive data,

- Have 3 copies of each piece of data.
- Store these on two separate media such as tape and CD or something else.
- Have one of your backup media located offsite.

IMPLEMENTING FIREWALL PRACTICES

Apple Mac OS X firewall is a software program that protects itself from unauthorised users. When you turn the firewall protection on, it is similar to locking your front door and limiting access only to known and friendly people that you know.

The firewall as such scans incoming network traffic and rejects or accepts these packets based on rules.

To enable firewall on your Mac OS X:

- Apple Menu -> System Preferences -> Security & Privacy -> Firewall tab
- Click **Turn On Firewall**

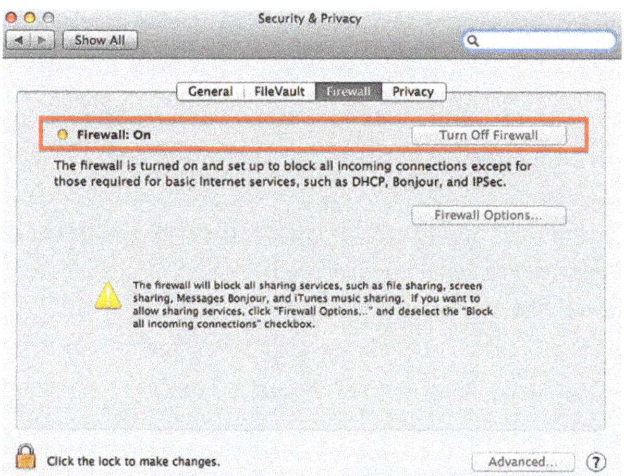

- Never connect your computer directly to the Internet. Always connect behind a firewall (software or hardware) before connecting to the Internet.
- Should you choose a firewall appliance, ensure that you change its default password.
- Should you chose a UTM as your gateway, make sure that it is properly configured.

Apple Gatekeeper

Apple Mac OS X 10.8 and newer versions comes with a new feature called Gatekeeper. Gatekeeper is designed to protect users from downloading malicious applications.

Gatekeeper gives you three security options. Just like today, you can download and install applications from anywhere on the web. Alternatively, you can choose the safest option and download and install apps only from the Mac App Store. Otherwise, use the default option, which allows you to download apps from the Mac App Store as well as those signed with a Developer ID.

If an app is unsigned, Gatekeeper blocks the app from being installed, and warns you that it did not come from an identified developer. If you're sure the app is safe, you can manually override Gatekeeper by Control-clicking the app and choosing to open it.

The default is the second option, which uses a signature system that checks with Apple to make sure the app was created by someone with a valid Apple developer ID.

When a user tries to install that app for the first time, the system will check to make sure it has not been previously identified as malware, has not been altered since being signed, and that the developer is not a known distributor of malware.

- Apple Menu -> System Preferences -> Security & Privacy -> General tab

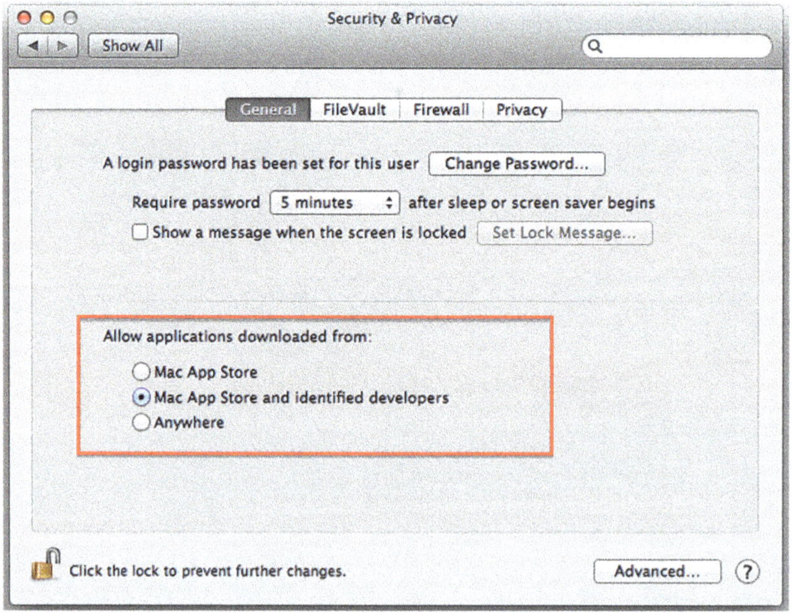

IMPLEMENTING LAPTOP LOCKDOWN PRACTICES

With an increasingly mobile work force, there is an increasing use of laptops within an organisation and consequentially a rise in the amount of confidential data stored on these machines.

If a laptop is stolen, confidential data stored on the device is lost. There are numerous tools that can be used to minimise the loss of data when a laptop is lost or stolen.

File Encryption

Using Apple's latest version of FileVault, you can protect the files on your disk from being seen or copied. FileVault disk encryption encodes the information stored on your disk so it can't be read unless the login password is entered.

If you store sensitive information on your computer, you should consider using FileVault disk encryption. For example, if you carry all your company's financial data on your portable computer, losing it could allow someone to access sensitive data that might hurt your business. If you are logged out of your account when your computer is lost but the data is encrypted, your information is protected.

- Apple Menu -> System Preferences -> Security & Privacy
- Click **FileVault** tab
- Click **Turn on FileVault**

When you turn on FileVault, you are given a recovery key. You can use the recovery key as a safety measure to unlock the disk if the administrator's login password is forgotten.

To ensure security when you turn on FileVault, other security features are also turned on. For example, a password will be required to log in after waking from sleep, and after leaving the screen saver. After the initial startup, only users enabled in FileVault will be able to log in; other users will need an administrator to log in first.

!

Don't forget your administrator password. If you turn FileVault on and then forget both your login password, your Apple ID, and your recovery key, you won't be able to log in to your account, and your files and settings are lost forever.

When you do decide to turn FileVault on, you have the choice to store the recovery key with Apple.

- For the inexperienced user, I would recommend storing your keys with Apple. Realise that this is a potential vulnerability.
- For the serious security-conscious user, I would suggest you to manage the keys yourself in a safe storage.

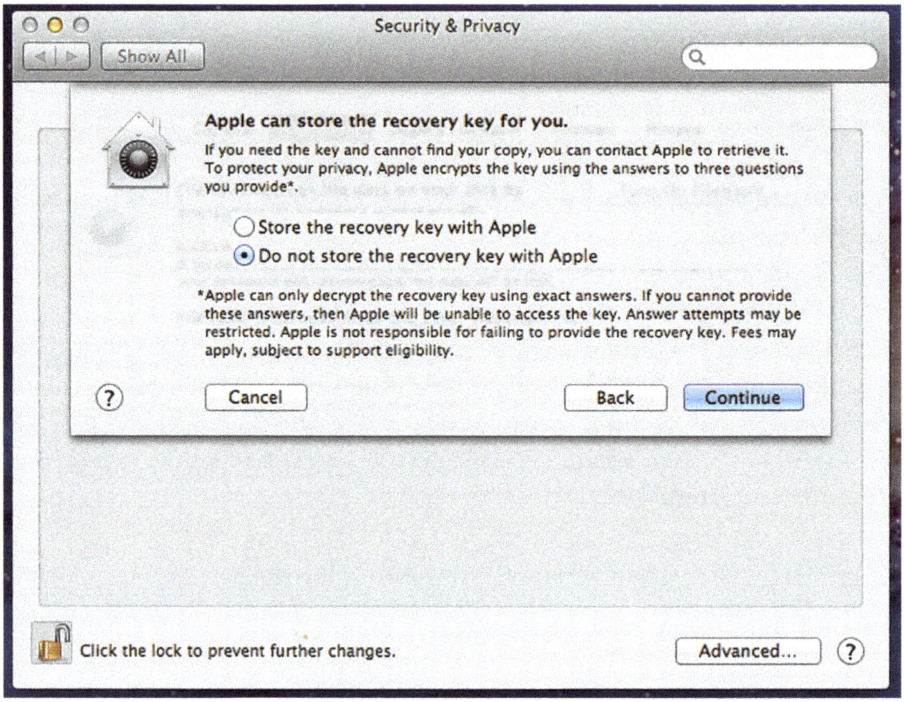

FileVault can encrypt any removable drive, helping you secure Time Machine backups or other external drives.

Another useful feature, FileVault makes it easy to clean data off your Mac. Instant wipe removes the encryption key from your Mac, making the data completely inaccessible. It then proceeds with a thorough wipe of all data from the disk.

However, FileVault disk encryption cannot be used with some highly partitioned disk configurations such as RAID disk sets.

Screen Saver

Mac OS X comes with a built-in screen saver that includes password locking. This should be enabled to stop someone from using your computer when you step away from it.
To enable the screen-saver:

- Apple Menu -> System Preferences -> Desktop & Screen Saver -> Screen Saver (select a screen saver)
- Change Start screen saver to 5 minutes

To require a password to exit the screen saver:

- Apple → System Preferences → Security& Privacy → General tab
- Check **Require password** to wake this computer from sleep or screen saver

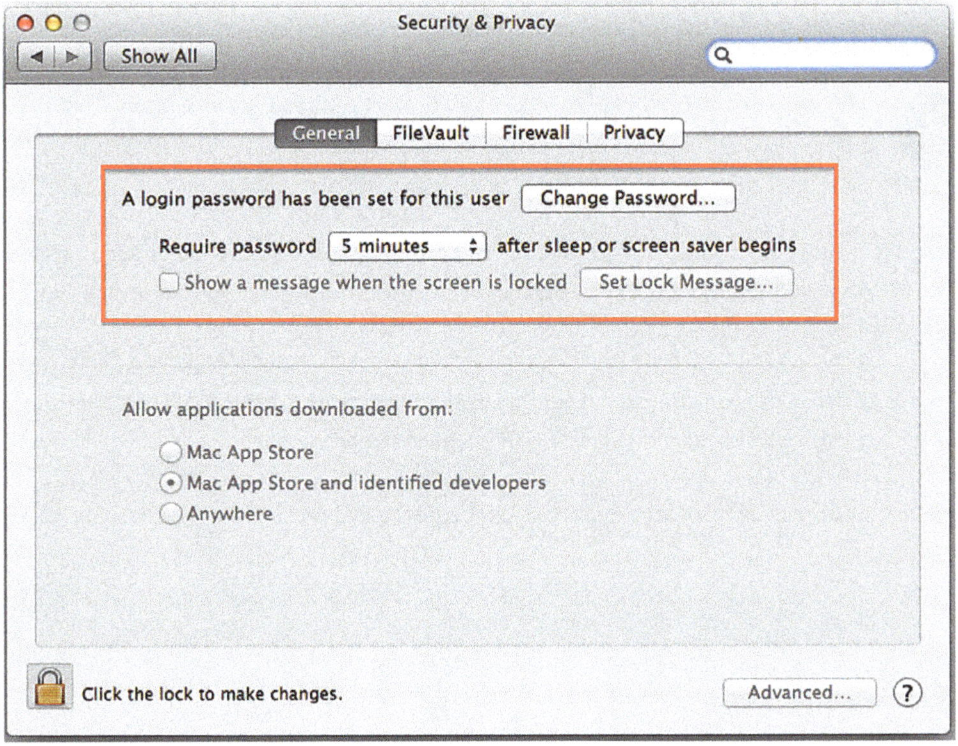

ANTIVIRUS PROTECTION

As Apple products grow in popularity, they're increasingly attractive targets to the "bad guys."

With the continual outbreak of new malware, a lot of attention has been brought to potential viruses and trojans hitting the Mac platform.

Should You Run Mac Antivirus Software? Good question. Typically, most Mac users don't believe that their Apple system requires virus protection, as they are impervious to any malware. But, such thoughts are based on false understanding.

Having said that, the Mac is designed with built-in technologies that provide protection against malicious software and security threats. It is important to note that no system is 100% immune from every threat.

Unlike most other software, virus protection typically requires a yearly fee to keep protection active. If you stay away from the "red light district" on the Internet, you are much less likely to get infected.

Antivirus implementation on your Apple machine is just one additional step to ensure that your system is further protected and is highly recommended.

There are a number of firms that offer free and commercial antivirus tools that you can take advantage of.

APPLYING ADDITIONAL SECURITY PRACTICES

This section articulates a number of additional security measures that can be taken.

Removing Other Local Users

To ensure the security of your Mac OS X machine, you should avoid allowing any other local user accessing your machine.

- Apple menu -> System Preferences ->Users & Groups
- Select user (In the following diagram it's Michael)
- Click the minus "-" button -> Deletes user immediately

Disabling Bluetooth

Bluetooth allows a user to wirelessly connect numerous personal devices to allow communication between them. Bluetooth achieves what is sometimes referred to as a Personal Area Network (PAN), allowing you for example to have your mobile phone, hands-free kit, PDA, and computer all communicating wirelessly.

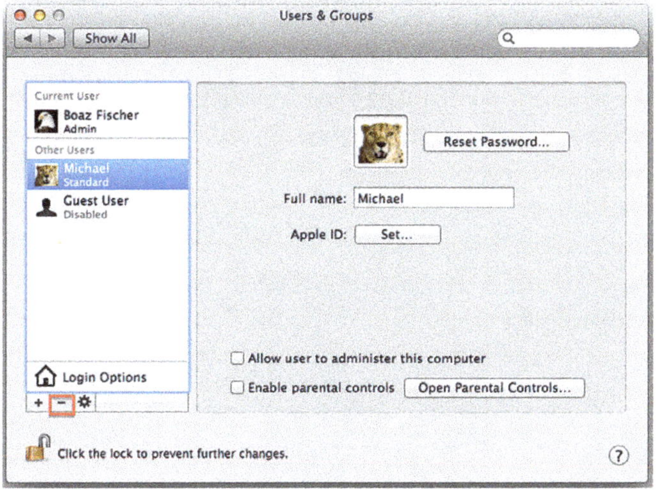

Unfortunately, Bluetooth has numerous security drawbacks. This section discusses a number of methods to help lock down Bluetooth on your Mac OS X machine.

Turn it off

If you are not using Bluetooth then don't have it on. Here is how to disable it.

- Apple menu -> System Preferences -> Bluetooth
- Turn Bluetooth Off

Should you require Bluetooth enabled, then your devices only need to be "visible" or "discoverable" mode when pairing them with your other Bluetooth devices. Once you have paired devices, you should disable "Discoverable." Paired devices are still able to communicate even when not in discoverable mode.

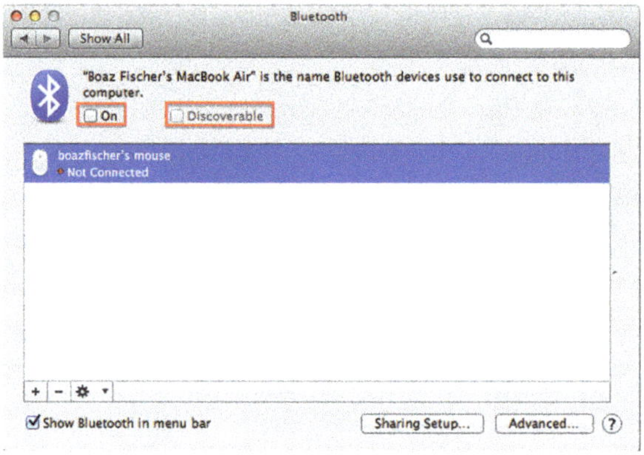

Disabling Services

By default, Mac OS X does not come with any network services enabled. However, some services may have been enabled unwittingly or by installing extra software.
By default, Mac OS X comes with all the **Sharing** network services turned off. However, some users may have enabled services unnecessarily.

To disable all services:

- Apple menu -> System Preferences -> Sharing
- Uncheck any checked service

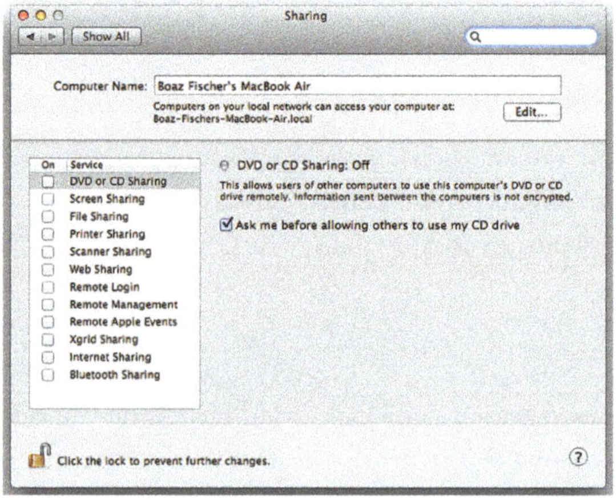

7 SIMPLE STEPS TO SECURING YOUR APPLE MAC FROM MALWARE

Wait, aren't Macs supposed to be immune from malware?
With the "Flashback" attacks targeting Macs, these have simply shown that it is possible to infect Mac systems.

Sophos (a well-credited security company) stated findings in their regular blog site—nakedsecurity.sophos.com—on April the 24th 2012, that approximately 1 in 36 Mac systems (2.7%) were found to have OS X based malware on their systems.

Malware can spread onto Macs via USB drives, email attachments, website download, or even a silent drive by installation where the user doesn't realise their Mac's security has been subverted.

Sadly, cybercriminals view Macs as a soft target, because their owners are less likely to be running antivirus software. "Bad guys" may also believe that Mac users are likely to have a higher level of disposable income than the typical Windows user. So, they might believe the potential for return is much higher.

Here are seven simple steps to secure a Mac from malware.

1. Ensure that your OS X and applications are at the latest version.
   Apple regularly issues Security Updates and many third party applications do as well. Therefore regularly updating both your OS X System Software and OS X apps is one of the single best preventative measures you can take to keep a Mac secure.

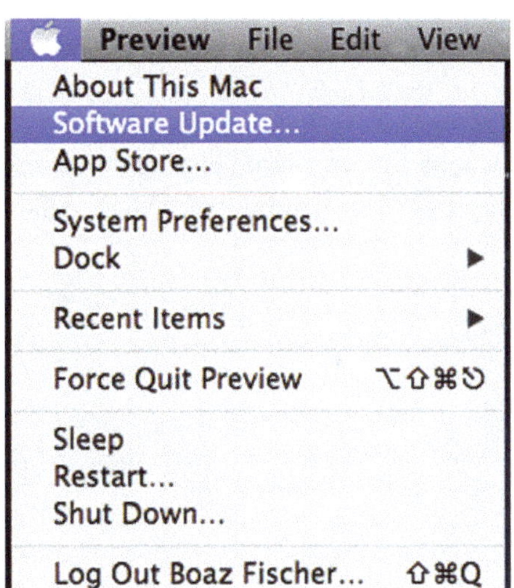

2. Update your antivirus software to the latest version

Run antivirus software on your system and make sure

- It's up to date.
- Regularly scan your machine for malware on a weekly basis.

3. Ensure Your Firewall is Turned On

Ensure that your firewall is turned on. This should provide you with immediate protection against incoming connections, except for those required for basic Internet services.

4. Disable Automatic File Opening

Safari defaults to automatically opening "safe" files after they're downloaded. For added security, disable this feature and manage the opening of downloads yourself:

- Open Safari Preferences and click the General tab
- Uncheck the box next to "Open 'safe' files after downloading

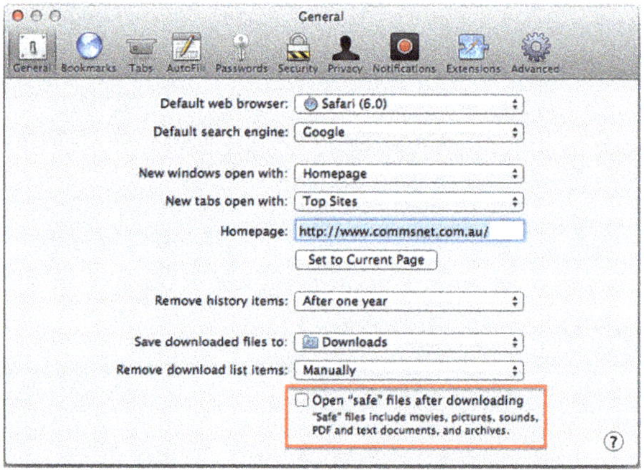

5. Enable Automatic Update of Safe List

Apple keeps an updated list of unsafe malware that may try to compromise the security of your computer. Your computer is set, by default, to automatically update this information.

- Apple menu -> System Preferences -> Security & Privacy
- Under the General Tab, click **Advanced**—You will need to authenticate first…

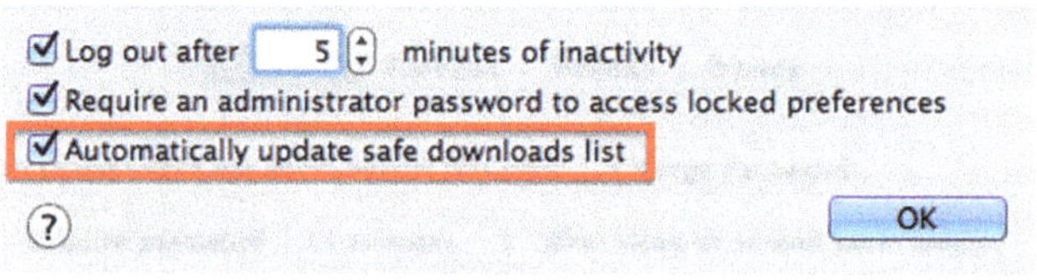

6. Don't install random applications you didn't ask for!

Keep your wits about you and stay informed! If you keep clued-up about security threats, you are less likely to be tricked by a cybercriminal into making a poor decision.

Don't install random applications! If you come across a "pop up window" asking you to install a program on your machine that you didn't initially request, don't install it.

Exercise caution about the programs you install, the links you click on, and the attachments you open.

7. Beware of What You CLICK

Beware of hype. Beware of amazing offers. Beware of astonishing or shocking news. Beware of requests. Beware of simply clicking on links because they may inadvertently take you to a site that has malicious content.

Beware of what you click on! Have you heard of Clickjacking? Clickjacking is a malicious technique of tricking you into clicking on something different to what you perceive you are clicking on, with the potentially revealing confidential information or taking control of your computer while clicking on seemingly innocuous web pages.

For The More Security-Conscious User

8. Disable Adobe Flash

Flash has been used as an attack vector in the past, and Macs stopped shipping with Flash installed for a reason. Flash is typically used for video and games. It is prone to security breaches.

- Open Safari
- From the Safari menu tab, click **Preferences**
- Click **Extensions** as can be seen from the following diagram.
- Then click **Get Extensions**. These plugins are free and available for every major browser. For Apple Safari visit the following website —https://extensions.apple.com

I will recommend using a Flash block plugin for your web browser. This causes all Flash to be disabled by default until you click to allow individual plugins and instances of the Flash plugin to run, preventing unauthorised Flash, from running in a web browser completely.

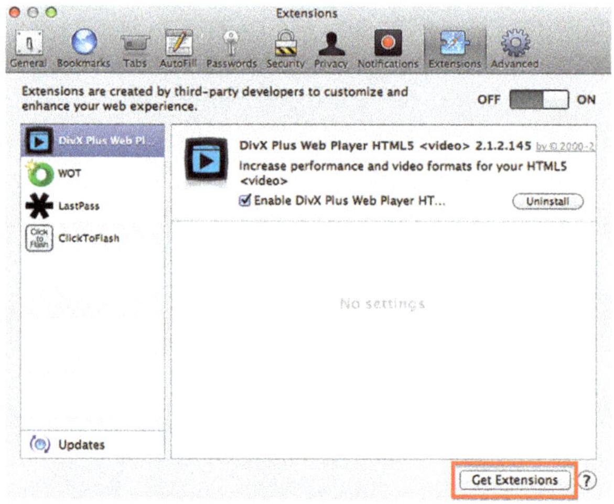

9. **Disable Java**

Java is a set of several computer software products and specifications from Oracle Corporation that together provide a system for developing application software. Java is used in a wide variety of computing platforms from embedded devices and mobile phones on the low end, to enterprise servers and supercomputers on the high end. Java applets are sometimes used to provide improved and secure functions while browsing the World Wide Web.

In 2010, targeting of Java security exploits increased significantly, resulting in Java becoming a common target.

Most typical users won't need java installed on their Mac, let alone on their web browser. I would therefore highly recommend disabling it.

Disabling Java in Safari

- Open Safari and pull down the Safari menu, selecting **Preferences**
- Click on the **Security** tab and uncheck the box next to **Enable Java** and **Enable JavaScript**

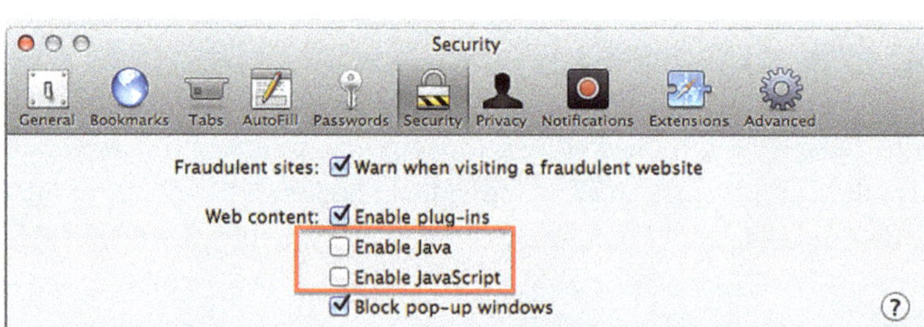

REMINDER! Don't forget to register at www.pi10m.com

By registering your details, we will be able to provide you with free updates to the book, critical security alerts, valuable security tools that you can start using right now for free, answer your questions and much much more.

SUMMARY OF POINTS

This chapter presents a number of considerations and attention steps for you to follow. They are not difficult. Some actions are automated. Some may require manual intervention.

- **Patch Your System** — Ensure that your systems and applications are regularly updated with the latest patches and updates.
- **Set Strong Password** — Longer passwords are better. Do not use the same password for all your access accounts.
- Also make sure that you change your entire Internet facing passwords. That means changing your "default" password on your firewall, router, and Wi-Fiappliances.
- **Regular and Consistent Backups** — Backup your data regularly and on different devices. Get into the habit of doing that regularly. Test your backup to ensure that data can be recovered.
- **Laptop Lockdown** — Encrypt your machine either using Mac OS X native FileVault or some other reputable encryption. Make sure your laptop is encrypted!
- **Antivirus** — Ensure that your antivirus software is up-to-date. Regularly run a scan against your system.
- **Firewall** — Make sure that your firewall is enabled.
- **Disable Bluetooth** when not needed.
- **Close your machine down** when not in use.

FOR THE MORE SECURITY-CONSCIOUS USER

If security is a great concern, here are some additional steps for your consideration:

- **Daily scan your machine for malware**
- **Use a Hardware Firewall Device** — Use a hardware firewall device unit rather than a software firewall. You want to separate your computer from the direct connection from the Internet and let the firewall provide you with the protection.
- **Disable services that you don't need.** Disable IPv6 and AirPort when not needed.
- **Create a non-admin account for everyday activities** — Like Windows, your default account on Mac OS X is an administrator user, and malware writers can take advantage of that to infect your computer. For everyday activities, we recommend you create a non admin user and you only log in as administrator when you need to perform administrative tasks.
- **Disable Adobe Flash and Oracle Java.**
- **Cover up your webcam when not in use.**

4

Web Browser Protection Guidelines

"There is no security on this earth. Only Opportunity."

– GENERAL DOUGLAS MCARTHUR

SETTING WEB BROWSER SECURITY

The Internet is a risky place.

The world relies on extensively intertwined websites, web applications, web services, and rich Internet applications, all running on the web browser.

Your web browser is your primary connection to the rest of the Internet, and multiple applications may rely on your browser, or elements within your browser to function.

The web browser has become the transition application to the web.

- Cloud computing is gaining more and more visibility and acceptability. traditionally in-house applications are moved to the Internet which requires a web browser.
- The Web 2.0 has truly opened up for social networking, social interaction, and social collaboration.
- Remote accessibility to the corporate business systems is now being accessed using just a web browser, thereby providing the flexibility to connect from anywhere at any time and from any device.
- Many of the client–server applications are being transitioned to web interface due to independence of the end user platform.

The discovery of the first web browser vulnerabilities changed the game. Once hackers found web browser vulnerabilities, they started breaking the browser. Web browser developers were left scrambling to patch the browser vulnerabilities, while security teams and the public frequently never got around to applying the patches. Breaking the browser has now grown into a motivated profit-driven activity by cyber hackers.

There are many ways the humble web browser can be compromised, including but not limited to the following:

- Visiting websites that automatically install malware on our system.
- Tricking us to visit websites that install malware on our systems.
- Tricking us into clicking on something different to what we perceive it to be.
- Forcing the browser to run a script that gives remote access to the system.
- By abusing vulnerabilities in the web browser and in the operating system, an attacker can remotely get access to files on an innocent user's hard drive and network shares.

There is one immediate conclusion from the above: even if you have a firewall in place and antivirus software installed, you are still exposed to a variety of identity theft and web attacks.

By configuring your browser as we outline in this section of the book and running the recommended extensions, you can significantly reduce the threats arising through using your web browser. In this section we are covering the four most common web browsers—Microsoft Internet Explorer; Mozilla Firefox; Google Chrome; Apple Safari.

INTERNET EXPLORER 9

Microsoft Internet Explorer (IE) is a web browser that is integrated into the Microsoft operating system.

First thing first, to ensure you are running the correct version of Internet Explorer, choose

- Tools-> About Internet Explorer, it should produce a screen similar to the following

If your version of Internet Explorer is below 9, unless there is a specific reason to run a lower version of the browser, we recommend that you upgrade either to Internet Explorer 9 for Windows 7 and Internet Explorer 10 for Windows 8.

- Open up your Internet Explorer browser and select **Internet Options** from the **Tools** menu.

- Choose the **Security** tab, and then select the Internet button and drag this to "**High**" under Security level for this zone.

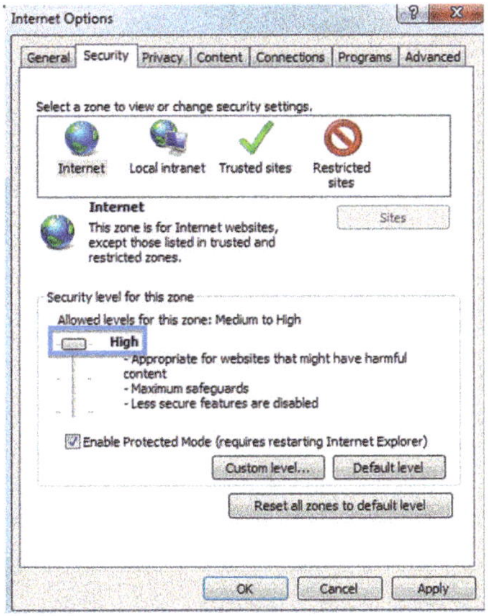

If this causes some of the websites you visit not to function, you can add them to the trusted sites list.

Next click the **Trusted sites** icon and set the security level to "**Medium High,**" then the screen you see should look similar to the following:

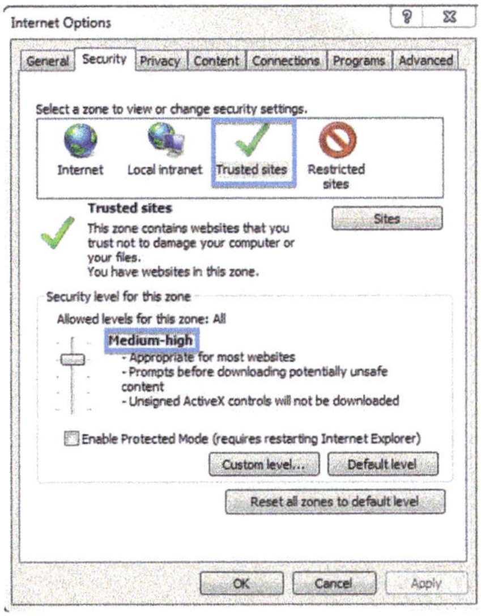

If you have any sites on the Internet that do not function properly due to the high security setting, you can fix this by clicking the **Sites** button and adding the site URL there.

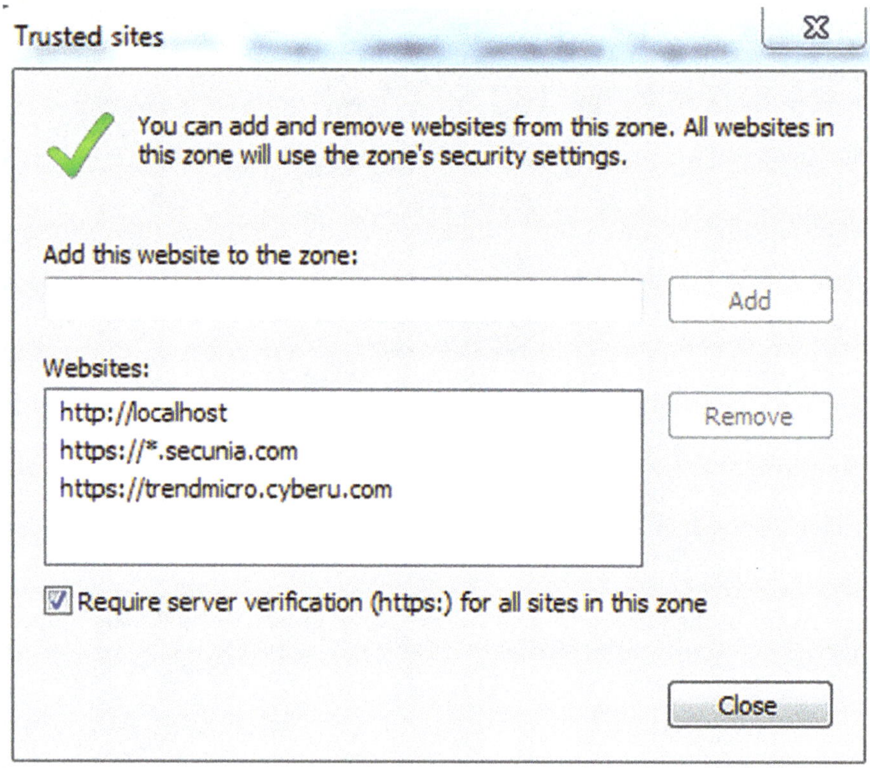

Next choose the **Privacy** tab and set the privacy level to **Medium.**

The Privacy tab contains settings for cookies. Cookies are text files placed on your computer by various sites that you visit either directly or indirectly. A cookie can contain any data that a site wishes to store, and they often are used to track your computer as you move through the website and store as preference or credentials.

We strongly recommend checking the following:

- **Never allow websites to request your physical location**– This ensures that your location privacy remains confidential from third party websites
- **Turn on Pop-Blocker**
- **Disable toolbars and extensions when InPrivate Browsing starts**

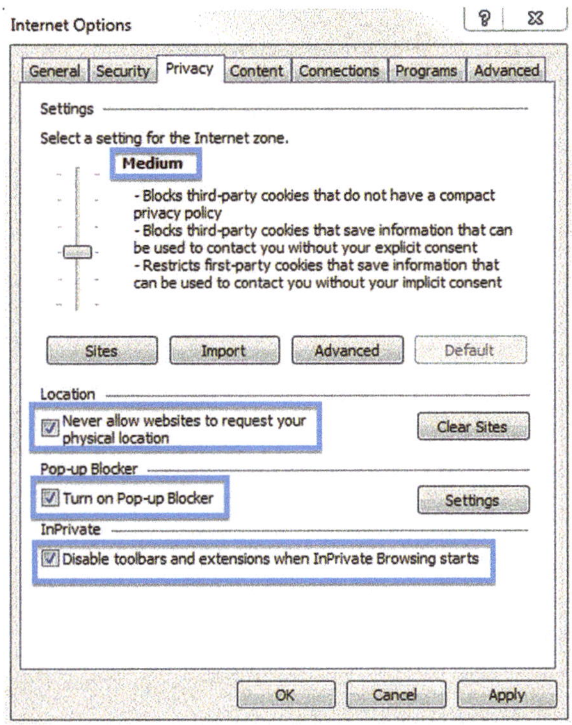

Next click the **Advanced** button and set the options as follows:

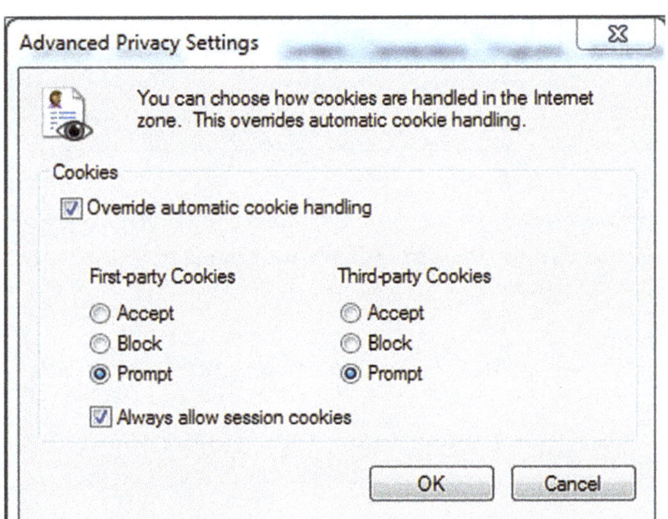

Next click the **Advanced** tab and uncheck **Enable third party browser extensions** radio button.

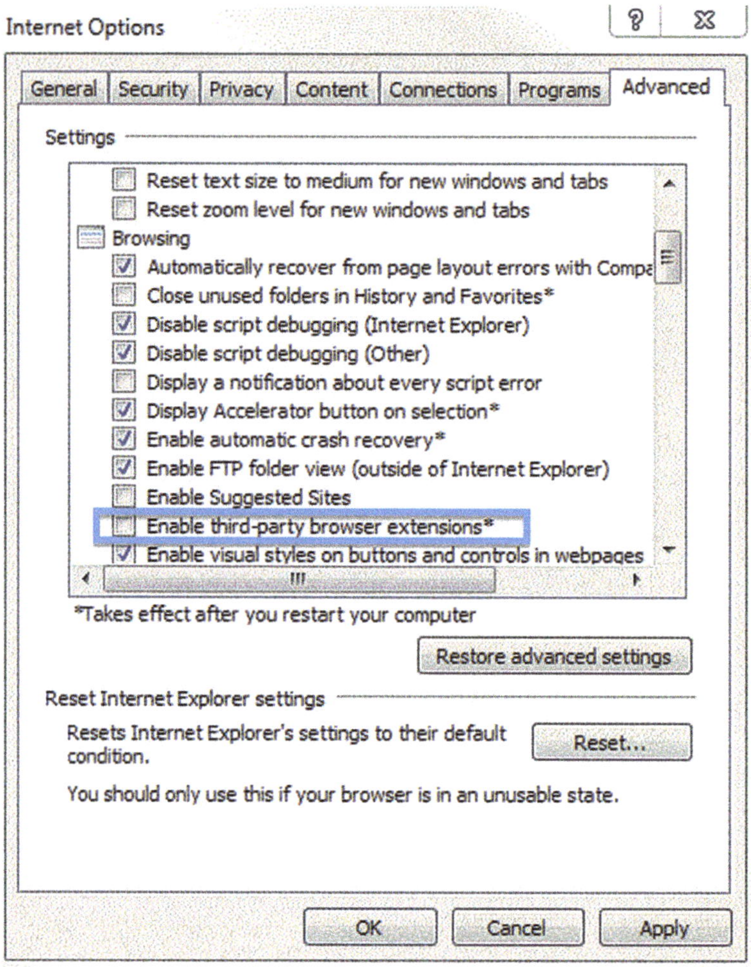

While in this Windows, scroll down the page. I would recommend that you click **Always show encoded addresses** and unclick **Play sounds on web pages** as can be seen in the following diagram. This

1. Reduces the chance of you executing malware contained in audio files embedded in web pages.

2. Reduces the chances of you being sent to malware-infested domains that are hidden by the encoding.

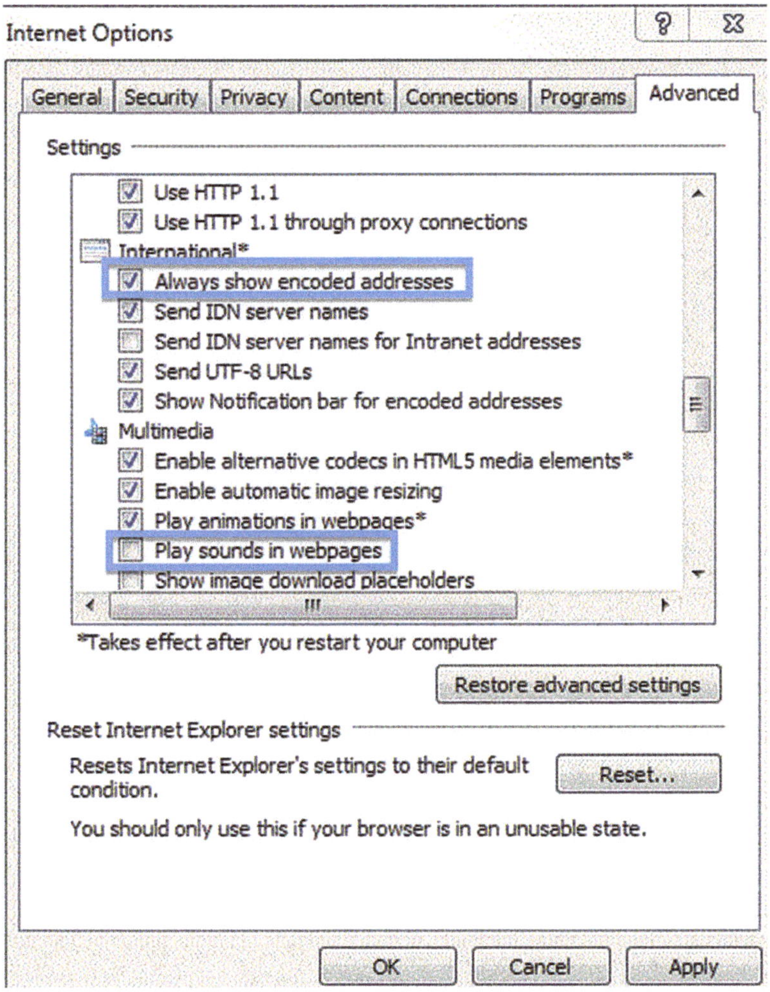
Internet Options
General
Security
Privacy
Content
Connections
Programs
Advanced
Settings
Use HTTP 1.1
Use HTTP 1.1 through proxy connections
International*
Always show encoded addresses
Send IDN server names
Send IDN server names for Intranet addresses
Send UTF-8 URLs
Show Notification bar for encoded addresses
Multimedia
Enable alternative codecs in HTML5 media elements*
Enable automatic image resizing
Play animations in webpages*
Play sounds in webpages
Show image download placeholders
*Takes effect after you restart your computer
Restore advanced settings
Reset Internet Explorer settings
Resets Internet Explorer's settings to their default condition.
Reset...
You should only use this if your browser is in an unusable state.
OK
Cancel
Apply

INTERNET EXPLORER 10

To determine that you are running IE 10

- Open up Internet Explorer. Select **Help** Tab, then click **About Internet Explorer**; this will produce a screen similar to the following:

To set the security of the browser:

- Select **Tools** tab, then click **Internet Options**, then select the **Security** tab, and this will present a screen similar to the following:

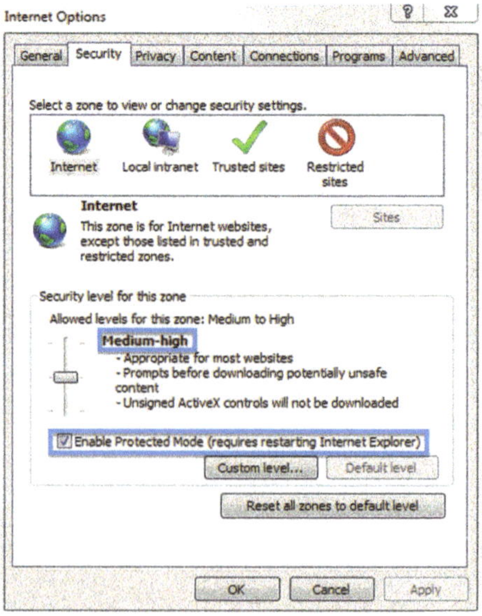

- Drag the security slider on the left to "**Medium-High**"and ensure **Enable Protected Mode** is checked.

I recommend configuring IE10 using the same settings as for IE9.

INTERNET EXPLORER 11

IE11 is the default browser of Windows 8. Although there isn't much difference between IE11 from its previous versions, IE11 is a worthy upgrade for anyone using Windows 7.

It is important to note that it doesn't run on operating systems versions earlier than Windows 7.

Internet Explorer 11 is all about performance. Improved page loading times and faster JavaScript performance are joined by the promise of reduced CPU usage and better battery life for laptops and netbooks running Windows 7.

From a security point of view, the key difference between IE10 and IE11 is Privacy settings. The check box for Do Not Track set to "on" by default.

And by far more powerful is IE11 tracking protection feature, which actually blocks third-party interactions and cookie placing based on tracking protection lists created by independent privacy organisations, which you subscribe to.

For more information about IE11 Privacy and security settings, visit —www.pi10m.com/b1/13

MOZILLA FIREFOX

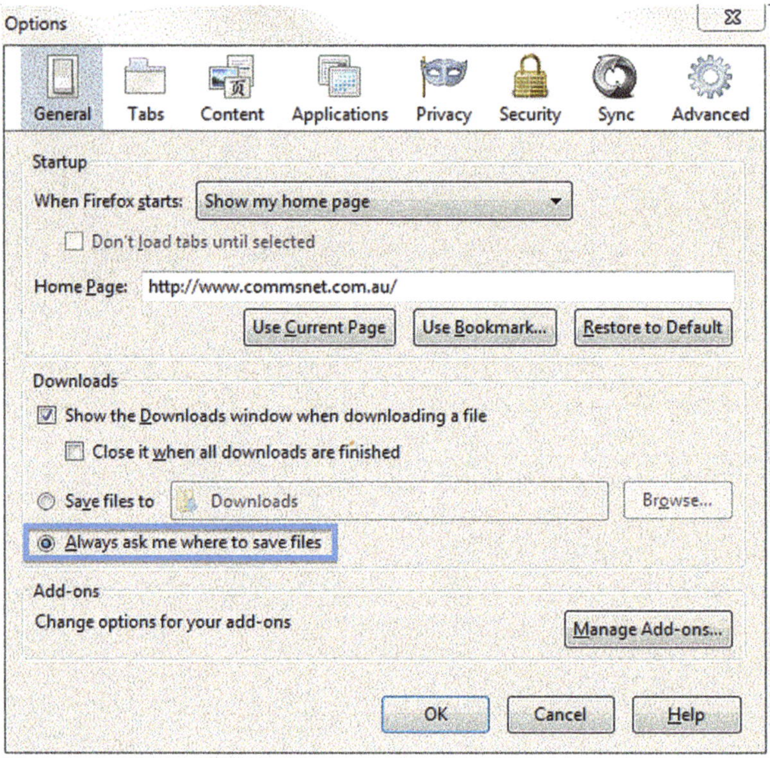

Firefox is a web browser favoured by security professionals because of the low number of bugs found in the browser and the speed that bug fixes are released. Firefox can be downloaded from the following URL: http://www.mozilla.org

If you have already installed Firefox, you should ensure you have the latest version. This is very easy to do, for when you start Firefox it automatically checks that the version installed is the most current. If not, it will prompt you to download and install the latest version.

The following configuration changes to Firefox will ensure that your browsing experience is as safe as possible.

Select the **Options** menu entry from the **Firefox** drop down menu within Windows or Preference from the drop down **Safari Tab** within an Apple Mac. This will present a screen similar to the following:

As a suggested option, check **Always ask me where to save files**. This prevents Firefox from the possibility of automatically downloading files that may contain malware.

Next click the **Privacy** tab. This will present a screen similar to the following:

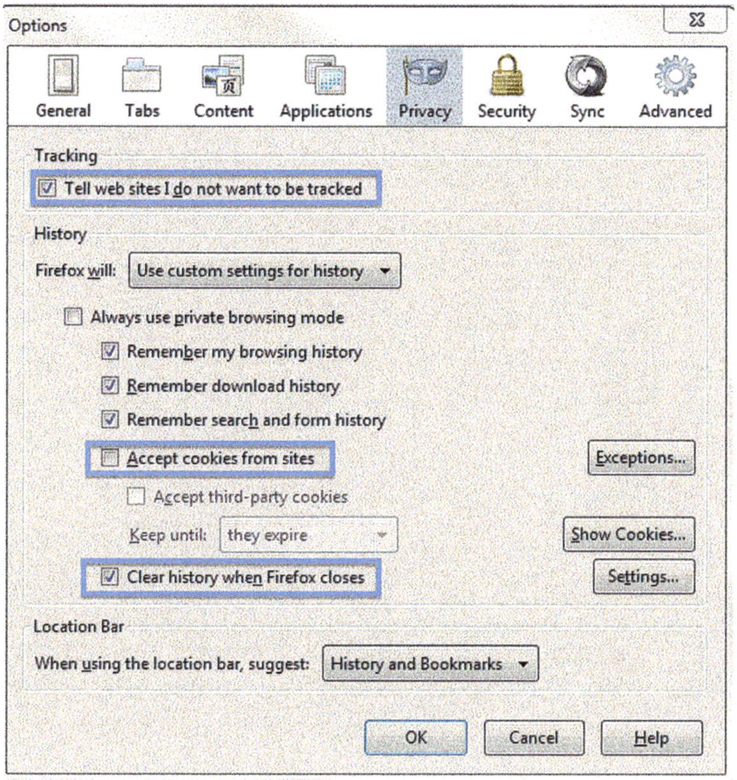

Ensure that the settings are as shown here. These are recommended suggestions:

- Web Tracking is explained in more detail in the next chapter. Checking this box will tell websites that you wish to opt-out of tracking by advertisers and other third-parties.
- **Cookie Definition**: This is also known as a browser cookie or web cookie. This is usually a bit of data sent from a website and stored on a web browser. When you browse the same website in the future, the data stored in the cookie can be retrieved by the website to notify the website of the user's previous activity. By unchecking, you therefore don't accept cookies from sites.
- **Third-Party Tracking:** Although cookies cannot carry viruses and cannot install malware on the host computer, tracking cookies and especially third-party tracking cookies are commonly used as ways to compile long term records of individual's browsing histories, which may be a major privacy concern.
- Once your Firefox closes, certain items will be deleted. Click Settings to find out what items will be deleted

Next click the **Security tab**. This will present a screen similar to the following:

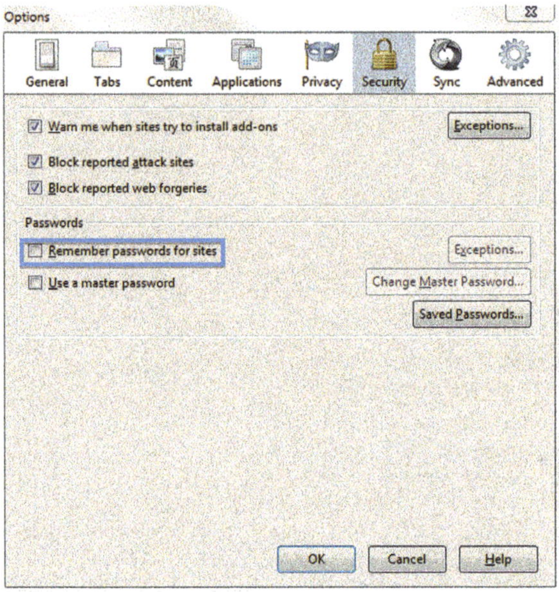

Generally I would highly recommend disabling the **Remember password for sites** option. This prevents someone who has compromised your machine from automatically logging into the web accounts you have used on the compromised machine.

If you do not want to do this, then enable the master password option. This will encrypt all remembered passwords stored in the browser. However if you lose the master password, there is no way to recover your web account passwords.

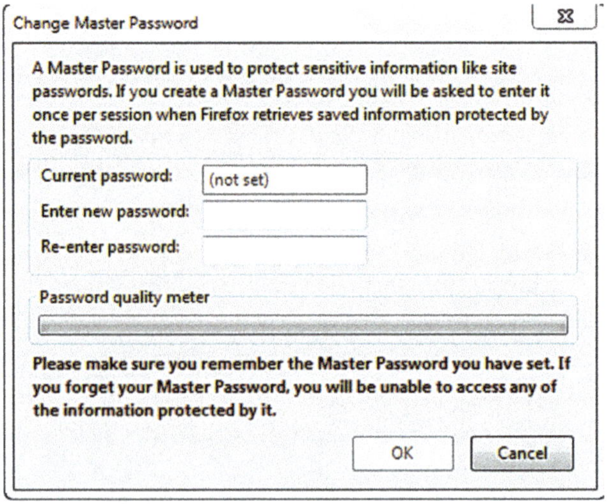

Next choose the **Content** tab and disable java script.

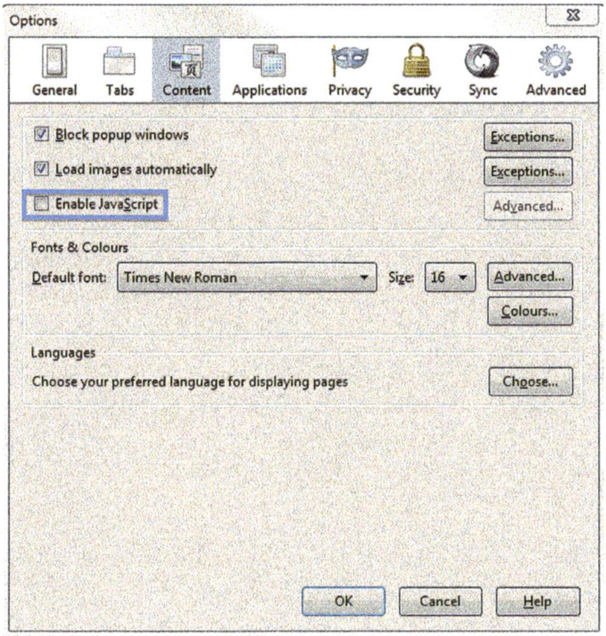

- Uncheck **Enable JavaScript**
  - JavaScript is a scripting language commonly used to make web pages interactive.
  - If you need to run Java or JavaScript for specific sites, we recommend that you consider installing the extension "NoScript." This is described in the recommended extension section below.

For the more security-conscious user

The following extensions to Firefox are recommended for enhancing the security of your Firefox Browser.

From the General tab, click Manage Add-ons button if you are using Firefox within Windows.

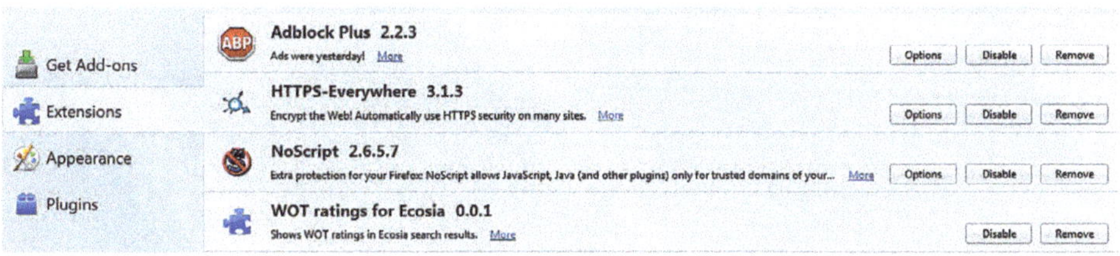

Recommended Add-ons

1. **Addblock Plus** - Blocks all adds automatically and has a database of known malware domains which can be blocked automatically. Details of this extension can be found at the following site—www.pi10m.com/b1/14

2. **HTTPS Everywhere** - Checks if a site supports https. If it does every time you visit that site, this extension forces you to use the more secure https connection. Details about this extension can be found at the following site www.pi10m.com/b1/16

3. **NoScript** - Allows you to control the running of JavaScript, Java, and Flash on Firefox on a domain by domain basis. This will greatly reduce the risk associated with these three technologies on the web. NoScript can be found at the following site www.pi10m.com/b1/15

4. **Web of Trust** - This add-on extension is available for Mozilla, Google Chrome, as well as Internet Explorer. It provides a graphical rating of the trust-worthiness of websites before you visit the site. Details of this extension can be found at the following site www.pi10m.com/b1/17

As Mozilla Firefox has a very configurable security capability, I would recommend visiting the following site - www.pi10m.com/b1/20

GOOGLE CHROME

Google Chrome is the most recent addition to the browser market. You can download Google Chrome from the following site: http://chrome.google.com

Once installed, ensure that you have the latest version of the browser. You can verify the version of Chrome by clicking the **folder** icon on the top right hand corner of Google Chrome.

Select the drop down option **About Google Chrome** and you will see a pop up window similar to the following for Google Chrome.

This web popup will identify the version of the software and whether your software is the most up-to-date version. If it is not up-to-date, you will be prompted to download the latest version.

Google Chrome in its default configuration will provide a very secure browsing experience.

Please follow the security recommended settings (highlighted in blue in the following image).

Click on the **folder** icon and select the drop down menu section **Settings.** Then click on **Show Advanced Settings** link right at the bottom of the page. This will then open further information.

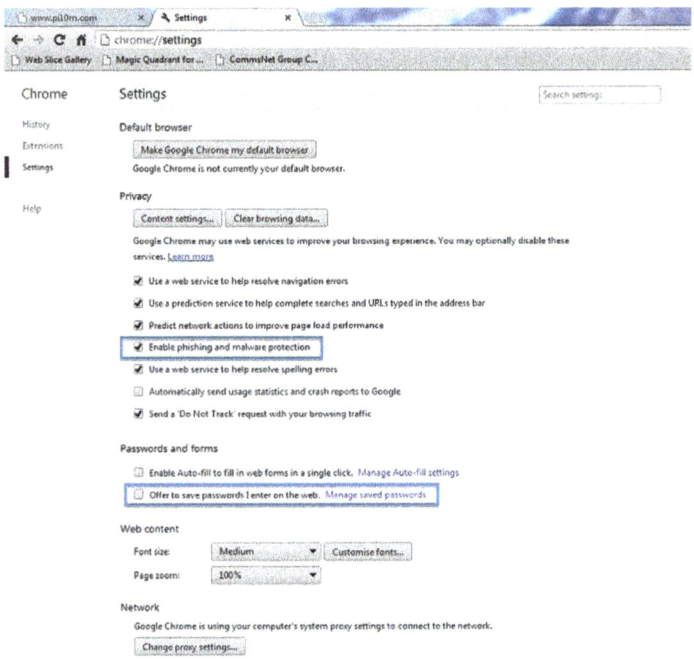

Continue to scroll down.

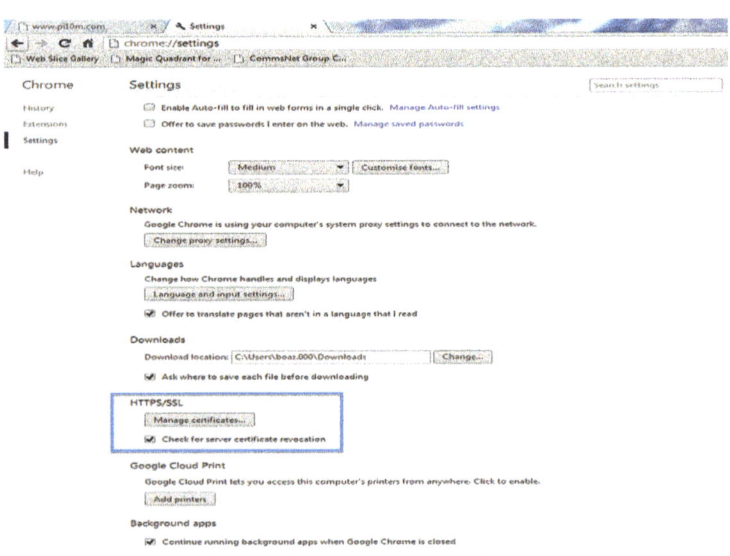

For the more security-conscious user

Along with the default set-up, we recommend the following extensions to further boost the security of Google Chrome.

Click **Folder** icon. Then click **Settings**. Then click **Extensions**.

1. **Web of Trust** - gives a graphical trust worthiness rating to websites before you visit the site. Details for this application can be found in the section on secure web browsing www.pi10m.com/b1/17

2. **KB SSL Enforcer** - detects if a website support SSL and redirect the URL entered to the secured SSL equivalent. This extension can be found at the following site www.pi10m.com/b1/18

3. **Flash Block** - Flash is a major source of web-based security vulnerabilities. This Chrome extension allows you to block Flash content on a site by site basis. This extension can be obtained from the following site - www.pi10m.com/b1/19

4. **View Thru** - Many sites especially social media sites such as twitter use shorted URLs that could point to malware infected sites. The view through extension allows the shorted URL to be expanded in full, before you visit that web site. This extension can be found at the following site - www.pi10m.com/b1/21

Click **Folder** icon. Then click **Tools**. Then click **Extensions**.

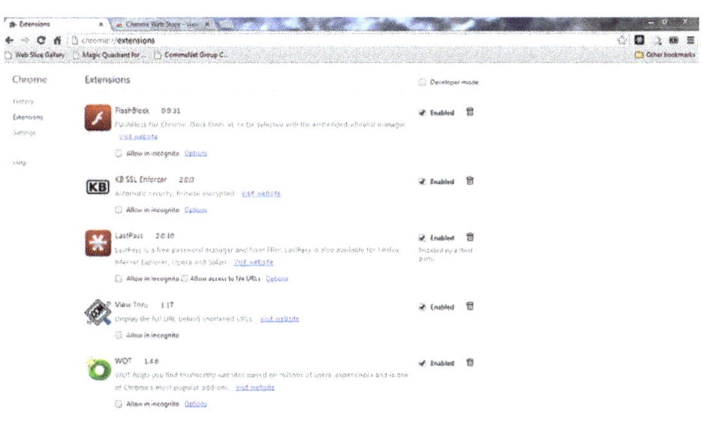

As Google Chrome has a very configurable security capability, I would recommend visiting the following site—www.pi10m.com/b1/22

APPLE SAFARI

Apple has come a long way in increasing its security within its Safari web browser. Should you chose Safari as your preferred browser, then the following information will make your browsing experience with the Safari browser more secure.

Firstly, make sure you have installed the latest version of Safari. To determine if your browser is up-to-date, follow the following steps:

From Windows

- Access All Programs from within Windows and then click Apple Software Update.

If you have the latest version of the software, then you will see a screen similar to the following.

From Apple Mac

- Click the Apple Logo (top left corner)
- Click Software Update

Next you can view the security settings by clicking the right hand **cog** icon on the browser and choosing **Preferences** for Windows or Click **Safari** tab → **Preferences** for Apple Mac.

The following screens will appear:

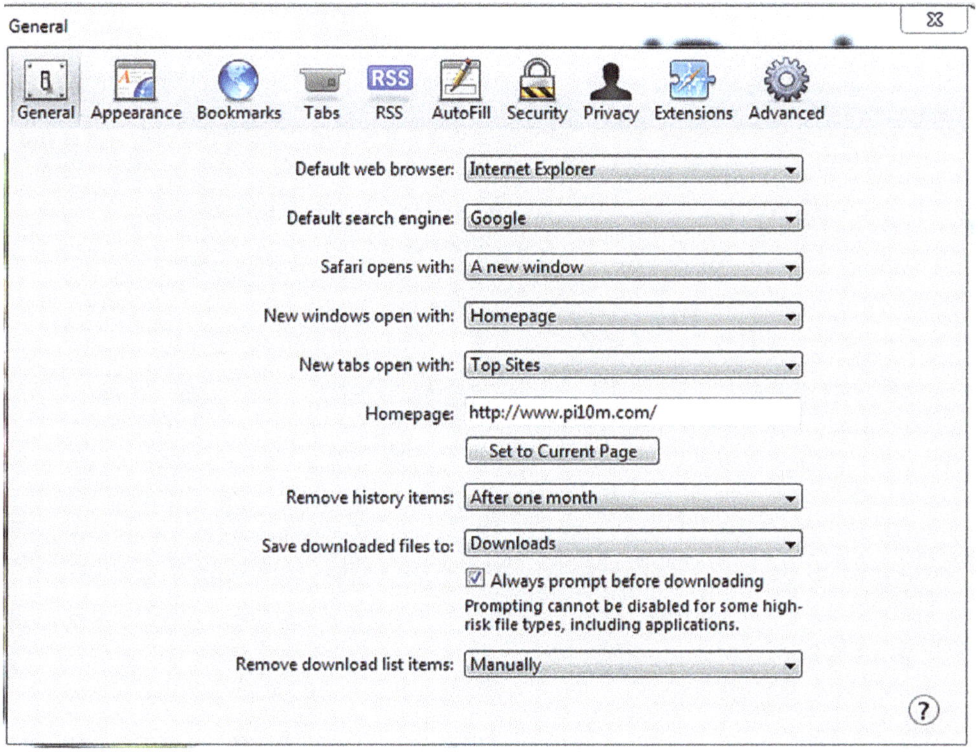

- From the preference window click the **Security** tab.

Uncheck the first three selections in the **Web Content** section and re-enable them on a case by case basis if required.

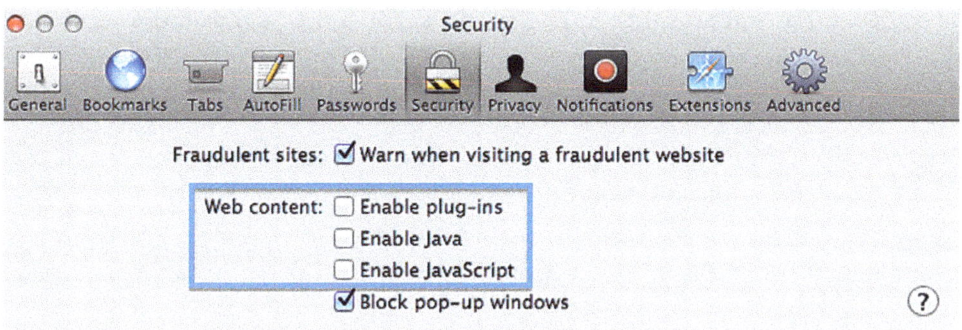

Next click the **Privacy** tab. This will present a screen similar to the following.

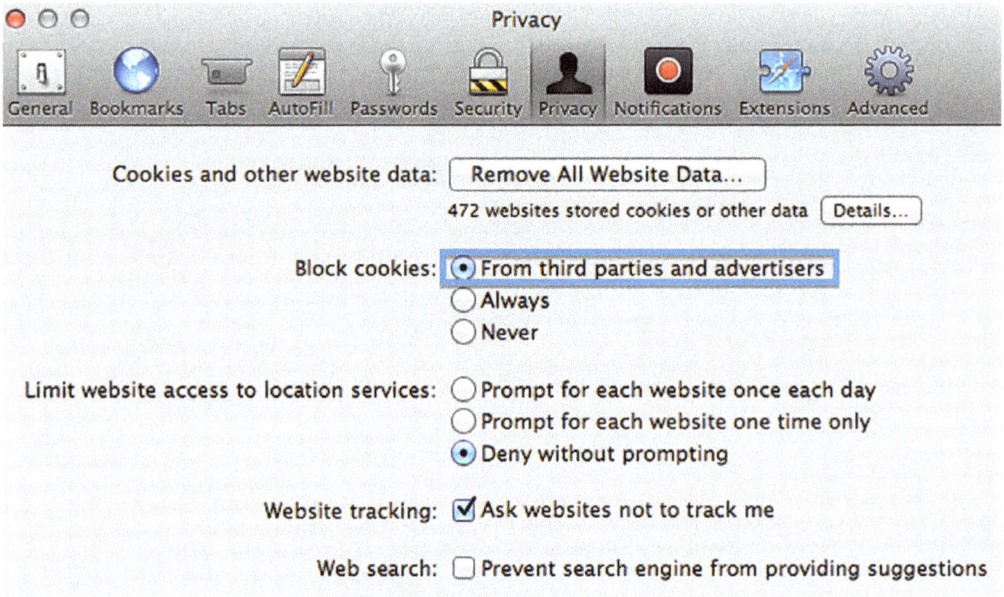

Ensure that the **Block cookies: From third parties and advertisers** is checked

Cookie Definition: This is also known as a browser cookie or web cookie. This is usually a bit of data sent from a website and stored on a web browser. When you browse the same website in the future, the data stored in the cookie can be retrieved by the website to notify the website of the user's previous activity.

Third-Party Tracking—Although cookies cannot carry viruses, and cannot install malware on the host computer, tracking cookies and especially third-party tracking cookies are commonly used as ways to compile long term records of individuals browsing histories, which may be a major privacy concern.

Disable Safari Auto Open

Safari, Apple's web-browser, includes a feature where it will automatically launch a number of different file types with their associated application. This could potentially pose a risk with the user unwittingly opening a file without realizing it.

To disable the feature:

- In **Safari**, chose **Safari > Preferences -> General**
- Uncheck **Open "safe" files after downloading**

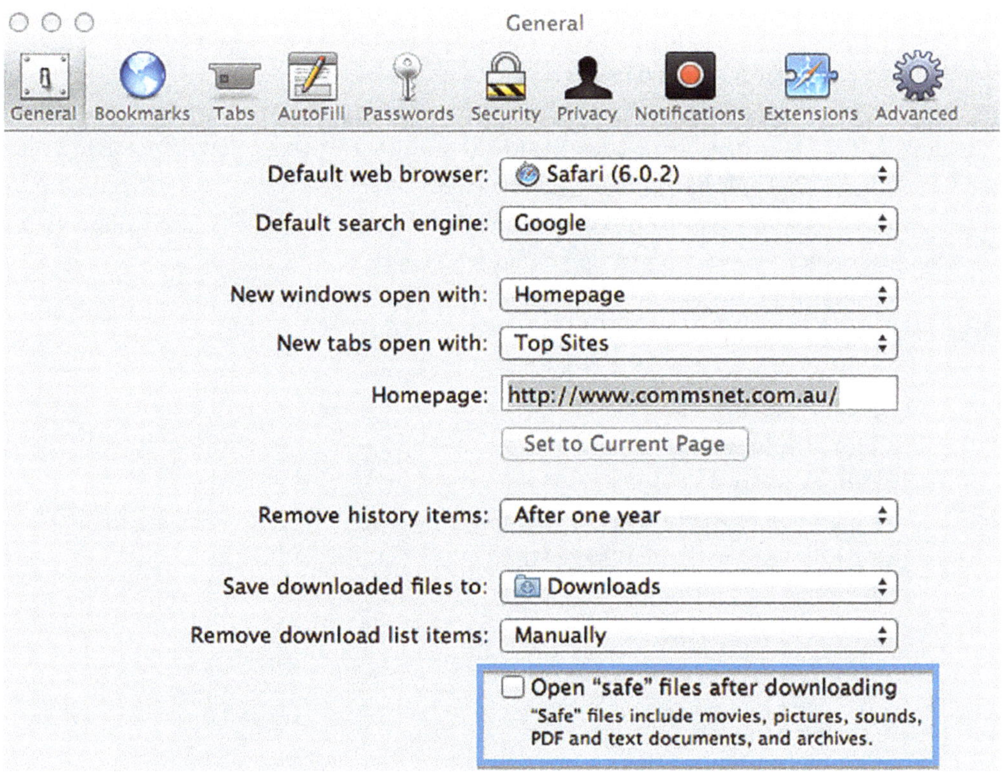

DISABLING JAVA

Java is widely used platform for development and deployment of portable and versatile applications. Java is one of the most popular programming languages in use, particularly for client-server web applications.

Unfortunately Java has its security flaws and it has become one of the weakest links in Windows and Mac's defence against external malware.

Numerous critical Java flaws have been identified and Oracle seems slow in resolving these issues. In April 2012, Apple has said that they are removing Java software from their computers. Starting with OS X 10.7 Apple stopped including a Java runtime in OS X, but still provides a quick link to install it if you run a program that requires Java.

Disabling Java Within Windows

- Open your **Control Panel**
- Double Click **Java** Icon
- Click the **Security** Tab

Uncheck the box Saying **Enable Java content in the browser**. If you do not want to disable it, I suggest you set the security level to **Very High.**

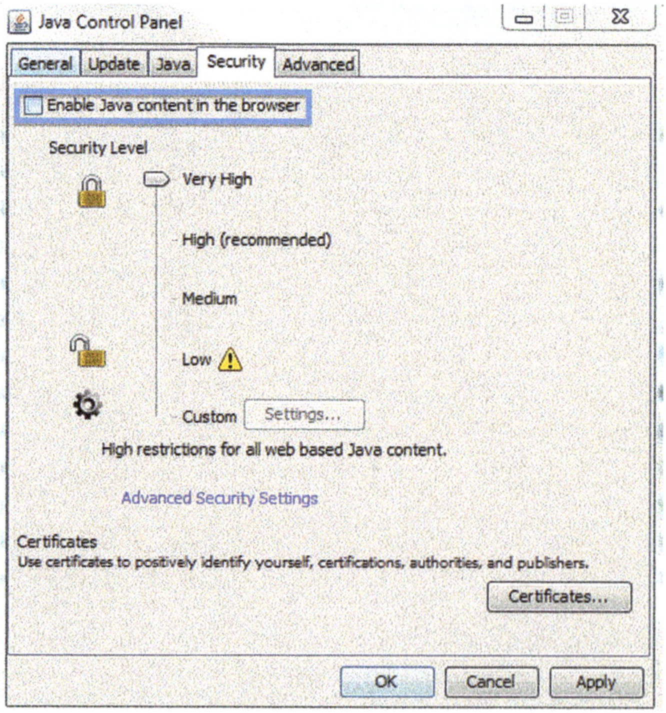

To disable Java in Safari

- In Safari, choose **Safari > Preferences**
- Click **Security** tab.
- Uncheck **Enable Java**.
- Close the Safari preferences window.

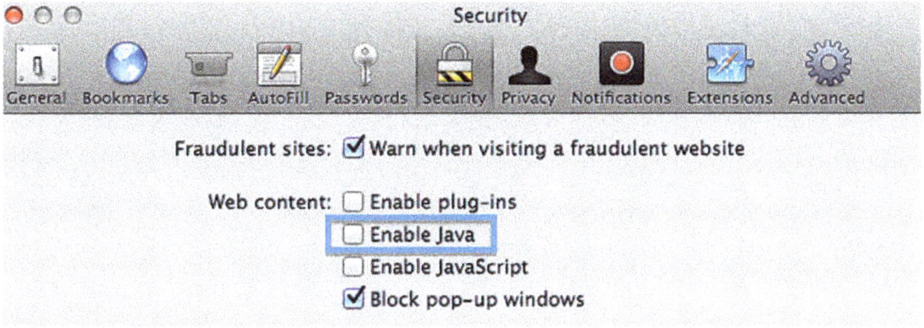

Disabling Java within Mac OS X

Another recommended option is to disable Java from your System Preference.

- Click on your Apple icon (top left corner)
- Click on **System Preference**
- Click **Java** icon
- Click **Security** tab
- Uncheck **Enable Java Content in the browser**
- Click **Apply**

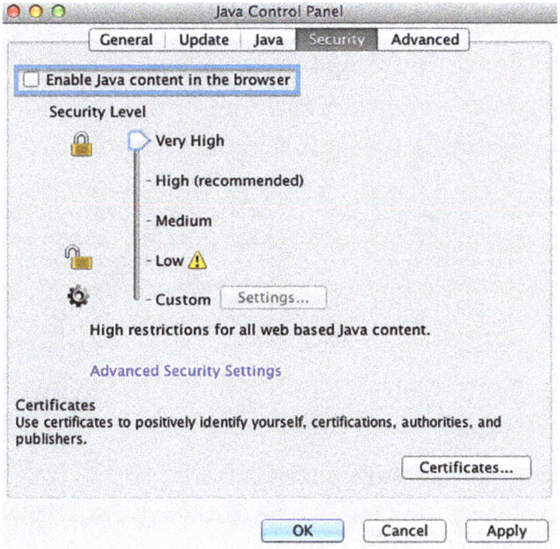

PRIVATE BROWSING

When you browse the web, your web browser stores information about the websites you visit. If you have allowed your browser to save your password, it will store any user names and passwords that you enter.

Many websites also store information on your computer, in cookies, and other places. As will be mentioned in the next chapter in more detail, some websites store tracking cookies and other data so advertisers can show you ads for products that match your interests. To inhibit third parties from viewing this kind of information, use Private Browsing.
If you browse the web that's also used by other people such as at an Internet café or airport lounges, they can view your browsing behavior by reading the history list or the list of stored passwords. This becomes quite invasive and dangerous. To prevent others from gaining access to this information, use Private Browsing.

When Private Browsing is on, web pages are not added to the history list, the names of downloads are removed from the Downloads window, user names and passwords are not saved, and searches are not added to the search field's pop-up menu.

What is interesting is that websites can't modify information stored on your computer, so services normally available at such sites may work differently until you turn off Private Browsing.

Turning Private Browsing - Safari

Turn On Private Browsing

While browsing a webpage using Safari,

- Choose **Safari > Private Browsing** OR within Windows, select **Cog Wheel → Private Browsing**
- When you see a confirmation message, click **OK.**

A Private button appears in the address field to indicate that private browsing is on.

Turn Off Private Browsing

While browsing a webpage using Safari within Apple Mac,

- Choose **Safari > Private Browsing** (so the checkmark disappears), or click the Private button in the address field. Within Windows, select **Cog Wheel → Private Browsing.**

Close any Safari windows you used to view private information. If you don't close the windows, other users can view those pages using the Back and Forward buttons.
Private Browsing is always turned off when you open Safari, even if it was on when you last quit Safari.

If you downloaded any items from websites, Private Browsing only removes the names of the items you downloaded from the Downloads window. To get rid of the items themselves, delete them from your computer.

If you use a shared or public computer, I suggest you reset Safari before and after use. This will deter other people from seeing which web pages you visited and other information about how you used Safari.

- Within Apple Mac, choose **Safari** > **Reset Safari** OR **Cog Wheel → Reset Safari**.

Turning Private Browsing - Internet Explorer

Turn On Private Browsing

- Within IE, select **Tools → InPrivate Browsing** or **Ctrl+Shift+P**

This opens a new dedicated browser as seen below. Internet Explorer will not store data about your browsing sessions.

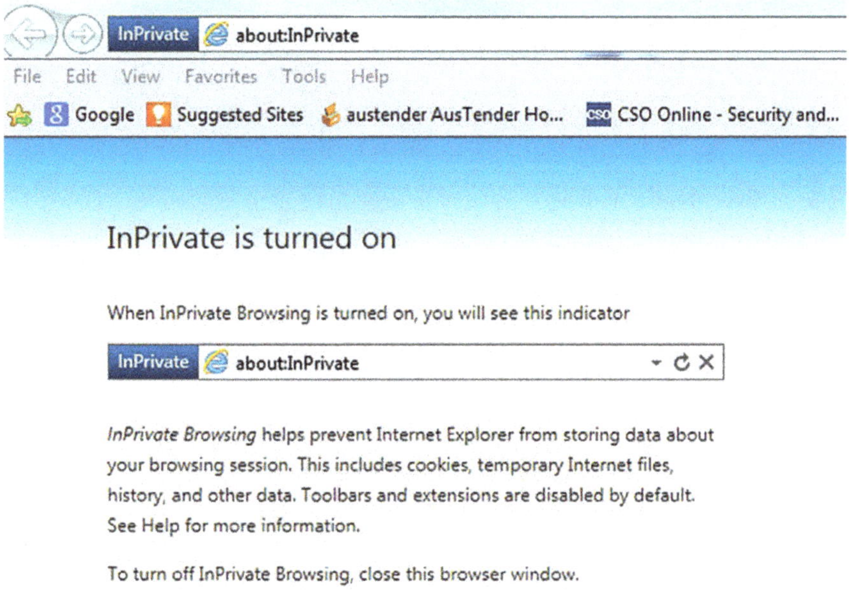

Turn Off Private Browsing

- Just close this browser window

Turning Private Browsing - Firefox

Turn On Private Browsing in a Windows environment

- Within Firefox, select **Firefox → Start Private Browsing**

The following Dialog box will appear.

- Click button **Start Private Browsing**

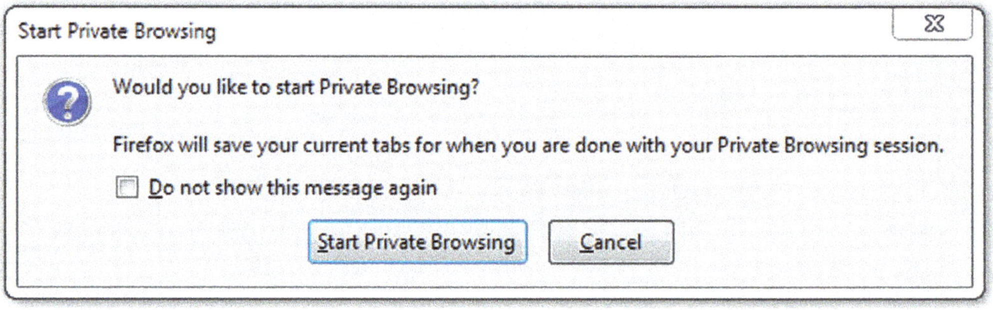

A new Firefox browser will appear.

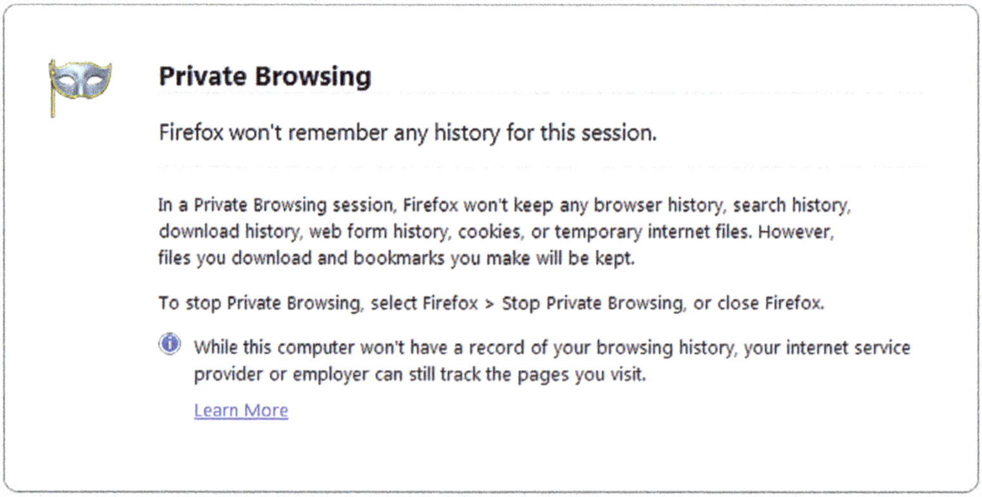

Turn Off Private Browsing

- Select **Firefox ->Stop Private Browsing** or close browser.

Turn On Private Browsing—Google Chrome

Turn On Private Browsing

- Within Chrome, select **Folder** icon and click **New incognito windows**

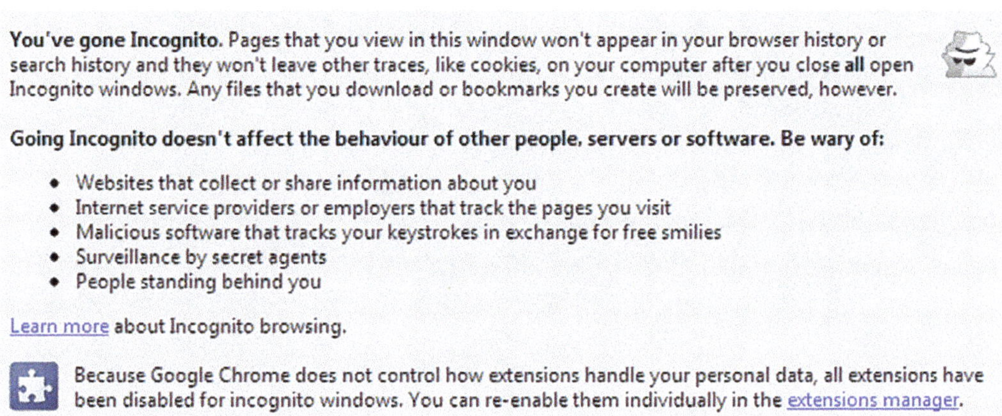

Turn Off Private Browsing

- Close Window

REMINDER! Don't forget to register at www.pi10m.com

By registering your details, we will be able to provide you with free updates to the book, critical security alerts, valuable security tools that you can start using right now for free, answer your questions and much much more.

SUMMARY OF POINTS

Your web browser is an untrusted application. It constantly reaches out to the wide global Internet, seeking the appropriate information from foreign systems all the time. As a result, this is your most vulnerable situation and a source for many security problems.

Should you visit a site that has some form of malicious malware and your browser is vulnerable, your browser may be exploited and infected. This is often referred as Drive-by download. There is nothing more that a hacker wants than to be able to run any program of their choosing on any machine that clicks a link in an email or visits a website.

- **Browse Safely** - Be smart about websites that you want to visit.
- **Use Strong Passwords when Authenticating.**
- **Close Web Browser when Not in Use.**
- **Always uncheck the "stay logged" in and "save password"** - Many browsers automatically save your password or login by default. If you don't opt out, you risk that others may access those services, using your identity.
- **Disable Java & Flash within your Browser** - These are full-fledged programming languages that are extremely powerful and do have vulnerabilities. If you give your browser that right to invoke such programs, you are asking for problems. They are just not safe.
- Ensure Firewall is turned On.
- **Use a dedicated web browser to perform your web banking**. For example, use Firefox to do all your online banking. Use Internet Explorer, Safari, or Google Chrome to access other non-banking websites.

FOR THE MORE SECURITY - CONSCIOUS USER / ORGANISATION

- **Utilise a Third Part Web Security Gateway** - There are a number of well-recognised web security programs that will handle the web security as your first line of defence. Such systems should be able to protect you from malware, phishing, malicious websites, click fraud, and other dangers. These solutions can also be found as Cloud Services.
- **Utilise an Application Whitelisting** - Implement Application Whitelisting to help prevent malicious software and other unapproved programs from running without your authority.
- **Web Domain Whitelisting** - Domain Whitelisting ensures that users can only visit authorised websites.
- **Develop Acceptable Internet Usage Policies** - Policies are a collection of guidelines that you can undertake to ensure your business runs with consistency, efficiency, effectiveness, confidentiality, and integrity. This is explained in detail in Chapter10.
- **User Education** - Proactively help and engage with users about Internet best practices.

5

Internet Usage Protection Guidelines

"Raising our security conscious awareness is the best and simplest way to minimise the exposure to security threats."

– JONATHAN ZITTRAIN

THE INTERNET THREAT LANDSCAPE

Like the real world, technology and the Internet present dangers as well as benefits. Software has vulnerabilities and attackers will target you as soon as your computer is connected to the Internet.

Furthermore, by exploring popular places on the Internet such as search engines, social networks, popular websites, and online email, you are now keenly targeted by cyber attackers. Just as you take precautions to protect yourself in the real world, you need to take precautions to protect yourself online. For many users, computers and the Internet are unfamiliar and intimidating, so it is appropriate to approach them the same way.

The rise of threats demands a new type of security to protect against data loss, financial or identity theft, and other costly consequences. You need to be a proactive in your thinking and quickly adapt to the changing threats. The key to this type of defence is to understand your vulnerabilities and increase your security awareness. Security technology will go so far.

Today, more than ever, cyber hackers aren't just producing malware for notoriety! No, they are producing primarily for financial gain and the secondary gain is about stealing your data / intellectual property.

The web is by far the biggest opportunity for malware infection. It transmits emails bearing malicious links and attachments, websites carrying exploits targeting browsers and other software, drive-by downloads, phishing scams, questionable storefront operations, and all other malice of the cyber world.

The success of mitigation of the attack will depend on you. Yes, You! Irrespective on what security tools you employ, a silly click of a button may inadvertently download malware to your system.

How well you manage not to be tricked by such scams and trickeries is often referred to as "Social Engineering." It will depend on you being alert, vigilant, and attentive.
In this chapter we will start to help you raise you awareness starting with the **7 Myths of Safe Web Browsing**.

7 FALLACIES OF SAFE WEB BROWSING

Safe web browsing practices is about being smart and vigilant. Here are 7 fallacies that we encounter in our conversations with many people that we talk with.

Fallacy #1: I haven't been infected so far, so I'm not a target and unlikely to be infected in the future.

Many people take this view predominantly due to ignorance. How would you know whether you have been infected or not? These days malware infection are highly unlikely to advertise themselves to you. They will sit in the background, listening and recording any information that it deems confidential. Such information is then communicated unbeknown to you. A collector will then leverage this information to access your bank accounts and then steal your money or steal your identity.

In a study conducted by McAfee (Operation Shady RAT), the report identified 71 compromised parties—US Government, Utilities, Communications Defence, Finance and others. The report went on to say that some of these parties have had an intrusion duration for up to 28 months and the party hadn't recognised the intrusion.

Fallacy #2: My computer WAS infected, but I managed to clean it and NOW it should be fine.

If you were lucky enough to clean it, congratulations! However, most malware leaves many open doors. You may have successfully removed that virus, that trojan or that keylogger program, but are you aware of what other software it may have downloaded? Are you aware of what configurations it may have accomplished on your system? Are you aware of what registry settings it has manipulated?

I would suggest that you format your systems and re-install your applications from scratch. Yes, it's frustrating. Yes, it is time-consuming. And yes, it is the best way forward to gain some confidence that your system is most likely clean.

Fallacy #3: Only porn, gambling, and other dangerous websites are infected.

According to Websense, 82% of malicious websites are hosted on compromised hosts (Websense Threat Report 2012).

In essence, Web 2.0 applications were created to provide a venue for publishing user-generated content from multiple sources. These technologies allow users to share and exchange information online easily through company-sponsored and social media sites.

In short, organisations are adding more Web 2.0 content such as RSS feeds, blogs, user forums, third-party ads, and web applications to enhance their visitors' online experiences. Because legitimate sites are trusted by most users, cybercriminals prefer to infect them with malware and increase the potential number of victims. Some of the websites recently affected include Walmart, The New York Times, and The Wall Street Journal. It's not just about porn and gambling sites. It's not just Twitter, Facebook, or YouTube. This is a universal web problem!

Fallacy #4: One can only get infected if one downloads a file.

If you have decided to download a program without an understanding of the consequences, then you leave yourself open for possible malware infection.

However, this is NOT the only way one can get infected. Have you come across the term called "drive-by download?" Drive-by downloads may happen when visiting a website, viewing an e-mail message, or by clicking on a deceptive pop-up window.

By visiting that website or clicking on the window in the mistaken belief that it was fine, you have "consented" to the download although actually unaware of having started an unwanted or malicious software download and thereby being infected.

There are many other ways of being infected. Be vigilant and wary of the type of websites you visit, what information you are passing on when you are responding, and not being drawn into the latest exciting celebrity news item.

Fallacy #5: I use an Apple Mac. Apple Macs are safe because they are not targeted.

It's worth recognizing that malware on the Mac is a subject which raises strong emotions. There are some who believe that the problem is overhyped (or even non-existent!) and others who believe that the malware problem on Macs is underestimated by the Apple community.
The fact that there have been a number of mass exploits for the Apple Mac lately means that an individual user needs to take some precaution.

And as Apple Mac systems become more and more entrenched in our daily lives, expect to see increased attention and focus in the number of attacks.

Like any software vendor, Apple will have some shortcomings. Don't rest on your laurels. Even with an Apple Mac, find the necessary protection.

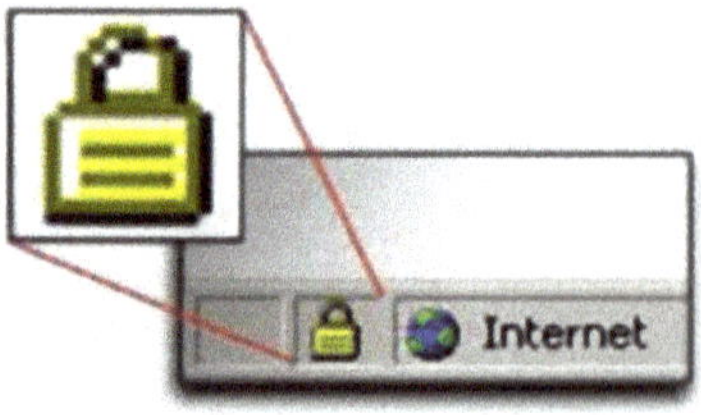

Fallacy #6: When the "Lock" icon appears on the web, it must be secure.

The lock icon indicates there is an SSL encrypted connection between the browser and the server to protect the interception of personal sensitive information.

It does not provide any security from malware. In fact, it's the opposite because most web security products are completely blind to encrypted connections. It's the perfect vehicle for malware to infiltrate a machine.

Furthermore, some malware can exploit vulnerabilities to spoof SSL certificates to make users feel more secure or enable devious connections to fake banking sites. There are numerous recent examples of hackers creating elaborate phishing schemes that emulate bank, credit card, or PayPal sites complete with spoofed SSL certificates that are extremely difficult for the average user to identify as fraudulent.

What can you do? Pay careful attention to the website. Look for any noticeable signs that it is maybe a fake.

Fallacy #7: I'm always up to date with my patches. Therefore I'm secure!

That's great and a very important step forwards in minimizing potential risk. However, if you do intend to download a program without understanding the consequences, then you leave yourself open for possible malware infection irrespective of what security measures you have taken.

Malware infections tend to occur frequently because users are not careful in their actions. They either clicked on something that they shouldn't have or they either downloaded something that they shouldn't have.

Remember, your secure fortification is only as secure as your weakest point. New malware is being introduced in the thousands each day to take advantage of new vulnerabilities that get found every day. The term "Zero-Day Attacks" or "Zero-Hour Attacks" is a threat that tries to exploit vulnerabilities that are unknown to others and before security vendors have had an opportunity to develop a security fix.

WEB TRACKING

Just how bad is it?

The marketers are spying on you, me, and all of us. It's called web tracking and behavioral profiling. Every search that you make, every email, every chat message, and every page that you visit is then combined by the big marketers (Google, Facebook, Amazon, Apple, Microsoft, etc.) to create an accurate profile of you! This is then sold to advertisers who are then better able to target you as a customer.

Every time you go shopping, you share intimate details about your consumption patterns with retailers. Many of those retailers are studying those details to figure out what you like, what you need, and which coupons are most likely to make you happy.

So what is Web Tracking? Web Tracking is the analysis of your behavior on a website. When you visit a website, you are allowing that site to access a lot of information about your computer's configuration. The information collected can then be used to deliver you content based on your preference during the visit or in the future.

How are you tracked? Today, as you visit website, you are sharing information with more websites than the ones you see in the address bar in your browser. This is inherent in the design of the web and simply how the web works, and it has potentially unintended consequences. As you visit one site, many other sites receive information about your activities. For example, when a webpage includes a third-party image file—such as a "web bug," IP address information, cookies, and referrer data can be sent.

So what is a Cookie? A **cookie**, also known as **aweb cookie** or **browser cookie**, is a piece of data stored by a website within a browser, and then subsequently sent back to the same website by the browser. Cookies were designed to be a reliable mechanism for websites to remember things that a browser had done there in the past, which can include having clicked particular buttons, logging in, or having read pages on that site months or years ago.
Tracking cookies and third party cookies are commonly used as a way to compile records of individual browsing histories.

Advertising companies use third party cookies to track a user across multiple sites. In particular, an advertising company can track a user across all pages where it has placed advertising images or web bugs. Knowledge of the pages visited by a user allows the advertising company to target advertisements to the user's presumed preferences.

So what is a Web Bug? A web bug is any one of a number of techniques used to track who is reading a web page or email, when, and from what computer. They can also be used to see if an email was read or forwarded to someone else, or if a web page was copied to another website.

Web bugs are frequently used in spamming (sending unsolicited commercial email) as a way of "pinging" to find which spam recipients opened (and presumably read) before deleting it.

So what is Facebook Like Button? A Like Button is described by Facebook as a way to give positive feedback and connect with things that you care about.
Users can "like" status updates, comments, photos, and links posted by their friends as well as adverts by clicking the "like" button. This makes the content appear in their friend's "news feed."

The information that Facebook gathers every time any user is visiting a site is the following: date, time, URL, and "other technical information" including the IP address, browser information, and operation system information.

The Like Button is also available for use on non-Facebook websites. When the user clicks the Like button on a site, a story appears in the user's friends' News Feeds with a link back to the website. At the same time when any visitor, including non-Facebook members and logged out users, visit a site with the Like Button, their presence on the site is recorded by Facebook. A "Like Box" also allows Facebook page owners to see how many users and which of their friends like the page.

What can you do?

1. Close your browsers when not in use and delete your cookies.

2. Configure your browser to "Do Not Track." Most web browsers provide you this feature, and we have described it on the following pages.

    - Although this probably will not stop websites tracking from you, it merely indicates that you do not want to be tracked.
    - This is important, as it approaches the practice of web tracking from two sides: Technology and policy. Solely relying on technological solutions to suppress/evade web tracking could never be fully successful. Marketers will always find ways around your technical defences, while publicly arguing that web users want to be tracked because it provides a better online (purchasing) experience. But Do Not Track has a policy side as well: It allows regulatory bodies to nudge marketers to honour the Do Not Track setting.

Setting up "do not track on" your web browsers

Enabling Tracking Protection for Internet Explorer 9.

- Click on the **Tools** tab and then click **Tracking Protection.**
- In the Manage Add-on dialog box, click a **Tracking Protection**, and then click **Enable** as indicated below.

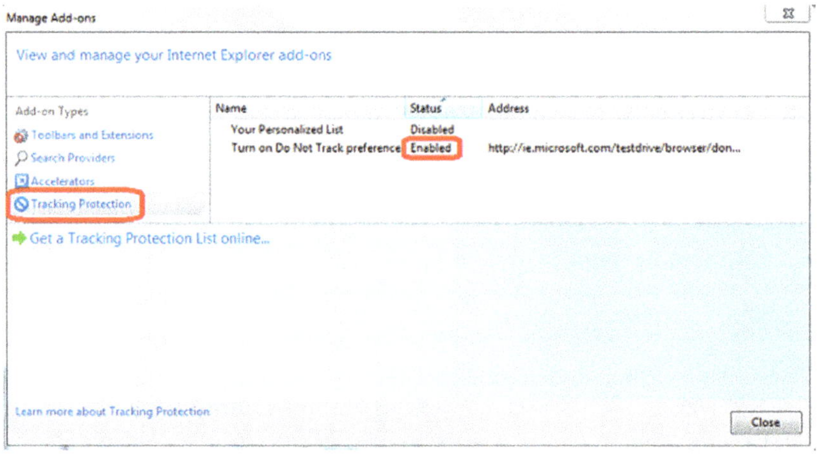

- If you wish to enhance your privacy against third party content, you can add additional "Tracking Protection."
- In the Manage Add-on dialog box, click **Get a Tracking Protection List Online**.

Enabling Tracking Protection for Internet Explorer 10.

- By default, Internet Explorer 10 turns on a feature called Do Not Track. Should you wish to check the status of it, follow the process below.
- Click **Tools** tab, then click **Tracking Protection**
- Ensure **Enabled** status is on for **Turn on Do Not Track Preference**

Enabling Tracking Protection for Internet Explorer 11.

- For more information about tracking IE11 as well as all other previous IE versions, visit the following site—www.pi10m.com/b1/23

Enabling Tracking Protection in Firefox 10 and above.

- At the top of the Firefox window, click on the **Firefox** button and then click **Options.**
- Select the **Privacy** tab.
- Check **Tell websites I do not want to be tracked.**
- Click **OK** to close the Options window.

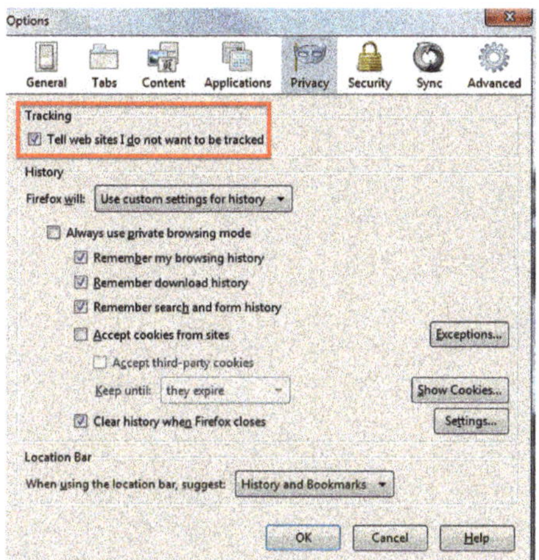

Enabling Tracking Protection in Safari.

Tracking protection is supported only in the Mac OSX version.

- Within Safari, click on the **Safari tab** and then select **Preference.**
- Click on the **Privacy** tab.

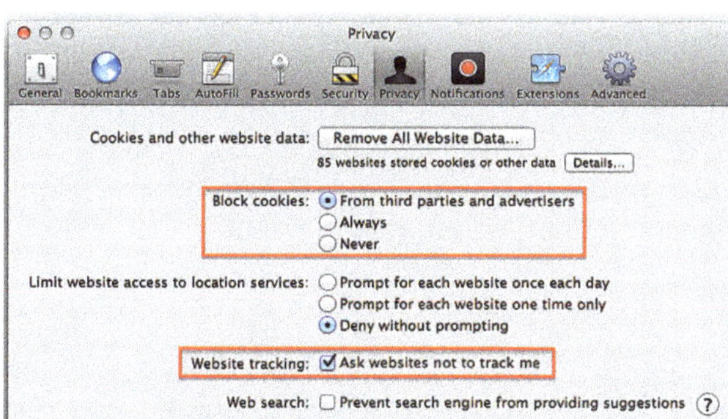

- Select **Block cookies** from **third parties and advertisers.** This might help prevent certain advertisers from storing cookies on your computer.
- Uncheck **Ask websites not to track me.** If this option is selected, each time Safari fetches content from a website, Safari adds a request not to track you.

Enabling Tracking Protection in Google Chrome.

- Within Chrome, click **Folder icon,** then select **Settings.**
- Check **Send a 'Do Not Track' request with your browsing traffic.**

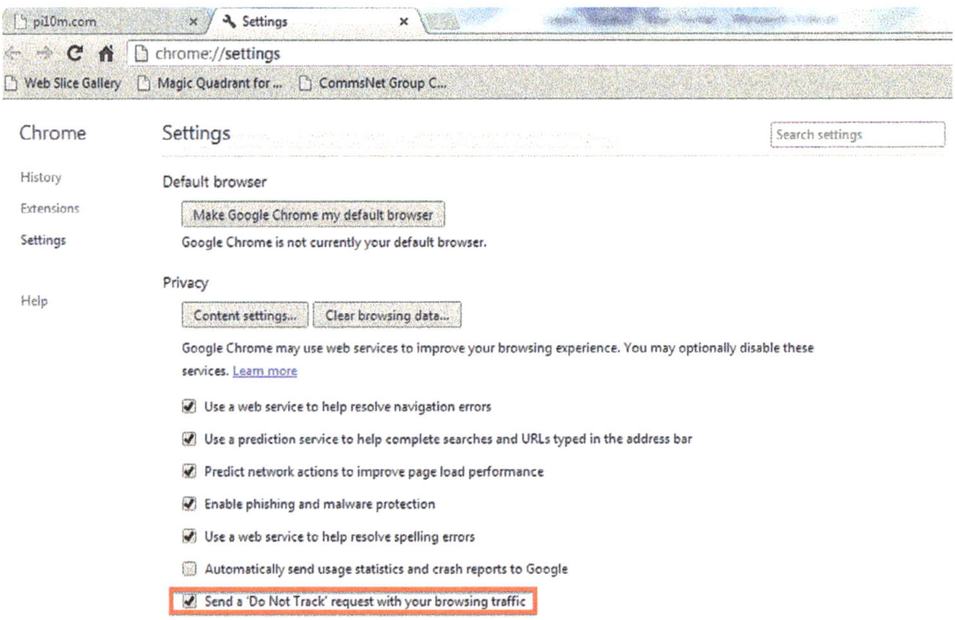

> *If what you are getting online is for free, you are not the customer, you are the product!*
>
> – JONATHAN ZITTRAIN

BEHAVIOUR PROFILE

Not so long ago, there was a familiar product called software. It was sold in stores, in shrink-wrapped boxes. When you bought it, all that you gave away was your credit card number or a stack of bills.

Now there are "apps" (short for applications)—stylish, distinct chunks of software that live online or in your smartphone and notebooks. To "buy" an app, all you have to do is click a button. Sometimes they cost a few dollars, but many apps are free, at least in monetary terms. You often pay in another way. Apps are gateways, and when you buy an app, there is a strong chance that you are supplying its developers with one of the most coveted commodities in today's economy: your personal data.

Some of the most widely used apps on Facebook—the games, quizzes, and sharing services that define the social networking site and give it such appeal, are gathering volumes of personal information.

A *Wall Street Journal* examination of 100 of the most popular Facebook apps found that some seek the email addresses, current location, and sexual preference, amongst other details, not only of app users but also those of their Facebook friends. One Yahoo service powered by Facebook requests access to a person's religious and political leanings as a condition for using it. The popular Skype service for making online phone calls seeks the Facebook photos and birthdays of its users and their friends.

Yahoo and Skype say that they seek the information to customise their services for users and that they are committed to protecting privacy. "Data that is shared with Yahoo is managed carefully," a Yahoo spokeswoman said.

This appetite for personal data reflects a fundamental truth about Facebook and by extension, the Internet economy as a whole. Facebook provides a free service that users pay for, in effect, by providing details about their lives, friendships, interests, and activities. Facebook, in turn, uses that trove of information to attract advertisers, app makers, and other business opportunities.

Up until a few years ago, such vast and easily accessible sources of personal information were all but nonexistent. Their arrival is driving a profound debate over the definition of privacy in an era when most people now carry information-transmitting devices with them all the time.

Facebook requires apps to ask permission before accessing a user's personal details. However, a user's friends aren't notified if information about them is used by a friend's app. An examination of the apps' activities also suggests that Facebook occasionally isn't enforcing its own rules on data privacy.

It's no surprise that when Facebook is queried about its practice, its response: "We're focused on helping people make informed decisions about the apps they choose to use.

App developers agree to our policies when they register. If we find an app has violated our policies, through our automated systems, internal policy teams, or user reports, we take action."

In short, Facebook can gain deep knowledge of people's lives. It is, after all, a social network where users voluntarily share their names, closest friendships, snapshots, sexual preferences ("interested in men," "interested in women"), schools attended and countless other details, including moment-to-moment thoughts in the form of "status updates."

By default, Facebook applications you approve get access to your Facebook ID, name, profile photo, gender, list of friends, networks, locale, age range, and anything you have made 'Public'.

The "app economy," which includes Facebook as well as smartphone apps, is estimated to have generated $20 billion in revenue in 2011 by selling downloads, advertising, "virtual goods" and other products, according to estimates from Rubinson Partners, a market researcher.

By virtue of its sheer size and user base of 1.19 billion monthly active users as of 30th of October 2013, Facebook is at the heart of the personal data economy. Popular apps can quickly go "viral" there and gain millions of users, but can also flame out just as quickly. This explains why some apps seek to cash in by gathering as much data as possible and hoping to find ways to make money from it.

Facebook profiles are now set by default to let apps obtain all data from a user's friends except sexual preference, religion, and political views. That means, for instance, even if a user has set his or her birthday, location, and "online status" messages to be private to friends, their friends can approve an app that will also obtain that information.

Case Study:

In an article published by Forbes on the 16th of February 2012, Kashmir Hill headline was— **"How Target Figured Out A Teen Girl Was Pregnant Before Her Father Did."** A very interesting article describing how Target (one of the largest retailers in the world) gathered information on their shoppers, analyzed the data and predicted with a fairly high degree of certainty whether the woman was pregnant and in what stage and whether the child was a boy or a girl.

Target has figured out how to data mine its way into your womb. And based on its "pregnancy score," Target started sending coupons for baby items to its customers.

The store's bull's-eye logo has more connotations than what you might think. Visit the following website to read the article in more detail www.pi10m.com/b1/24

What can you do?

1. Close your browsers when not in use and delete your cookies.

2. Configure your browser to automatically do the following upon closing your browser:

    - Delete Internet temporary files
    - Delete your browsing history
    - Delete your recent searches

3. Be careful what applications you use.

4. Be careful what information you give out. This is covered in more details in Chapter 7—Social Networking Protection Guidelines.

For the more serious and conscious security user

1. Facebook have developed a number of applications that monitor application and data tracking. It's a good way of gaining a better understanding of what these applications do.

    - Visit Privacy Score—www.pi10m.com/b1/26 to ascertain the privacy risk of using a website based on how they handle your personal and tracking data.
    - Visit Privacy Choice—www.pi10m.com/b1/27 to gain an understanding of the different Facebook applications and their privacy relevance.

2. The *Wall Street Journal* have developed and analysed 100 of the most used applications that connect to Facebook's social-networking platform to see what data they sought from people—http://www.pi10m.com/b1/25

THE INTERNET ADDRESS (URL)

Uniform Resource Locator (URL) is the global address of documents and other resources on the World Wide Web. Whenever you visit a site, it has a unique address, like your postal address.

One of the biggest sources of malware infection for computers is visiting websites. Malware installed on the offending website is automatically installed on your computer.
However when someone sends you an email with an attached Internet link, how do you know that this is a valid website and not a malicious one?

According to Websense, the web has become increasingly more "malicious" in 2012. Websense recorded nearly a 6-fold increase in malicious sites overall. Moreover, 85% of these sites were found on legitimate web hosts that had been compromised (Websense 2013 Threat Report).

What can you do?

1. If you think the Internet link is not viable, then you are probably right. Don't bother clicking.

2. When assessing whether the Internet link is viable, evaluate the link by placing the mouse over the link. Compare the highlighted link with the URL link. Is it the same?

Here are is an example: www.paypal.com

Can you spot the problem in the following website?

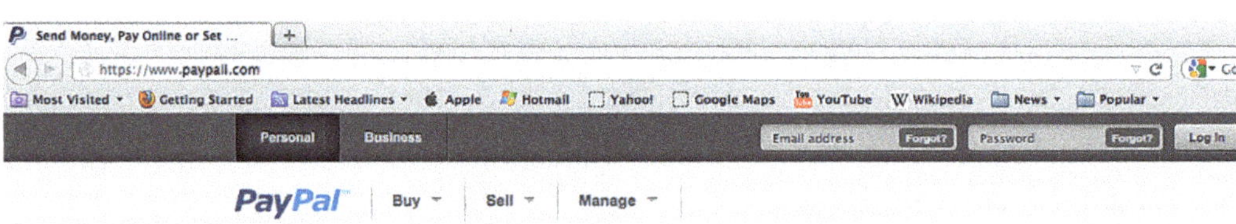

The URL above has an incorrect link. Its URL has an extra "l" on PayPal. Therefore this site should be avoided. Do not click it to verify.

Can you spot the problems with the following URLs?

- www.paypa1.com
- www.paypal.c0m

- www.paypal.con
- www.poypal.com
- www.payme.com
- www.paypalonline.com

3. Ignore requests.

- Ignore headlines. Such headlines are often ways to entice you to visit a malicious website.
- Ignore messages asking you to visit popular websites requesting you to verify or change your preference. For example: Facebook is offering its users the ability to change its colour interface from blue to bright pink.
- Ignore messages that you have become an instant winner, overnight millionaire, congratulations awards, etc. These are all ways to get you emotionally involved to click the link.
- Ignore survey messages. They are just another way to scam your identity.

4. Importantly, make sure that your antivirus has recently been updated.

For the more serious and conscious security user

There are a few tools that you can utilise to help you identify whether the site has its reputation evaluated and whether it contains any malicious content. Remember, these are tools that may provide more visibility, but do not rely on them 100%.

- **Websense Ace Insight** have a real-time reputation analysis of over 1 billion pieces of content daily—www.pi10m.com/b1/28
- **Zscaler URL Risk Analyzer** is a dynamic assessment engine that scores the safety of your website—www.pi10m.com/b1/29

There are other tools that can help you assess the Internet link reputation.

- **WOT** is one of our favourites in the web-of-trust application that can be found at the following site—www.pi10m.com/b1/17

If you undertake a web search without such an add-on, you get a web page that looks like the following images below. There is no way to determine if the websites are malicious or not.

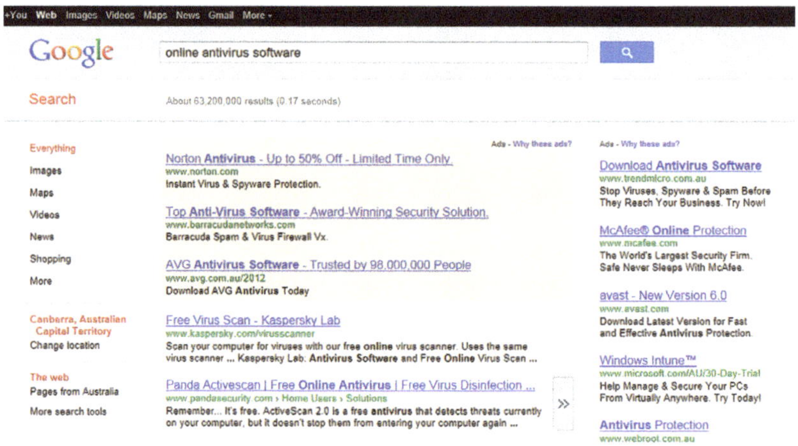

Let's look at the query if the web of trust add-on is installed. We get the same entries but now each site has a coloured circle based on its reputation allowing the home user to make an informed decision if the website is dangerous to visit or use.

WOT's traffic-light style rating system can be understood by the smallest of web surfers. Green means safe, yellow means caution, and red means Don't GO There!

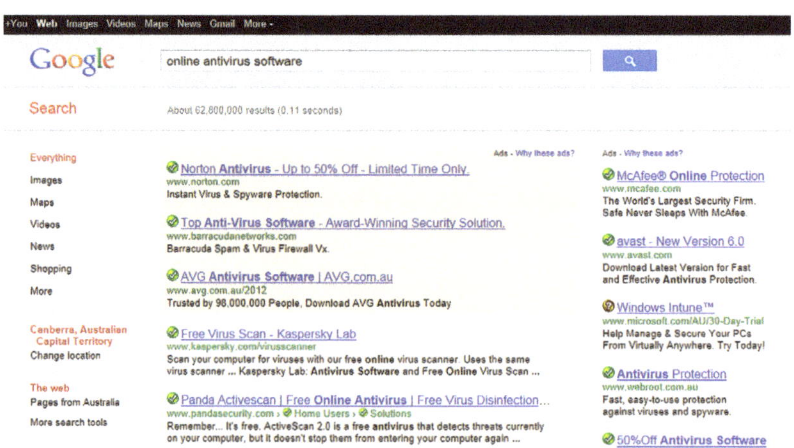

- **Trustwave** offers a free browser plugin that analyses web pages in real-time for Malware www.pi10m.com/b1/30

WEB EMAIL GUIDELINES

There are risks in using Cloud email services such as Hotmail, Yahoo, Gmail, and others. While you may think that access to these email tools is necessary for your productivity, think otherwise.

For example, you may be thinking that you are being a good agent of your company by sending data home to work on at night or over the weekend, but spare a thought to the following risk:

1. The information you transmitted is not necessarily encrypted.

2. The security of the email systems may not be on par with your corporate security requirements.

3. Your email mailbox content is constantly scanned, so that appropriate advertising can reach you. You have no controls on who can see your email.

4. The data may reside on various servers in various countries.

What can you do?

If you must use a web-based email system then we suggest you take the following steps:

1. Always use 'https' when accessing your web email. Hypertext Transfer Protocol Secure (HTTPS) is a widely used communications protocol for secure communication over a computer network, with especially wide deployment on the Internet.
   - When accessing your web email service, instead of typing http://www. gmail.com, type https://www.gmail.com.
   - Most email vendors do this automatically for you. This ensures that data is encrypted in transit.

2. Consider the use of encryption technology to protect the contents of the email sent by these services. One such product is Symantec's PGP, www.pi10m.com/b1/34. An open source solution is GnuPG www.pi10m.com/b1/35. You create your email in a text editor and use one of the above mentioned products to encrypt the text and paste the encrypted text back into your web browser. The receiver of the email has to repeat the process for decrypting the email.

3. If you have Microsoft Outlook or Outlook Express installed, consider configuring it to be the email user agent for the web-based email services. This will ensure integration with installed antivirus solutions and encryption technologies.

4. Unless the email is encrypted, because it could be stored anywhere in the world, do not send any confidential information in web-based email.

For the more serious and conscious security user

1. If you intend to send sensitive files or large attachments, utilise programs that are able to secure file transfer services such as

    - Citrix ShareFile—www.pi10m.com/b1/31
    - Lockbox—www.pi10m.com/b1/32
    - Hightail—www.pi10m.com/b1/33

PROTECTING YOUR WEBSITES AND APPLICATIONS

In recent years the popularity of websites and web applications has grown dramatically. Web-based applications allow an organisation to distribute services that can be accessed from any computer, notebooks, and smart mobile devices whether within or outside the organisation, equipped with a web browser of choice.

However, you need to pay attention: **Your website and its applications are under attack 24 hours a day!**

More than 50% of visitors to your website are non-human visitors, and that means one of two possibilities.

1. **There are good web crawlers** such as Google's search, Yahoo, or Microsoft Bing which are operated by well-known and commonly used services that regularly search your website and update their database.
2. **The bad web crawlers.** These include comment spammers, vulnerability scanners, and other malicious web crawlers (bots) that seek to take advantage of your website.

230 is the average number of vulnerabilities on a website (Imperva Web Application Attack Report—2011).

27 times per hour web applications on average are probed or attacked. That equates to once every two minutes (Imperva Web Application Attack Report—2011).

38,000 attacks per hour occur on web applications. That equates to ten per second (Imperva Web Application Attack Report 2012).

Web attacks are a serious challenge and threat facing organisations today. Typical firewall and antivirus solutions aren't capable of stopping web attacks. They are not designed to stop such threats. They cannot differentiate between web crawlers and human users, so they cannot block business logic attacks like site scraping (data extraction) and comment spam.

To make matters worse, predominantly these attacks are automated. Cyber-criminals are increasingly using automation to carry out their attacks on website and applications. If you thought that you wouldn't be targeted as you pose little relevance, then think otherwise. Automation attack doesn't discriminate!

You can no longer ignore the security of your web applications! Web applications collect personal, classified, and confidential information such as medical history, credit and bank account information, and user satisfaction feedback. Additionally, if your organisation is bound by legislation or industry compliance such as HIPAA, GLBA, PCI, or Sarbanes-Oxley to protect the privacy and security of personally identifiable information, and hackers can get at this sensitive information, you run the risk of being found guilty of non-compliance.

Threats and Challenges Facing Websites

The threat landscape for Internet and web applications is constantly changing. Key factors for this evolution are:

1. Huge motivation in successfully fleecing, stealing, and swindling the victim personal and/or corporate data.

2. Massive advancements made by attackers in developing even more crafty attack systems that are automated, persistent, and may be targeted as well.

3. New vulnerabilities are constantly discovered daily, due to software flaws.

As such, attackers can potentially use many different paths of attack through your web and applications to do harm to your business or organisation.

Many of these types of attacks are described in detail under the Open Web Application Security Project (OWASP)— http://www.owasp.org

The following seven steps will provide you with a high level strategic framework for you and your organisation to work with.

7 STEPS TO SECURING YOUR WEBSITE & APPLICATIONS

Step 1 > Security Assessment

Web application vulnerabilities remain the number one source of attacks. It's important to realise that:

- Web application software is notoriously full of exposures and vulnerabilities.
- Much in-house and even commercially developed web software often consider application security as an afterthought and is usually vulnerable to some of the types of attack as mentioned above.
- Attacking web applications is popular because it is often the easiest and most direct route to the corporate networks since almost all firewalls are configured to allow inbound port 80 and 443 TCP traffic.

Am I Vulnerable?

You are vulnerable as soon as you provide web services whether it is to the public or for internal business requirements.

How Do I Prevent This?

Preventing your website being successfully breached requires you to do the following:

- Run a comprehensive vulnerability assessment on your website and applications.
- Run a comprehensive framework for assessing the security of your web-based applications. This framework should include the following checks for:
  - Invalidated Input Parameters
  - Broken Access Control
  - Broken Authentication and Session Management
  - Cross Site Scripting
  - Cross Site Request Forgery
  - SQL and Command Injection
  - Improper Error Handling
  - Buffer Overflows
  - Insecure Configuration Management
- Importantly, include application security assessment as part of your Software Development Lifecycle.

Now, if this looks rather technical and "jargon talk," seek advice from a security expert.

- Develop a remediation strategy for those items discovered during the assessment.
- Ensure you understand their overall context within the framework of web application security.
- Regularly assess the above process on a continual basis.

Step 2 › Backup Management

What would happen if you woke up tomorrow and your web host had accidentally deleted your website?
What would you do if you found out that your host provider was no longer in operation?
What would you do if after any of the above situations occurred, that neither the host provider nor your business has a backup?

If your business relies heavily on online presence, then this could be a nightmare scenario.

Why are Website Backups so Important?

- **Don't assume your host provider has backup of your website**. In June 2011, a massive security breach with a large hosting provider resulted in the destruction of thousands of Australian websites. The company said that more than 4800 websites that were hosted on their computer servers had been destroyed with no chance of recovery.
- **Don't assume your host provider will be in business**.

Am I Vulnerable?

You are vulnerable if you do not keep an updated backup of your website.

What Can I Do?

If you developed your website on a test server or on your local computer, you may think that's enough as a backup protection. However, over time, websites are tweaked and changed and those changes often won't be reflected in the original version. If you run a forum, blog, or CRM system, much of your valuable content is uploaded by your users, and won't exist in any place other than on your website.

Here are recommended steps:

- Back up regularly.
- Test your backup. Test your recovery.
- Develop a Business Continuity Plan.
    - In the event your host provider is unable to recover your website
    - In the event your host provider is no longer viable
    - In the event you need to move your website to an alternative hosting provider.

Step 3 › Database Monitoring

Web applications are a prime target for attacks because they are easily accessible and they offer a lucrative entry point to valuable data, and most data resides in databases.

Database systems tend to be the principal business assets in an organisation. They store all the most critical company assets include client details, financial information, human resource details, product designs, and more—all the data that keeps your company in business and, as such, they need to be secure.

According to one recent Forrester study, 80 precent of data security breaches involve insiders, employees or those with internal access to an organisation, putting information at risk.

The big challenge for companies today, particularly as email and the Internet make sharing and distributing corporate information easier than ever, is to strike the right balance between providing workers with appropriate access and protecting sensitive information, as much as possible.

Am I Vulnerable?

If you hold a database and it contains sensitive, intellectual property or other valuable data, then it is extremely important to place protective measures.

What Can I Do?

In order to protect your key sensitive data, you will need to ensure the following key objectives are met:

- Audit all access to sensitive data by privileged and application users.
- Alert or block database attacks and abnormal access requests, in real time.
- Detect and virtually patch database software vulnerabilities, thereby reducing the window of exposure.
- Identify excessive and dormant user rights to sensitive data.
- Accelerate incident response and forensic investigation with advanced analytics.
- Utilise specialised database security technologies which should provide you with the following security features:
    - Database activity monitoring
    - Real time database protection
    - Aggregating and reviewing user rights
    - Providing vulnerability assessments
    - Auditing and reporting

Step 4—Web Application Firewall

The discovery of new web vulnerabilities and attacks on a daily basis confirms that web applications are not secure.

Vulnerabilities in the web infrastructure can appear when new features are introduced to applications. Even if applications written by a company's Information Systems team are almost perfect, one must still consider the security issues, which can occur when running third party applications. Since building security into application code requires constant revisions, breaches can creep in when programmers implement security fixes.

In a September 2009 piece titled "The Top Cyber Security Risks," the SANS Institute stated that attacks against web applications constitute more than 60% of the total Internet attacks. During the past couple of years, the number of web-related threats to organisations has risen sharply. The increase in attacks is also due in part to the sheer number of web applications being developed, a number that is skyrocketing.

However, organisations relying on traditional security mechanisms such as intrusion protection systems (IPS) that are dependent on signature matching and creating blacklists of disallowed activities are becoming less and less effective. These IPS solutions provide only a rudimentary line of defence against some of the first application-centric attacks such as SQL Injection and Cross-site Scripting.

Am I Vulnerable?

Attacks are becoming even more automated, perpetrated by organisations of infected machines (bots). Every day, millions of bots all around the world are unwittingly enlisted into service. These infected machines can target a specific company, send spam, conduct Distributed Denial of Service (DDoS), SQL injections, propagate malware, and any number of malicious acts. What hope have you got if you are relying on traditional security practices?

What Can I Do?

In response, Web Application Firewalls (commonly known as WAF) is rapidly evolving to defend Web applications against increasingly sophisticated attacks, perpetrated by a growing number of attackers.

The hallmark of a Web Application Firewall:

- A web application firewall must understand application structure, elements, and expected user behaviour in order to accurately detect attacks.
- The web application firewall needs to combine multiple strategies together to stop the automated attacks like site-scraping, application DDoS, comment spam, and automated SQL injection attacks.
- The ability to identify and stop fraudulent transactions.
- The ability to patch vulnerabilities on the fly, sometimes called "virtual patching." Virtual patching reduces the window of exposure and the cost of emergency fix and test cycles.
- It requires the ability to correlate attacks with accurate protection against malicious activity by analysing multiple data points, including protocol violations, attack signa-

tures, data leak signatures, and variance from past behaviour. This capability delivers stronger protection against today's complex, multi-vector attacks.
- The ability to protect Web 2.0 applications and XML without requiring any application changes.

You may also want to consider "Cloud WAF." This is an easy and affordable Cloud-based Web Application Firewall service that offers businesses a powerful way to protect critical Web applications without the need of infrastructure investment and expertise.

Cloud WAF is provisioned as a service, enabling organisations to jumpstart their web application security initiative in a matter of minutes.

Cloud WAF should be integrated with Cloud DDoS which is described in Step

Step 5 › Distributed Denial of Service Attack Protection

What is a Distributed Denial of Service Attack? A Distributed Denial of Service Attack (DDoS) occurs when multiple systems flood the bandwidth or resources of a targeted system, usually one or more web servers.

If an attacker mounts an attack from a single host, it would be classified as a DoS attack. In fact, any attack against availability would be classed as a Denial of Service attack. On the other hand, if an attacker uses many systems to simultaneously launch attacks against a remote host, this would be classified as a Distributed DoS attack.

The major advantages to an attacker of using a DDoS attack are that multiple machines can generate more attack traffic than one machine. Multiple attack machines are harder to turn off than one attack machine, and that the behaviour of each attack machine can be stealthier, making it harder to track and shut down.

These attacker advantages cause challenges for defence protection. For example, merely purchasing more incoming bandwidth than the current volume of the attack might not help, because the attacker might be able to simply add more attack machines. The downside however is that you will be lumped with higher bandwidth costs.

DDoS attacks have become the weapon of choice for hackers, criminals, and political cyber-terrorists. They are inexpensive to perform and difficult to stop. For a mere $50, a malicious user can rent a botnet to launch a 24-hour long attack on any website of their choosing.

DDoS attacks are also more sophisticated than ever. Advanced attacks now evade firewall detection by targeting application resources and vulnerabilities. To demonstrate how pervasive

DDoS attacks are, 74% of organisations sustained at least one DDoS attack during a 12 month period, according to Forrester Research.

Am I Vulnerable?

Any organisation is vulnerable to such an attack. It does not discriminate between the small business and an enterprise organisation.

What Can I Do?

There are very few solutions that can counter DDoS Attacks. Traditionally, organisations had to address the issue with their Internet Service Provider with little success. ISPs have little if no motivation to provide clean bandwidth services unless it provides this as an additional chargeable service.

However, one of the most effective ways in dealing with DDoS attacks is utilising Cloud DDoS protection.

Cloud DDoS Protection should offer a complete defence against all types of DDoS threats, including network-based attacks and application attacks that attempt to overwhelm server resources.

The other main benefit with Cloud DDoS Protection is that it can be rolled out without any hardware, software, or web application code changes. This effortless deployment allows organisations to be protected in a matter of minutes while maintaining their existing hosting provider and application infrastructure.

Step 6 > Visibility and Understanding

Simply knowing where web applications are and their details have been difficult tasks. This process is actually getting harder to manage because of several factors, including organisation expansion, mergers and acquisitions, and more frequent department restructuring, not to mention the prolific growth in web applications in general.

Gaining visibility of the type of applications that are running on your environment is critically important. You will never succeed in placing protection frameworks and policies, unless you know about them.

Equally important is having sufficient forensic evidence to analyse and build in new security controls. This is why audit information is such a critical part of any security strategy. Should you experience a security incident or breach, you can then address this question along with other pressing points such as:

- How long have they been doing this?
- What else have they been doing?
- Who else might be doing something similar?

Importantly, audits should lead to the understanding and visibility of usage trends, bandwidth utilization, and performance levels. It will also need to provide visibility into web transactions from the application level and at the business abstraction level.

Detailed investigations as such will be able to yield patterns, anomalies, and behavioural interactions that can then in turn be used to generate more exacting security policies, reports, and remediation efforts.

Am I Vulnerable?

The saying goes "you cannot manage what you can't measure. And you can't secure what you can't manage."

What Can I Do?

Threats have evolved and become industrialised. Attackers are targeting web applications to get data. In order to protect your organisation, it is important to have the visibility, understanding, and the insight of what applications are running in your own environment.

Step 7—Domain Name Management

The security of your domain name data is no different from other sensitive business information. Any breach of security can leave your business vulnerable to external threats and potential loss of confidential information.

Am I Vulnerable?

Yes. Should you be managing your corporate online services, you need to ensure the protection of your domain name.

What Can I Do?

1. **Your Domain Name Password.** Each domain name in the registry database is password protected. Anyone who has access to your domain name password may be able to use it to access to your domain name, including your website and emails. Setting up a strong and secure authentication credentials is imperative.

2. **Your Domain Name Registration Details.** If you do not maintain accurate and up-

to-date domain name registration details, including contact details, you may risk losing your domain name. You can check your domain name registration details at anytime, by doing a **WHOIS** search on your domain name registration

3. **Your Domain Name Expiry Date**. All domain names have a fixed license period, meaning that you must renew your domain every period. Typically, it is around two years. You should keep a record of your domain name expiry date and make sure to renew it when the time comes. If you fail to renew your domain name, it will become available for registration on a first come, first served basis and you do not have any automatic rights to get it back.

For the more security-conscious practitioner and Web Developer

1. Setting up good password policies for your web application
   - Make sure that password length is at least 8 characters which should include upper, lower , number and special characters
   - Block account after 10 authentication failures
   - Provide onscreen advice on how to chose a strong password during setup
   - Provide users with an onscreen assessment of password strength while they are selecting a password
2. Effective management of your Domain Name System (DNS). Think of it like a post box. For example, the domain name www.example.com hypothetically translates to the addresses 192.0.43.10 (IPv4) and 2620:0:2d0:200::10 (IPv6).

By tricking the principle provider of the DNS for your website name www.example.com to a rogue site, a mechanism is provided for leaking information about the internal structure and setup of your website infrastructure. This could be used to facilitate attacks of numerous kinds. Similarly, by tricking the DNS server to redirect requests from your website to a site set up by a hacker, inappropriate content could be displayed or attacks launched from the rogue website against your customers. Both of which could cause incalculable damage to your brand and its reputation.

The use of Domain Name System Security Extension (DNSSEC) by your DNS provider can greatly mitigate this risk. DNSSEC was designed to protect the public by ensuring that websites visited are the real deal and not imposters. Phony websites aim to steal users' login names, passwords, and money, and DNSSEC technology helps prevent such thefts by blocking bogus page elements and flagging pages whose DNS identity has been hijacked.

The use of DNSSEC is becoming more common with DNS providers. The US government has strongly invested with DNSSEC and many other government agencies will follow suit.

REMINDER! Don't forget to register at www.pi10m.com

By registering your details, we will be able to provide you with free updates to the book, critical security alerts, valuable security tools that you can start using right now for free, answer your questions and much much more.

SUMMARY OF POINTS

As mentioned, the Internet threat landscape is constantly changing. Just as you take precautions to protect yourself in the real world, you need to take precautions to protect yourself and your business online.

This chapter therefore presents a number of important considerations and steps for you to follow. They are not difficult. However, it is well advisable that you go over this chapter carefully as it presents some important points about Internet best security practices.

- **Patch Your System**—Ensure that your systems and applications are regularly updated with the latest patches and updates, including your browser.
- **Browse Safely**—Be smart about websites that you want to visit and close your browser when not in use.
- **Delete Internet temporary files.**
- **Use Strong Passwords when Authenticating.**
- **Use two-factor authentication if possible.** This might be slightly inconvenient when you log in, but it pales in comparison if your personal data ends up in the wrong hands.
- **Ensure your Firewall is Turned On.**
- **Manage your Domain Name** – Keep track of when it expires and renew it well in advance.

FOR THE MORE SECURITY-CONSCIOUS USER / ORGANISATION

- Utilise a 3rd Part Web and Email Security Gateway—There are a number of well-recognised web and email security programs that will handle the web and email security as your first line of defence. Such systems should be able to protect you from malware, phishing, malicious websites, click fraud, and other dangers for Web. It should also protect you from viruses, spam, and other spoofing attacks for email. These solutions can also be obtained as a Cloud Service.
- **Employ an Application Web Firewall (WAF) for your Web Servers**—This will protect your web servers and applications from security threats. Utilise a Cloud WAF for simplicity and effectiveness.
- **Employ Data Base Security**—Monitor and secure sensitive data stored in databases.
- **Develop Acceptable Usage Policies**—Policies are a collectionof guidelines that you can undertake to ensure business runs consistency, efficiency, effectiveness, confidentiality, and integrity. This is explained in Chapter 10.
- **User Education**—Proactively help and engage with users about Internet best practices.

6

Internet Fraud Protection Guidelines

Consumer - Online shopping is practical and convenient, why would anyone target me?
Cyber Criminal - The money's the same, whether you earn it or scam it.

– BOAZ FISCHER

Every day, consumers receive offers that just sound too good to be true. In the past, these offers came through the mail or by telephone. Now the bad guys have found a new avenue to pitch their frauds, the Internet. The on-line scams know no national borders or boundaries and they respect no investigative jurisdictions. But, as with all scammers, they have one objective and that is to separate you from your money and steal your data.

The doors that provide entry to good customers online are the same doors that fraudsters use to gain entry—logins, new account registration, and online purchases. The keys that enable people to pass through these doors are credentials, identities, account numbers, credit cards, and personal information. The bad guys steal this information by tricking unsuspecting consumers into giving it to them innocently, or using technology to silently take over their computers and impersonate them or capture their keystrokes.

An interesting point about fraud is that it is a crime in which you decide on whether to participate. Online fraud is a game of deception, but the strategy and tactics employed by a scammer can be quite different depending on the target, the industry, and the objective.
Hanging up the phone or not responding to shady mailings or emails makes it difficult for the scammer to commit fraud. But, con artists are very persuasive, using all types of excuses, explanations, and offers to lead you and your money away from common sense.

The Challenge

Fraudsters are increasingly innovative in their methods to trick online users and to hide their own tracks while executing their fraudulent activities. They are also increasingly targeting attacks to web applications, embedding with malware, and malicious code in the event of stealing user credentials, infecting end users' devices when visiting, or both. Consequently, this allows hackers to collect critical information from users as well as the ability to fully control any Internet session initiated from the end user device.

What are the common scams?

- Charity
- Overseas Mortgage Investment
- Romance
- Telemarketing
- Distribution of rogue software such as fake antivirus software

What to look for?

- Being asked for personal financial information such as bank account information or credit card numbers via the telephone or by email.

- Using high pressure sales tactics so as not to give you time to think about the information you are providing.
- Being told you have won a lottery or sweepstakes.
- Being asked to help transfer funds out of a foreign country for a share of the money.
- Being offered help in repairing credit scores for an advanced fee.
- Receiving a counterfeit cashier's check or money order for more than the cost of the item you are selling.

Looks to be good to be true?

Education, good judgment, and a healthy dose of skepticism are the best defences against becoming a victim. Remember, if it looks too good to be true, it probably is!

There are two classes of Internet fraud.

1. Technical

   With this type of fraud, malware is either installed on your system to capture you Internet banking details, identity, or online credentials, or it is accomplished by tricking you to enter this personal identification typically into a website masquerading as a financial institution website.

2. Social Engineering

   This type of money fraud is much more subtle and essentially involves you being deceived in parting with your money. These can range from the infamous "Nigerian Scam" to selling you goods and not delivering the items once you have paid for the goods.

How much is fraud costing your business?

- Estimate $3.4 Billion lost to online merchant fraud (2012 Online Fraud Report CyberSource).
- According to the Federal Trade Commission, as many as 9 million Americans have their identities stolen each year.
- Fraudsters exploited weak internal controls—up 74% (KPMG Analysis of Global Patterns of Fraud).
- Fraud takes longer to detect. North America averages 4.2 years; Australia 4.3 years; Western Europe 3.7 years; South America 2.1 years. And 1 in 7 workplace frauds are discovered by chance. (KPMG Analysis of Global Patterns of Fraud)

- One in 10 Australian Internet users have lost money to online identity fraud over the past year with losses totalling $1.286 billion, according to the VeriSign Online Fraud Barometer figures released in July 2010 (VeriSign is now owned by Symantec).
- More than 11.6 million Americans were victims of identity fraud in 2011, an increase of 13% over 2010 (Javelin Strategy and Research. Identity Fraud Survey Report, February 2012).

Here is an overview of some of the more common types of Internet fraud.

Online Automotive Fraud

A fraudster posts a non existent vehicle for sale to a website, advertised for well below its market value. An interested buyer, hopeful for a bargain, emails the fraudster, who responds saying the car is still available but is located overseas. Or, the scammer will say that he is out of the country but the car is with a shipping company. The scam artist then instructs the victim to send a deposit or full payment via wire transfer to initiate the "shipping" process. To make the transaction seem more legitimate, the fraudster will ask the buyer to send money to a fake agent of a third party that offers purchase protection. The unwitting victims wire the funds, and subsequently discover they have been scammed.

Purchase Fraud

Defrauders negotiate large purchases with the victim (e.g. ordering $50,000 to $200,000 worth of goods) agreeing to an advance payment via bank wire transfer. After ordering, the fraudster claims that paying via wire transfer is impractical, and instead sends a counterfeit check drawn on the account of a real, uninvolved organisation as an alternate payment. After the check clears, the victim company ships the goods. When the uninvolved organisation notices the fraudulent transaction against their account, they request a chargeback, resulting in the victim losing both the money and the goods. The fraudster is taking advantage of the lag between the cashing and clearing of the check.

Money Transfer Fraud

I'm sure you have seen the Nigerian Scam. Other more sophisticated money frauds will offer you the opportunity to earn an income from transferring funds. Here is an example:

> Dear Sir/Madam, I am XXXXX XXXXX, Human Resources Manager of XXXXX located in XXXX. We deal in XXXXXXX articles such XXXXXX worldwide. Our website is XXXXXX. We are currently in search of a book-keeper/company representative who would assist us in receiving payment from our customers in America/Canada/Asia and other part of Europe. This offer is absolutely legal and

> you do not need any capital to start. Your Job description is as follows: (1) You would receive payment on our behalf from our various clients which would come in the form of cashier's checks, traveler's checks and official checks. (2) You then get the payments deposited/cashed at your bank. (3) You then deduct a commission of 10% of each payment you would be receiving, as been our representative and then send the balance money via western union to any of our agent or offices that you would be instructed. HOW MUCH WILL YOU EARN? 10% from each operation! For instance: you receive 7000 USD via checks on our behalf. You will cash the money and keep $700 (10% from $7000) for yourself! At the beginning your commission will equal 10%, though later it will increase up to 12%! Our payments will be issued out in your name, as we would inform our clients to do so. If you are interested in this offer, kindly provide us with the below details. 1) Full name 2) Full house address Street/Ave, City, State and Zip Cope 3) Phone numbers 4) Age & Sex 5) Present Occupation PLEASE NOTE THAT ALL REPLIES SHOULD BE SENT THIS E-MAIL ADDRESS: XXXXXXXXXXXX Thanks for your anticipated action. And we hope to hear back from you. XXXXXX XXXXXX (Human Resources Manager)

The fraudsters then send fake checks or postal money orders in the hope that the victims will cash the fake money instruments, and send money to the scammers before the fraud is discovered.

Dating Fraud

Online dating frauds often referred to as a "sweetheart swindle." The con artist develops a relationship with his victim and convinces them to send money to the fraudster. The requests for money can be a one-time event, or repeated over an extended period of time, but they typically ask for some form of help:

- Requests for money, or for the victim to cash a check or money order
- Claims to be a US citizen who is abroad, well off, or a person of importance
- Claims to be a contractor needing help with a business deal
- Claims to need money for a parent's "operation in the hospital"

Most online dating services experience difficulties dealing with fraudsters and issue warnings to their users.

SEO Fraud

Search Engine Optimization fraud involves a supposed Internet marketing specialist presenting a prospective client with detailed graphs and charts indicating that the client's website receives some number of "hits" per month. The specialist claims his services will increase web traffic, thus increasing the site's sales revenue. After payment, the scammer does not provide the proposed services.

Auction Fraud

Auction fraud involves fraud attributable to the misrepresentation of a product advertised for sale through an Internet auction site or the non-delivery of products purchased through an Internet auction site. Typically the auction exhibits the following characteristics

1. The seller posts the auction as if he resides in the United States, then responds to victims with a congratulatory email stating he is outside the United States for business reasons, family emergency, etc.
2. The subject requests funds to be wired directly to him/her via Western Union, MoneyGram, or bank-to-bank wire transfer. By using these services, the money is virtually unrecoverable with no recourse for the victim.
3. Sellers acting as authorised dealers or factory representatives in countries where there would be no such dealers should be avoided.
4. Buyers who ask for the purchase to be shipped using a certain method to avoid customs or taxes inside another country should be avoided.
5. Credit card purchases where the address of the card holder does not match the shipping address.

Counterfeit Cashier's Check

The counterfeit cashier's check scheme targets individuals who use Internet classified advertisements to sell merchandise. Typically, an interested party located outside the United States contacts a seller. The seller is told that the buyer has an associate in the United States who owes him money. As such, he will have the associate send the seller a cashier's check for the amount owed to the buyer.

The amount of the cashier's check will be considerably more than the price of the merchandise and the seller is told the excess amount will be used to pay the shipping costs associated with getting the merchandise to his location. The seller is instructed to deposit the check, and as soon as it clears, to wire the excess funds back to the buyer or to another associate identified as a shipping agent. In most instances, the money is sent to locations in West Africa.

Because a cashier's check is used, a bank will typically release the funds immediately, or after a one or two day hold. Falsely believing the check has cleared, the seller wires the money as instructed.

Credit Card Fraud

The seller, usually foreign subjects, uses fraudulent credit cards. The unauthorised use of a credit/debit card, or card number, to fraudulently obtain money or property is considered credit card fraud. Credit/debit card numbers can be stolen from unsecured websites, or can be obtained in an identity theft scheme.

Debt Elimination Fraud

Debt elimination schemes involve websites advertising a legal way to dispose of mortgage loans and credit card debts. Most often, all that is required of the participant is to send $1,500 to $2,000 to the subject, along with all the particulars of the participant's loan information and a special power of attorney authorizing the subject to enter into transactions regarding the title of the participant's home on their behalf. The subject then issues bonds and promissory notes to the lenders that purport to legally satisfy the debts of the participant. In exchange, the participant is then required to pay a certain percentage of the value of the satisfied debts to the subject.

Escrow Services Fraud

In an effort to persuade a wary Internet auction participant, the perpetrator will propose the use of a third-party escrow service to facilitate the exchange of money and merchandise. The victim is unaware the perpetrator has actually compromised a true escrow site and, in actuality, created one that closely resembles a legitimate escrow service. The victim sends payment to the phony escrow and receives nothing in return. Or the victim sends merchandise to the subject and waits for his/her payment through the escrow site which is never received because it is not a legitimate service.

Internet Extortion

Internet extortion involves hacking into and controlling various industry databases, promising to release control back to the company if funds are received, or the subjects are given web administrator jobs. Similarly, the subject will threaten to compromise information about consumers in the industry database unless funds are received.

Investment Fraud

Investment fraud is an offer using false or fraudulent claims to solicit investments or loans, or providing for the purchase, use, or trade of forged or counterfeit securities.

Lottery Fraud

The lottery scheme deals with persons randomly contacting email addresses advising them they have been selected as the winner of an international lottery.

The email message usually reads similar to the following:

"This is to inform you of the release of money winnings to you. Your email was randomly selected as the winner and therefore you have been approved for a lump sum payout of $500,000. To begin your lottery claim, please contact the processing company selected to process your winnings."

An agency name follows this body of text with a point of contact, phone number, fax number, and an email address. An initial fee ranging from $1,000 to $5,000 is often requested to initiate the process and additional fee requests follow after the process has begun. These emails may also list a United States point of contact and address while also indicating the point of contact at a foreign address.

Phishing / Spoofing

Phishing and spoofing are somewhat synonymous in that they refer to forged or faked electronic documents. Spoofing generally refers to the dissemination of email which is forged to appear as though it was sent by someone other than the actual source. Phishing, often utilised in conjunction with a spoofed email, is the act of sending an email falsely claiming to be an established legitimate business in an attempt to dupe the unsuspecting recipient into divulging personal, sensitive information such as passwords, credit card numbers, and bank account information after directing the user to visit a specified website. The website, however, is not genuine and was set up only as an attempt to steal the user's information.

Ponzi / Pyramid Fraud

Ponzi or pyramid schemes are investment scams in which investors are promised abnormally high profits on their investments. No investment is actually made. Early investors are paid returns with the investment money received from the later investors. The system usually collapses. The later investors do not receive dividends and lose their initial investment.

Spam

With improved technology and worldwide Internet access, spam, or unsolicited bulk email, is now a widely used medium for committing traditional white-collar crimes including financial institution fraud, credit card fraud, and identity theft, among others. It is usually considered unsolicited because the recipients have not opted to receive the email.

When fraudsters use computers to steal money, they don't usually go after private individuals. The average person doesn't keep a sizable sum in a retail banking account.
Instead, most computer fraudsters target commercial banking accounts. Small and medium sized business accounts carry much heftier balances.

When they send out malicious spam more often than not, it is made to attract the attention of small business owners and employees. Getting malware installed on the right business computer can result in a huge payoff for the crooks. Typically, spam email wording is a bit vague, probably because these emails aren't intended to convey any real information. They are designed to spark users' curiosity and make them act upon the contents, thereby infecting the computer or getting them to respond to the email indicating that the user is actually real.

Click Fraud

Click fraud is a type of Internet crime that occurs in pay-per-click online advertising when a person, automated script, or computer program imitates a legitimate user of a web browser. Each time a (believed to be) valid web user clicks on an ad, the advertiser pays the advertising network, who in turn pays the publisher a share of this money. This revenue-sharing system is seen as an incentive for click fraud.

The protections from these types of fraud are as follows:

1. If you want to invest wisely and stay clear of frauds, you must get the facts.

2. If the offer seems too good to be true, then it generally is and is best avoided.

3. When you are buying goods on the Internet, unless you can absolutely trust whom you are paying, always pay using a method with protection against non-delivery of goods such as a credit card or a payment service such as PayPal (www.paypal.com).

4. Always be aware of your bank balance and flag any unusual transactions with your financial institution.

5. The types of investment fraud seen online mirror the frauds perpetrated over the phone or through the mail. Consider all offers with skepticism.

6. For online auctions, you need to know how the auction works and how the company will act if a problem occurs. Keep in mind that the method of payment is critical when you have to send a payment.

7. Feedback from previous customers is another thing to consider.

8. Watch out for unexpected costs such as shipping and handling.

9. Be vigilant in receiving unsolicited messages whether it comes as an email, sms, Social Network messages, or any others. Best is to completely ignore such messages.

10. Be attentive when receiving some form of voice communications getting you to act to reveal personal information or do something for them.

SAFE BANKING GUIDELINES

If you have ever received an email from a bank asking you to confirm your credentials as they have had a security update to their system, then presume it is most likely a phishing attack. Banks don't send such notifications!

The simple purpose of such emails is to capture your authentication credential details, hijack your browser session, and to leave some malware on your system.

Once they have those details, they can fleece your account.

Criminals today can hijack active online banking sessions, and new malware can fake the account balance to prevent victims from seeing that they're being defrauded.

Users are constantly are under attack. 45% of machines are crimeware infected, 75% go undetected by anti-malware—with an annual cost of $350 billion per year (Anti-Phishing Working Group (APWG)).

Banks take pride on being able to offer their customers the convenience of online banking, but they face a serious challenge on their hands. How much investment in security technology is required to provide acceptable protection standards? How much investment can they offer to raise user awareness of online banking risk? How much money are they willing to risk from fraudulent transactions?

Having said that, there are numerous things you can do increase the safety of your online banking experience:

- Use a dedicated computer to perform only banking transactions. Do not use work applications, e-mail, or visit nonbanking websites.
- Use a dedicated web browser to perform your web banking. For example, use Firefox to do all your online banking. Use Internet Explorer, Safari, or Google Chrome to access other non-banking websites.
- Conduct banking operations in a secured environment. If you can use Two-Factor Authentication to access your online account securely.
- Never store the banking credentials on the machine you are using to access the Internet unless those credentials are stored in an encrypted password management application such as LastPass—www.pi10m.com/b1/3.
- Remember, no legitimate bank will ask you to send your banking password via email.
- Always manually enter the URL of the bank every time you log in, never by clicking a link.

- Continue to obtain paper balances from the bank, and if the paper balance does not look correct, immediately refer the problem to your bank.
- Protect the computer with anti-malware software.
- Keep the computer refreshed with the latest software updates.
- Use strong, two-factor authentication for gaining online access (if such security features is provided by the bank).
- Unless it is an absolute emergency, never accesses the bank from a system you do not have full control over. You never know if the system has software installed that will record your online banking credentials. If you must, use such a system, but as soon as possible log on to your bank from a trusted computer system and change your password.

BUYING SAFELY ONLINE

Here are five simple steps that you need to take into consideration when purchasing goods and services online.

1. **Searching** - Whether you're just browsing or you have something specific in mind, keep an eye out for significantly undervalued items—if it seems too good to be true, it probably is.

2. **The Seller** - Once you've found something you're interested in, find out some more about it.
   a. Check that the supplier is legitimate.
   b. Get as much information that you can.

3. **Inspecting the Item** - The photos of the item might be fabulous, but nothing is as good as the real thing.
   a. Ask lots of questions about the product
   b. Be wary of sellers asking for a deposit at this stage. If you do choose to put a deposit down, make sure you get a receipt stamped with the date and time.

4. **Making a Deal** - Before you make an offer, know what your rights are.
   a. What is the warranty? Will the warranty be accepted in your country?
   b. What support is available?

5. **Payment** - Be safe when paying the seller. Use a method of payment that provides you with proof of purchase like a receipt or email confirmation directly from the provider.
   a. Never send cash in the mail to any financial institution.

SELLING SAFELY ONLINE

Here are five simple steps that you need to take into consideration when selling goods and services online.

1. **Creating Your Advertisement** - Make sure your advertisement has a strong security account.

2. **Answering Buyer's Questions** - Potential buyers will ask questions about the item and to make sure you're a legitimate seller.
    a. Be wary of buyers requesting specific personal details. You shouldn't need to provide them with your account details or any banking information.
    b. Be wary of buyers who offer you much more than the asking price or who ask you to pay for services such as shipping, agent fees, or customs charges.

3. **Inspecting the Item** - Buyers can ask to inspect the item prior to purchase so they can make sure they're happy with it.
    a. Is the buyer who they say they are? If you can, verify who they are.

4. **Making a Deal** - Before you accept an offer:
    a. Don't take your advertisement down until you are certain you have received payment from the buyer. It won't cost you anything to have it up longer.
    b. Ensure you have your transfer of ownership details ready to go.

5. **Payment** - Be safe when paying the seller.
    a. Don't rely on "proof" of payment from the buyer. Check with your bank, PayPal, or other provider that the money has been cleared and you can see the funds in your account before parting with your item.
    b. Give the buyer a receipt to confirm you've received their payment.

6. **Beware** of PayPal scams.

POINT OF SALES PROTECTION GUIDELINES

Typically, business people believe that "it will never happen to them" when it comes to hackers stealing their information and money, but you might be surprised to know that most attacks are directed against small companies as they are more easily breached, due to lack of security control.

Interestingly, such attacks can be prevented with a few small and relatively easy steps. Hackers are opportunists. Like computers, Point-of-Sales (POS) systems that process customer payments are also vulnerable. Increasingly, this has become an attractive target.

Below you'll find a few tips based on Point-of-Sale systems.

- **Change administrative passwords on all of your POS systems**—Hackers are scanning the Internet for easily guessable passwords.
- **Implement a firewall or access control list on remote access/administration services**—If hackers can't reach your system, they can't easily steal from it.
- **Avoid using your POS systems to browse the web**—If you do not use your POS for accessing the web, you reduce the chance of your system being infected.
- **Make sure your POS is a PCI-DSS compliant**—If you are unsure, ask your vendor.

Following these simple practices will save a lot of wasted money, time, and other troubles for your business and your customers.

RECOGNISING IDENTITY THEFT ATTACKS

Identity theft is a form of fraud or cheating of another person's identity in which someone pretends to be someone else by assuming that person's identity.

Identity fraud and theft are gaining significant ground. It is up to you to ensure your personal details are kept confidential and secure.

Identifying a Social Engineering Attack

Social engineering is the act of manipulating people into performing actions or divulging confidential information, rather than using technology to access your confidential information.

In a typical scenario, the attacker creates and uses an invented scenario to engage you in a manner that increases the chance that you will divulge information or perform actions.

In many cases, the attacker will use an emotional engagement trick that may be based on:

- Time—If they can get you to act now, thereby not providing you the time to think, judge, clarify, or verify makes it more compelling and easier to succeed.
- Loss—Human behaviour is driven by the loss of something. Therefore, if the attacker can create a scenario of the feelings of loss, you will more likely be motivated.
- Greed—Human behaviour is driven by greed or gain. Typical attacks have succeeded in convincing the victim that they will gain something from the transaction.

In the event that the person requests information from you whether it be financial (credit card details, bank access details), personal (birthday, passwords), business related or other

1. Verify who the person is. Use other means, other communication to verify if the story is true or false.
2. Stall for time and see how they react.
3. Call the police.

In the event that the person requests you to do something such as clicking on an attachment of an email, downloading a file to your computer, opening a bank account, sending or providing money or otherwise

1. Verify who the person is. Use other means, other communication to verify the story is true or false.
2. Stall for time and see how they react.
3. Call the police.
4. Checkout the scam watch website—www.scamwatch.gov.au. This is an Australian government setup website suitable for anyone in the world who is looking to gain some knowledge in protection against scams.

Spotting phishing attacks via email

Below is an example of an email that is used for a phishing attack. The attack is most likely to gain access to the potential victim's PayPal account and use the other information to commit identity fraud.

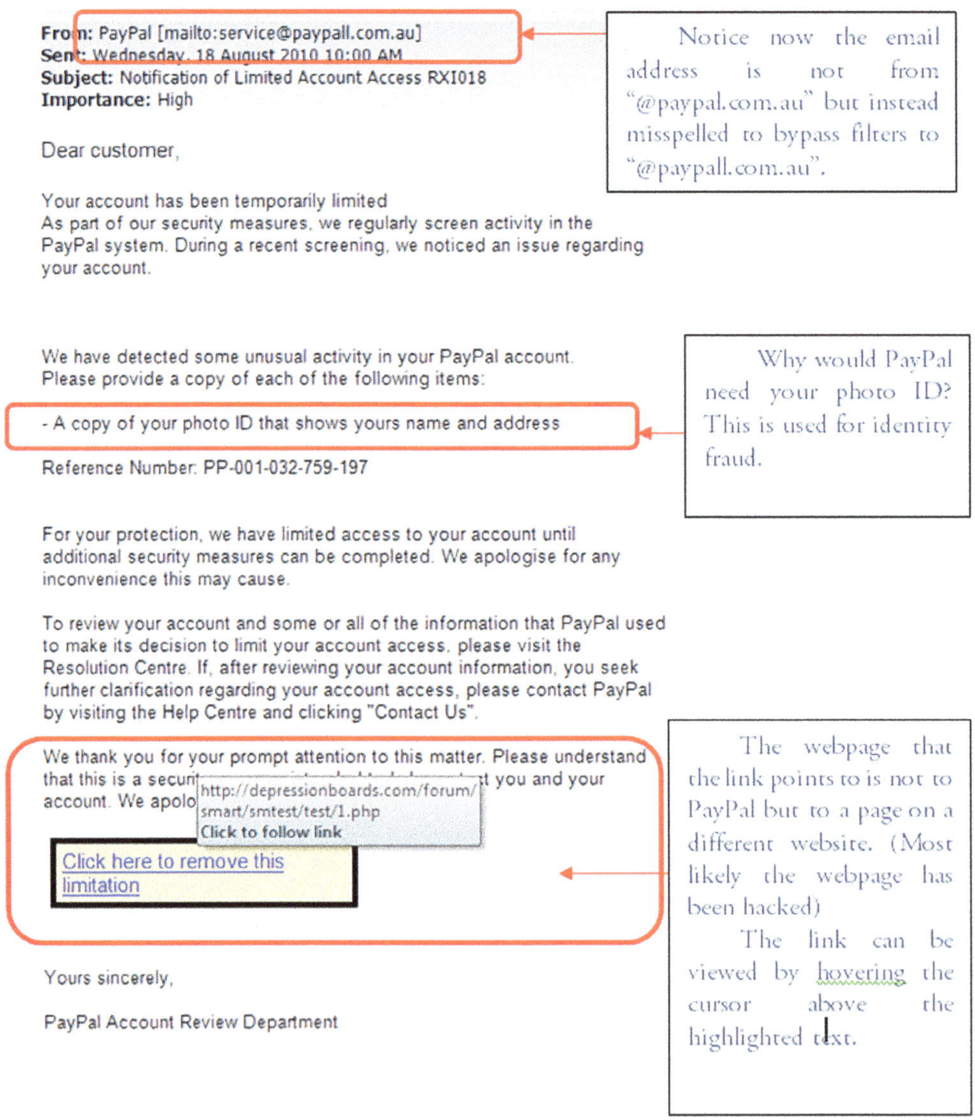

From: PayPal [mailto:service@paypall.com.au]
Sent: Wednesday, 18 August 2010 10:00 AM
Subject: Notification of Limited Account Access RXI018
Importance: High

Dear customer,

Your account has been temporarily limited
As part of our security measures, we regularly screen activity in the PayPal system. During a recent screening, we noticed an issue regarding your account.

We have detected some unusual activity in your PayPal account. Please provide a copy of each of the following items:

- A copy of your photo ID that shows yours name and address

Reference Number: PP-001-032-759-197

For your protection, we have limited access to your account until additional security measures can be completed. We apologise for any inconvenience this may cause.

To review your account and some or all of the information that PayPal used to make its decision to limit your account access, please visit the Resolution Centre. If, after reviewing your account information, you seek further clarification regarding your account access, please contact PayPal by visiting the Help Centre and clicking "Contact Us".

We thank you for your prompt attention to this matter. Please understand that this is a securi… t you and your account. We apolo…

http://depressionboards.com/forum/smart/smtest/test/1.php
Click to follow link

Click here to remove this limitation

Yours sincerely,

PayPal Account Review Department

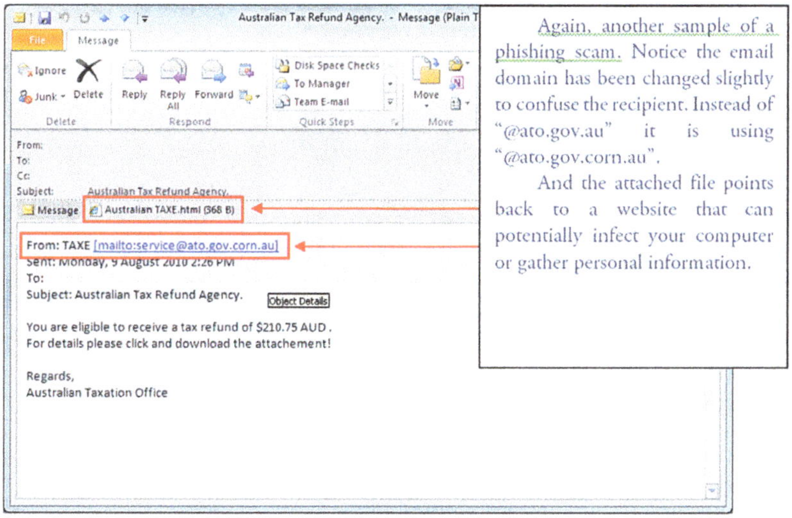

Spotting phishing attacks via voice communications

Vishing—uses social engineering attacks over the telephone system, most often using features facilitated by Voice over IP (VoIP), to gain access to private personal and financial information from the public Internet for the purpose of financial reward.
Vishing is very hard for legal authorities to monitor or trace.

Like email Phishing, the attacker exploits your emotions by getting you to act quickly. Here is an example

1. Typically, when the victim answers the call, an automated recording is played to alert the consumer that their credit card has had fraudulent activity or that their bank account has had unusual activity or that the bank has configured new security systems. The message instructs the victim to call a designated phone number immediately.

2. When the victim calls the number, it is answered by automated instructions to enter their credit card number or bank account number on the key pad.

3. Once the consumer enters their credit card number or bank account number, the attacker has the information necessary to make fraudulent use of the card or to access the account.

4. The call is often used to harvest additional details such as security PIN, expiration date, date of birth, etc.

To protect yourself from Voice attacks

1. Do not provide under any circumstance any details about yourself.

2. Be highly suspicious when receiving messages directing you to call and provide credit card or bank numbers.
    a. If speaking to a person, ask the incident number and then hang up.
    b. Contact the bank as printed on your credit card or bank statements that you have and verify the incident. **Do not use the phone number provided by the caller!**
    c. If the voice call is automated, contact the bank as printed on your credit card or bank statements that you have and verify incident. **Do not use the phone number provided by the caller!**

3. Be highly suspicious when receiving calls directing you to do something such as sending money to an account, opening an account.
    a. Verify who the caller is even if he or she appears to be a family member.
    b. Verify the story. Who else could you talk to confirm the story?
    c. Stall for time and see how they react.
    d. Call the bank and police to verify whether they know of any phone scams.

Spotting phishing attacks via sms communications (smishing)

With the rise in use of mobile phones, Smishing scams are growing in popularity with fraudsters. Mobile users are being targeted by text messages from seemingly legitimate sources. These messages, like phishing scams, seek to dupe users into providing personal details or communicating via email.

What can you do to avoid these scams?

1. Check to see if the message hasn't come from an overseas number. Legitimate looking messages from an international number are a tell-tale sign, and the text is a scam.

2. Be wary of text messages that encourage you to communicate via email. Now that you have the potential buyer phone number, we encourage you to communicate via a phone call rather than online.

3. Check the message hasn't come from an automated mobile number. Call the number to make sure it is active, rather than replying to the text.

4. Never click on links in text messages.

Here is an example of Smishing:

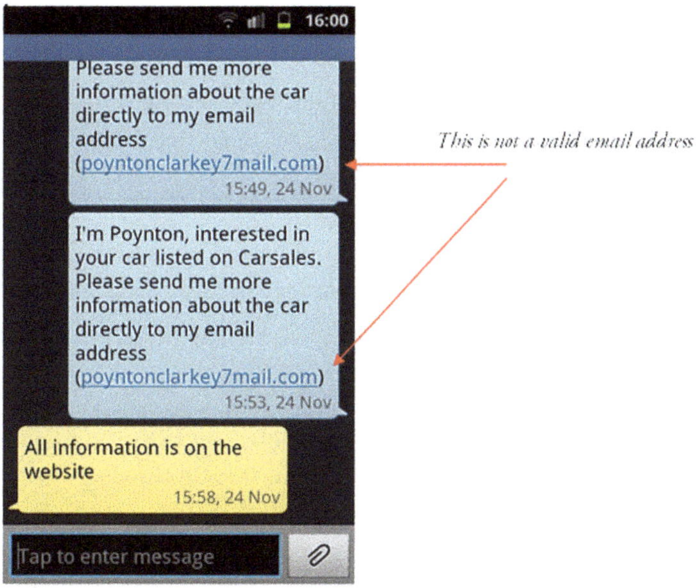

For the more security-conscious user

If security is a great concern, here are some additional steps for your consideration:

- You might want to consider using separate computers. Utilise a computer just for your business and Internet banking, while your regular computer could be used for general day-to-day Internet browsing purposes, games, emails, social media communications, and other non-business related activities.
- Consider using additional application security protection.
  - Website reputation and classification—Add-on software to your browser that will let you know whether websites have a good or a bad reputation.
  - Secure web gateway—That will provide your business with real-time analysis of web pages, content and data, and threat protection from malware; apply appropriate business policies.
  - Host base intrusion prevention system—Safeguard your business against complex security threats that may otherwise be unintentionally introduced or allowed.
  - Virtual web browser—A virtualised environment, isolated from malware and key loggers, to ensure that your browsing experience is secured.

SUMMARY OF POINTS

Before the Internet, fraud was mostly a paper-based scheme like check fraud, embezzlement, and forgery. But, the benefits that the Internet offers businesses and consumers are also available to fraudsters—speed, global reach, efficiency, convenience with opportunity, accessibility, and anonymity that have made fraud a top concern for consumers, governments, and businesses everywhere.

The motivation for the bad guys to commit online fraud places increasing pressure on consumers and the organisations that they engage with, to do more to prevent fraud. Consumer concern for becoming a victim of online fraud when they're banking, shopping, networking with friends,or dating is on the rise.

Unfortunately, consumers can and will shoulder only so much of the burden to protect themselves. They expect their providers to employ the latest technology that will keep them safe.

- Use a dedicated computer to perform only banking transactions. Do not use work applications, e-mail, or visit non-banking websites.
- Use a dedicated web browser to perform your web banking. For example, use Firefox to do all your online banking. Use Internet Explorer, Safari, or Google Chrome to access other non-banking websites.
- Conduct banking operations in a secured environment. Use strong, Two-Factor authentication for gaining access to an online bank securely (should the bank provide such facilities).
- Never store the banking credentials on the machine you are using to access the Internet unless those credentials are stored in an encrypted password management application as LastPass—www.pi10m.com/b1/3 .
- Always manually enter the URL of the bank every time your log in, never by clicking a link.
- Protect the computer with anti-malware software.
- Keep the computer updated with the latest software updates.
- Unless it is an absolute emergency, never access the bank from a system you do not have full control over it. You never know if the system has software installed that will record your online banking credentials. If you must, use such a system then as soon as possible, log on to your bankfrom a trusted computer system and change your password.
- Use two-factor authentication whenever this facility is provided.

FOR THE MORE SECURITY-CONSCIOUS USER / ORGANISATION

If security is a great concern, here are some additional steps for your consideration:

- You might want to consider using separate computers. Utilise a computer just for your business and Internet banking, while your regular computer could be used for general day-to-day Internet browsing purposes, games, emails, social media communications, and other non-business related activities.
- Consider using additional application security protection.
  - Website reputation and classification—Add-on software to your browser that will let you know whether websites have a good or a bad reputation.
  - Secure web gateway—Provide your business with real-time analysis of web pages, content and data, and threat protection from malware; apply appropriate business policies.
  - Host base intrusion prevention system—Safeguard your business against complex security threats that may otherwise be unintentionally introduced or allowed.
  - Virtual web browser—A virtualised environment, isolated from malware and key loggers, to ensure that your browsing experience is secured.

REMINDER! Don't forget to register at www.pi10m.com

By registering your details, we will be able to provide you with free updates to the book, critical security alerts, valuable security tools that you can start using right now for free, answer your questions and much much more.

7

Social Networking Protection Guidelines

*"Security is built on trust.
Yet we venture to the social web
revealing all our personal data,
and then we wonder why our trust is broken."*

– COMSCORE "IT'S A SOCIAL WORLD", DECEMBER 2011

With the widespread adoption of the Internet around the world came the rise of social networking and social media as a global phenomenon. In March 2007, Social Networking as a category had a global audience of less than 500 million users, representing just 56 percent of the world's online population.
Email reigned supreme as the king of communication channels online, and the word 'friend' was just beginning its transformation.

Since then, the digital landscape has changed immensely. Social networks, which provide platforms for online users to connect, share, and build relationships with others online, have forever altered the lives of individuals, communities, and societies all over the world. The growth in popularity of social networking has also created and engendered new online consumer behaviors.

According to comScore research (Top 10 Need-to-Knows About Social Networking and Where It's Headed Whitepaper—December 2011), social networking sites now reach 82 percent of the world's online population, representing 1.2 billion users around the world. The social networking adoption trend, largely mirrored the global Internet adoption curve, grew proportionately, showing that as people began to get connected, they immediately began connecting with one another.

Whether it is Facebook, LinkedIn, Twitter, Google+, Foursquare, MySpace, Pinterest or something else, it is becoming a way of life for millions of people to share information about themselves for personal or business reasons. The growth of social networking is a global cultural phenomenon. Despite significant differences in government, infrastructure, availability of Internet access, and cultural practices around the world, social networking is growing in every country.

"Social Networking is the most engaging online activity worldwide accounting for one in every seven minutes spent on the web."

– COMSCORE "IT'S A SOCIAL WORLD", DECEMBER 2011

The purpose of some networking sites may be purely social, allowing users to establish friendships or romantic relationships, while others may focus on establishing business connections or sharing information. The modern way of staying in touch with business and personal contacts is to be present on social networking sites and to communicate using email and other digital tools.

Social networking sites rely on connections and communication, so they encourage you to provide a certain amount of personal information. When deciding how much information to reveal, people may not exercise the same amount of caution as they would when meeting someone in person. This could be due to:

- Ego—creating a bigger image of themselves to impress others.
- Social networks encourage users to provide greater descriptions of themselves so that other users can benefit from interacting with them.
- Users believe that if they want any kind of interaction, they have to be engaged and reveal things about themselves.

While the majority of people using these sites do not pose a threat, fraudulent people are definitely drawn to them because of the accessibility and amount of personal information that's available.

The more information that gets posted, the greater opportunity, and mischievous people are able to take advantage of it. The personal information that users reveal about themselves can also be used to conduct a social engineering attack.

Additionally, because of the popularity of these sites, attackers may use them to distribute malicious malware. Sites that offer applications developed by third parties are particularly susceptible. Attackers may be able to create customised applications that appear to be innocent while infecting your computer without your knowledge.

Social networking challenges

The Value of Trust

Trust is about confidence. The opposite of trust is mistrust and suspicion. When you trust people, you have confidence in them. You are happy to transact with them. You feel that they have integrity, honesty, and are reliable.

In social networks, once a member becomes a friend, a connection, a member of your social network, there is an implied level of trust.

For example, LinkedIn networks you to others by degrees of separation. You know Bill, Bill knows you, Bill's friend Richard can be introduced to you. This works on the principle of personal relationships that is Trust.

Social engineering techniques that trick users into a false sense of trust have proven lucrative for attackers. Once a successful social network user is infected, the potential to infect others within that network is 10 times more successful at targeting users than e-mail-based attacks.

ComScore, a leader in measuring the digital world, has said that in the last year 57% of users have been spammed via social networks, an increase of 70.6%. Furthermore, 36% of users claim that they have been sent malware via social networking sites, which is a rise of 60.9% (Sophos Security Threat Report 2010).

Part of the problem is that people's comfort level with social networks makes them easy marks for cybercriminals who are jumping on these sites with gusto, dumping spam, launching phishing attacks, stealing identities, and installing malware. The same people who have learned to be very wary of phishing attacks, enticing links, and sales pitches for cheap Viagra in their mail inboxes, now allow themselves to be seduced on a social network purely based on TRUST.

Privacy & Confidentiality

Given the rising popularity of social networks, there is growing unease about privacy concerns ranging with these sites.

Let me explain: social networking sites lead a double life. On one hand, they encourage users to share as much personal information as possible, making it easy to post photos, videos, notes, and links. But at the same time, these sites have to safeguard that information and limit how it is shared between users and beyond their own walls.

Some social network sites (if not all) are also the public face of a much larger commercial organisation. The information that users post on sites allow social networking sites to leverage this information about where you live, what food you like, what shows you like, and what habits you might have, in order to specifically target advertising of products and services. Social networking sites are a gold mine for marketing activities and other dealings such as political interest groups, potential recruitment, and more.

The data a user posts is like completing a survey. With that information, others can make a decision about you, without your knowledge, consent, or ever being asked. In short, to the social network, your value increases the more data you share on the site.

Unfortunately, privacy means having a small number of friends, but that is not really consistent with being a fully engaged user. The reality is people are continuing to post material about themselves despite their concerns, especially Generation Y.

Furthermore, it is becoming quite apparent that many online users do not take the time to fully read and understand the user privacy agreements required by all social networks. Generally, online users are used to 'clicking' a box and completely ignoring the text inside.
It is becoming obvious that a lot of users are signing over their privacy rights to these companies in exchange for access to increasingly popular social networks.

Identity Theft

With the increased global use of social networks, there are more opportunities than ever before, to steal identities or perpetrate fraud online.

For example, status updates posted on Twitter, Facebook, and many other social network sites can be used for criminal activity. If you post that you're out of town on vacation, you've opened yourself up for burglary. If you mention that you're away on business for a weekend, you may leave your family open to assault or robbery. When it comes to stalking or stealing an identity, use of photo and video sharing sites like Instagram, Flickr, and YouTube provide deeper insights into you, your family and friends, your house, favorite hobbies, and interests.
It's simple, for example, to set up a phony ID on any of these sites to gain the trust of people in an organisation. For example, you could

- Request to be 'friends' with a dozen strangers on LinkedIn. Let's say half of them accept.
- Go to Facebook and search for those six people. Let's say you find four of them also on Facebook. Request to be their friends on Facebook. All accept because you're already an established friend in LinkedIn.
- With those two people who are not on Facebook, you could setup a fake but convincing user profile on Facebook by grabbing their information from LinkedIn and posting it in Facebook. And use these two users to send 'friend' requests to their friends on Facebook ("victims") and there you have it.

And as a bonus, Facebook itself will suggest you as a friend to those people and the probability is that they will accept to be your friend.
Think about the trust factor here. For these secondary victims, they not only feel they know you, but actually request 'friend' status. They sought you out.
Could you do the same process with Google+, Twitter, MySpace, or other social networks? Of course you can.

Now imagine what you could ask from them being a 'friend'.

Malware Threat

As social networking tools change the way we communicate, spammers have begun turning their attention to services such as the common social network sites Facebook, LinkedIn, Google+, and Twitter, tricking users into installing viruses, launching fraudulent websites, and deploying malware throughout their computers and networks.

Because of the nature of social networks, they're particularly attractive to hackers. The nature of user interaction within social networking sites is being exploited by malware authors and distributors and that's definitely on the rise.

While spamming via email services remains prevalent, spammers see social networks as the new horizon. Spammers have managed to set up phony social networking accounts (fake ID).

If you have over a billion users on Facebook, then why go to all the effort to infect users individually when it is by far easier to accomplish this via a social networking site.

It doesn't help that social networking users trust other users and accept messages from people on their friends list almost without thinking. Malware distributed via social networking sites is 10 times more effective than malware spread via email according to Kaspersky Lab Global Research.

This has enormous implications for the future of social networking because the popularity of social networking sites has not been ignored by cybercriminals.

Furthermore many of the social network sites have built an ecosystem of third party applications from games to widgets. Some applications have been shown to be completely fraudulent. Applications have been created to install malware on your computer and access your personal information. Some applications haven't been properly written and are exposed to malware.

While social network sites try to put a level of policing and assessment on these applications, the ecosystem is so big that it's hard to stop poor players. So users must be educated and cautious about installing applications. In general, watch for applications that bait you with learning a piece of information by clicking on a button, since this generally will initiate an install.

Data Leakage

Social networking is becoming the preferred way to manage personal data. It is an area where people take an active role in how their personal information is managed and displayed rather than being passive.

Social networks represent the world's largest body of personal data.
Data leakage occurs when intellectual property or sensitive information leaves the corporate network and is no longer under the corporation's control.
Data leakage has moved to the forefront of news in particular as seen by WikiLeaks' exposure of sensitive information.

Such bad or good news depending on your view can result in loss of customers, damaged reputation, ruin of organisations, and possible risk of lives. There is always a cost involved and it has been rising steadily.

What can you do?

Remember the Internet is a Public Resource. Only post information that you are comfortable with anyone seeing. This includes information and photos in your profile and in blogs and other forums. Keep in mind that at a later stage you might be confronted with the content you uploaded, e.g. in a job interview. Information and pictures you post online should be considered permanent. They can be copied and stored by other individuals and can resurface years later in search engines.

Once you post the information online, it is unlikely that you will be able to retract it. Even if you remove the information from a site or removed the user's saved information, a cached version may still exist on other people's computers. Furthermore, be aware that whatever you post is the property of the social network and not yours.

A very good example to illustrate this point occurred when two Domino's Pizza employees decided to post a crude and vulgar video onto YouTube. It went viral! Within 1 day, there had been approximately 1 million views. Needless to say, that these two employees got fired and charged. This created a disaster affecting brand reputation for Domino's Pizza.

A link to this video is available online if you look hard enough.

Secondly, do not post information that would make you vulnerable such as an address, birth date, financial data or information about your schedule or routine.

The question you should repeatedly ask, would you be comfortable with a stranger receiving the information that you posted? Also be considerate when posting information, including photos about your connections and friends.

The following seven points will help you take immediate stance in increasing your social networking protection.

7 ESSENTIAL POINTS TO TAKE IMMEDIATE CONTROL OF YOUR SOCIAL NETWORK SITES

1. Be Aware.

The Internet makes it easy for people to misrepresent their identities and motives. Consider limiting the people who are allowed to contact you on these sites. If you do need to interact with people that you don't know, be cautious about the amount of information you reveal.

You do not have to feel obliged to add someone to your friend's list. Politely refuse or simply ignore the request.

Should you want to interact, find out if anyone else knows this person? Where do they work? Can you verify what he or she is saying?

2. Be Sceptical.

Don't believe everything that you read online. It is really easy to post something that is false or misleading about various topics including identities. Whether this is done with malicious intent or unintentionally, take precautions and try to verify the authenticity of any information before taking action.

Fake identities have become a growing problem within dating sites. Dating members have become overly optimistic when self-describing their personal features and attributes such as height, weight, and particularly age, possibly something to expect given the situation and willingness to attract others.

There are some deluded members though who are disregarding the truth completely and create elaborate fake IDs to convince interested members of perceived wealth, responsibility, and success.

Confidence is key to creating the deception and its continued success can depend on how gullible the poor recipient is.

The more worrisome is the danger of a fraudster profiling themselves using images of porn actresses and models, looking to fleece another member of their hard-earned money.

3. Evaluate Your Settings.

Do you read every single "Terms of Service" or "Terms of Condition" you come across before clicking "I Agree" to? Most likely the answer is "no."

But as online industry grows, and we sign up for one social network after the other, we can't forget that we are trusting our sensitive information to corporations.

It's important therefore to understand and take advantage of a site's privacy settings. The default settings for some sites may allow anyone to see your profile. You can customise your settings to restrict access to only certain people.

Whether you use Facebook, LinkedIn, Google+, or otherwise, take your time to gain understanding of how you can lock down each of these social networking sites. Here is an overview of some key settings:

Facebook

With the growing use of Facebook as a communication tool and as business tool, it is imperative that you ensure the proper security settings on your Facebook account.
The biggest issue that any user who wishes to interact with Facebook is the level of trust and identity that user is willing to handle.

The following are recommended settings:

- **HTTPS browsing** is enabled by default (https://www.facebook.com). This is an important security protection step especially when accessing Facebook from public wireless networks such as McDonalds, libraries, restaurants, hotels, airport lounges, or other free Wi-Fi centre

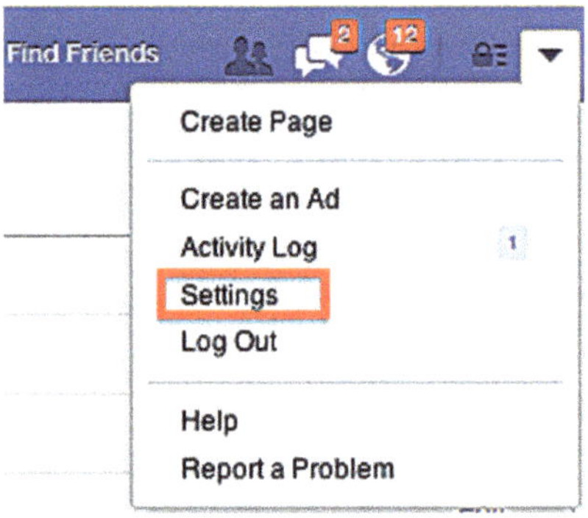

- Log into your Facebook account and choose **Settings**.
- Then click **Security**.
- To setup strong authentication, I would highly recommend using your phone as an extra layer of security. Click on **Login Approvals.** Think of this as a Two-Factor Authentication. This minimises the chance of someone accessing or stealing your account.

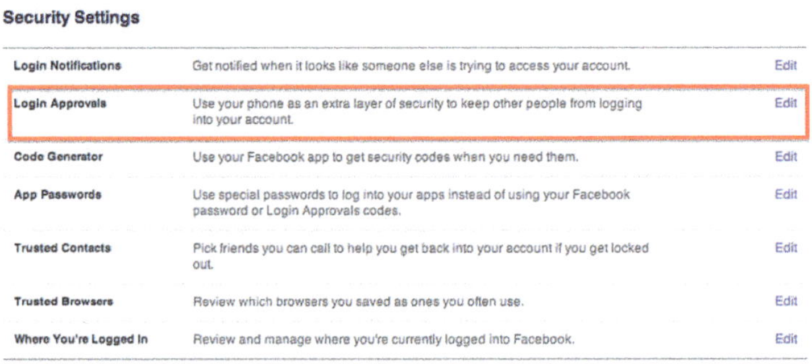

- Check **Require Security code to access my account from unknown browsers.** You have two options

- Can send a text message to your phone or
- You can use **Get codes.** Use a printed codes when you don't have a phone with you.

For the more security-conscious user.

Code Generator is Facebook addition to their Login Approvals feature, aimed at making it easier to confirm logins made on new devices. Before, if you had any difficulties receiving SMS or had poor cellular service, it was often tough to use Login Approvals easily. Now, using Code Generator, users will be able to receive Login Approval codes through your Facebook Application, without waiting on an SMS, and it will work regardless of whether you have cellular or Internet access.

- Then click on **Code Generator**

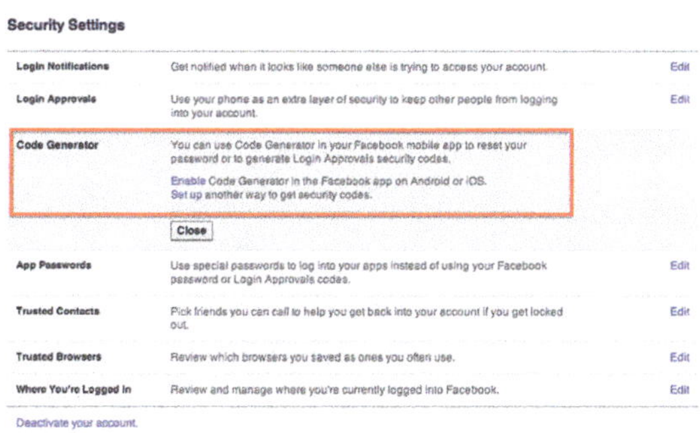

- **Login Notifications**. If you access Facebook from a limited number of devices, one of the first things you should enable is Facebook's ability to notify you if your Facebook account is accessed from another device.
- Under **Security Settings**, click **Login Notification**. And check Email and or Text to be notified.

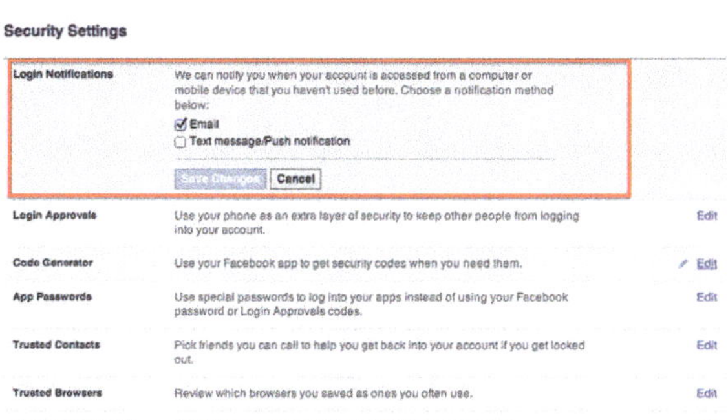

- Privacy Settings
  - Log into your Facebook account and choose **Privacy Settings.** This will present a screen similar to the following.

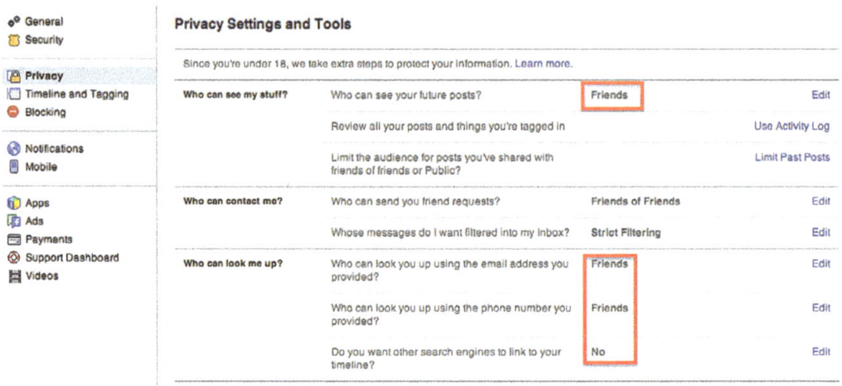

1. Recommend that you limit to **Friends** or **Close Friends** only who are able to see your posts.

2. Recommend that you limit to **Friends** or **Close Friends** only who are able to look you up using your email or phone number.

3. Recommend that you disable (**No**) search engines to be able to search on your timeline.

- Timeline and Tagging

Like Privacy settings, you want to control what can be tagged on your Timeline.

- Click **Timeline and Tagging.**
- Recommend that you limit to **Friends** or **Close Friends** only who are able to see or add to your Timeline, as can be seen by the following image.

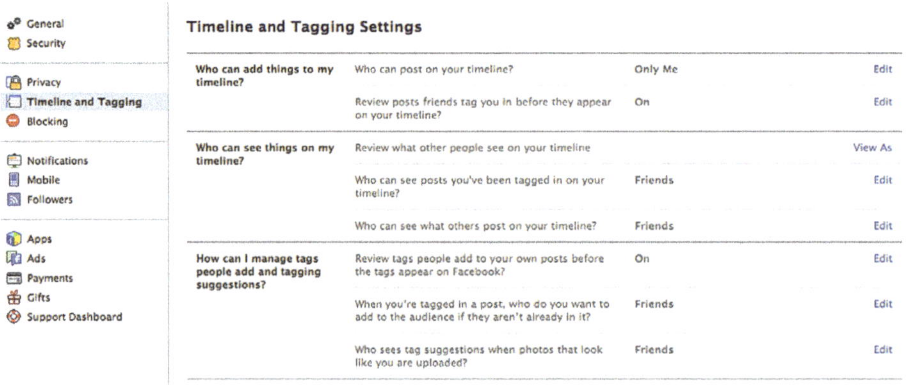

- Blocking

  In this page, you have the ability to either
  - Add friends to your Restricted List
  - Block Users that you do not want to associate with
  - Block App Invites from a specific user
  - Block Event Invites from a specific user
  - Block Apps which then can no longer contact you.

- **Data Use Policy** – www.pi10m.com/b1/70

  Learn about how Facebook manages your data.
  - Managing your information.
    - How your information is being used.
    - Get to know the privacy settings.
  - Website and applications—Learn how social plugins and information are shared with the games, applications, and websites you and your friends use off Facebook.
  - How advertising and sponsors work.
  - How cookies, pixels and other technologies are used.

- **For Additional Resources**
  - Facebook Privacy Page—www.pi10m.com/b1/71
  - Facebook Safety Page—www.pi10m.com/b1/72
  - Facebook Governance page—www.pi10m.com/b1/73

LinkedIn

Since its inception, the networking social media service LinkedIn has seen a growth in its usage that is simply phenomenal. It seems that a large part of the professional world is networking on LinkedIn.

By default everything in your LinkedIn profile is searchable by public search sites such as Google. This means that if someone does a search on your name, your entire profile will be given to them. This includes your picture, job, employment history, websites, Linked in groups, etc. To control what profile information will be returned in a public search, log into your LinkedIn account, and you will see a page similar to the following.

- Once you have authenticated into LinkedIn, you can access the settings, from the right hand corner under your name
- Click your **image** then click **Privacy & Settings.** Here, you have the choice to manage your profile more actively.
- Click **Account** and then click **Manage security settings**

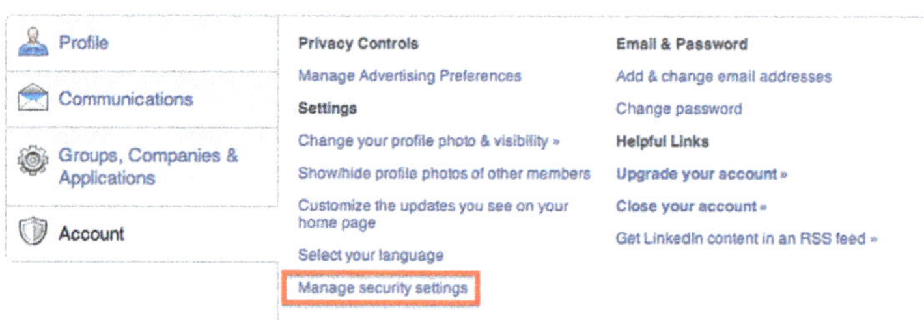

- Ensure that when you connect, you use a secure connection (https) to browse LinkedIn
- Next, **Turn OnTwo-step verification for sign-in**. This will add additional authentication protection. It will require a phone number to get verification codes via text (SMS).

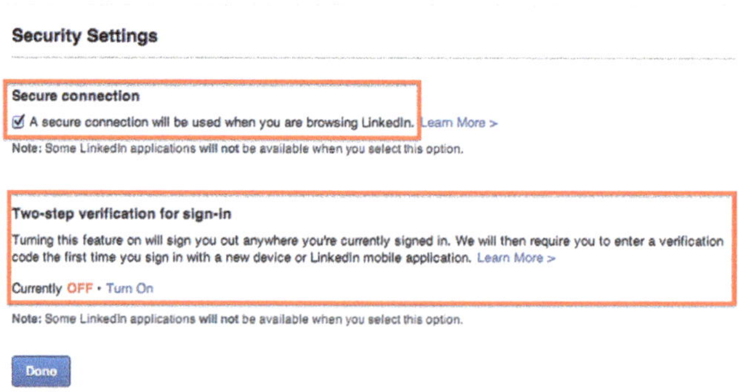

Google+

Google+ is a serious challenge for Facebook and like Facebook there is growing unease about privacy concerns ranging with this site.
Here are some settings that we recommend:

- if you wish to really secure your Google+ login, then consider the use of its built-in **one time password** systems where a password with limited life is sent to your mobile phone and you use this as your second setup verification.
    - Click on your image. Then click on **Account**
    - Should you click on **Privacy**, this will provide you with an overview of how Google treats your privacy and security.
    - Click the **Security** tab.

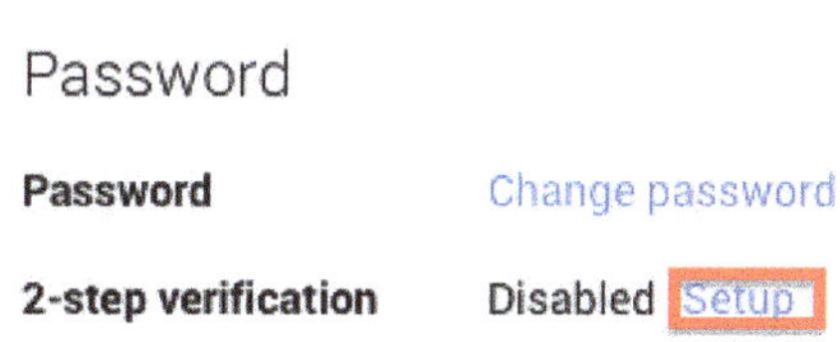

    - And now we want to make sure you enable 2-step verification. So click **Setup**

- Click **Start set up >>**
- Select your **Phone number.** Google will use this number for account security
- Now verify. You should receive a message on your phone with a 6 digit number.
- If you lose your phone, you have two options
    1. You can sign in from a trusted computer. Or
    2. You can create a backup option to another phone
- Also within the Security Tab, you can also
    - Control which apps and websites have access to your account
    - See recent related activities regarding your account. It's worthwhile checking regularly.
    - Recovery options.

Google Circles are groups of people with whom you share content. The names of your circles and who you add to them are visible only to you, though you can set whether the list of people in all of your circles is visible in your public profile. I suggest that the information that you share stays within in your circles and not the public.

- Click your **image** once again. Then click **View Profile**
- **Under Google+, Click on Profile** and scroll down to **Settings** which will allow you to manage how people interact with you.
  - Recommend that you allow only people within your circle to send you notifications or are able to comment on your profile. Choosing who is allowed to send you notifications or comment is important because it means that you can only be notified by the people that you trust.

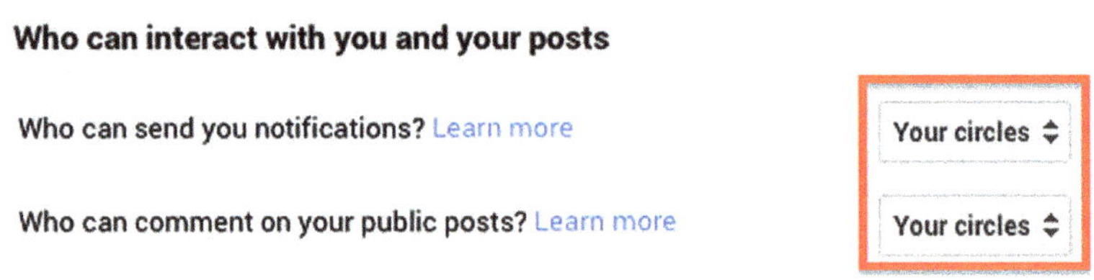

  - Next, make sure you check all notifications under **Receive Notifications.**
  - Under **Photos and Videos**, I highly recommend that you uncheck the following. Secondly, any tag needs your approval first

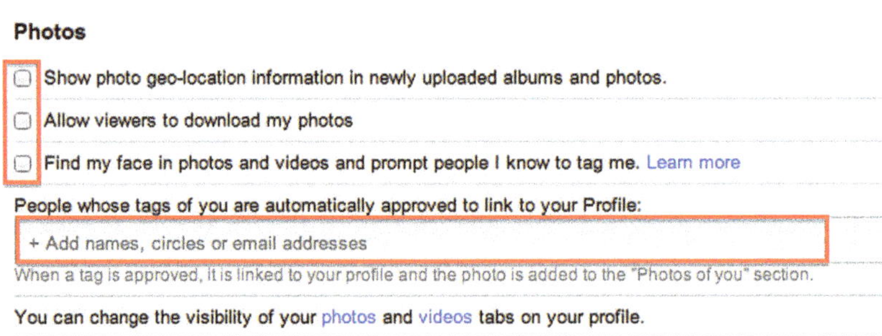

  - Under **Profile,** make sure that only people from your Circle are able to send communications to you. I would also recommend that you uncheck your profile from being searchable.

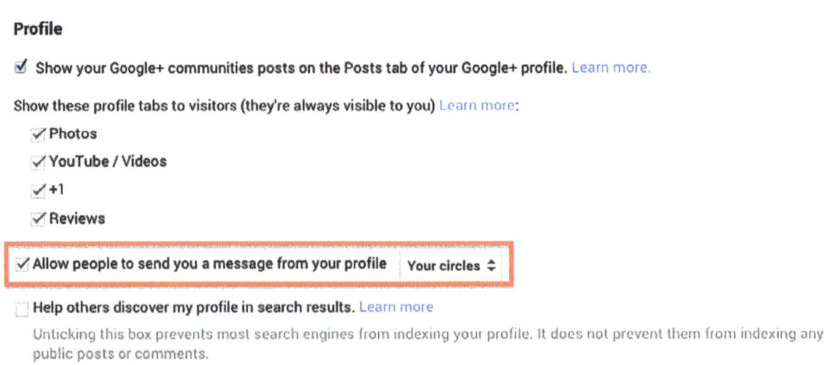

- → Under **Location Settings,** I would strongly recommend to uncheck your location setting. Secondly, no one else should know of your location.

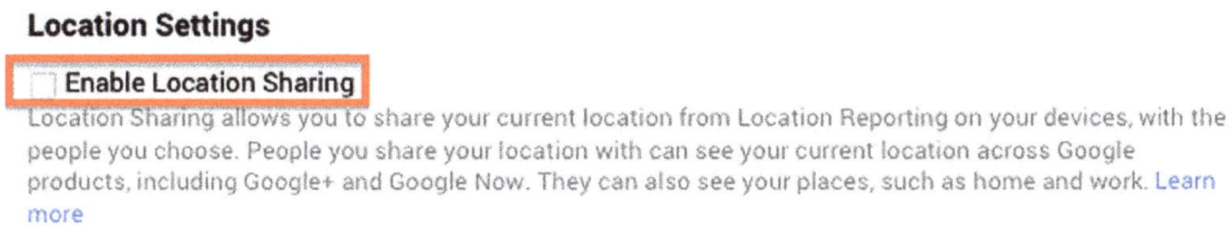

Another useful Google+ tool is their **Data tools.** Data tools provides you with information on how you use your account.

- Click your **image.** Then click **Data tools** tab
- Within Data tools you can do the following actions as can be seen by the following diagram
    - → Dashboard provides you with visibility of all your Google related relationships.
    - → Download will provide you with the ability to archive all or some of your Google data to your computer or selected device. Important: do not download it to a Public Computer.
    - → Ability to Delete your profile, account, data and products should you chose.
    - → "Me on the Web" provides you visibility of your profile on the web.
        - Click Search now of your name to see what Google has found about you.
        - Click Manage web alerts to receive notifications about you

Twitter

Since its inception, the micro-blogging service Twitter has seen a growth in its usage that is simply staggering. It seems that the whole world is now tweeting.

The Twitter service is very simple service that lets you send blogs at 140 characters a message. Consequently, the settings you can do to your twitter account are limited. The following are the recommended settings for protecting your privacy when using Twitter.

Once you log onto your Twitter account, click the **COG wheel**, then click **Settings**. I recommend the following settings:

- Twitter allows you to have **Login verification** which is a feature that helps you keep your account more secure. Instead of relying on just a password, login verification introduces a second check to make sure that you and only you can access your Twitter account. After you enable this feature, you will need both your password and your phone to log in to your account. When you log in to twitter.com you will receive a text message with a login code (SMS users with a supported carrier), or a push notification (iOS and Android users).

- If you have a supported carrier (www.pi10m.com/b1/74), check the login verification.

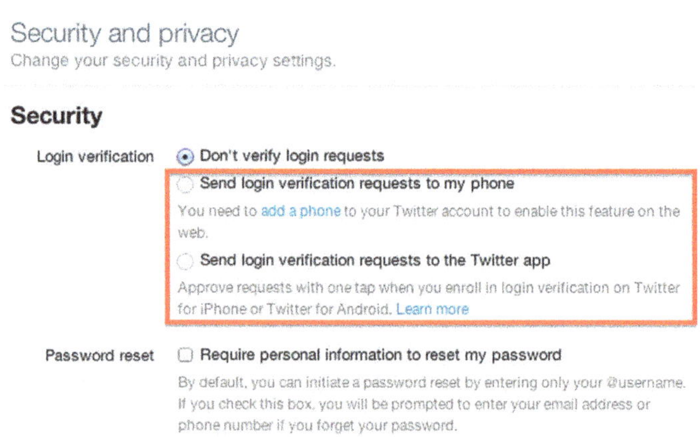

Two additional recommendations:

- Uncheck your **Tweet Location**. Tweet location is off by default. There may be some updates where you want to share your location and some updates where you want to keep your location private. Just like you might not want to tweet your home address, please be cautious in tweeting coordinates you don't want others to see.

- Check your **Tweet Privacy**. By checking this option, only those that you approve will receive your tweets. Tweets that have been posted previously with this option unchecked may still be visible to the public.

4. Be Cautious.

An increasing and growing concern is the increase in phishing attacks. Phishing is attempting to acquire information (and sometimes, indirectly, money) such as usernames, passwords, and credit card details by masquerading as a trustworthy entity.

Phishing scams come in variety of different formats and flavours. Typically, these scams like to use well-known global brands, celebrities, politicians, auction sites, Internet Service Providers (ISP's), social network sites, governments, and more.

The first part of the attack is to provide you with a communication, predominantly an email containing a link redirecting you to a fraudulent site.

In the second part of the attack, the fraudulent site attempts to steal your confidential information such as username, password, address, and credit card details.

Like most phishing pages, they look very believable to the average user. Considering that companies are moving every service they can to the Internet to reduce labour costs and other infrastructure expenses, this become a worrisome situation.

- Be cautious of any email requesting you to visit a site.
- Be cautious of any email requesting you to click or open an attachment.
- Be cautious of any email that the domain name doesn't match the vendor's name.
- Be cautious of any email proposing free offerings. There is no such thing as a free lunch!
- Be cautions of clicking on any links pertaining "amazing, miraculous, astonishing" news.
- Be cautious from applications that claim that your machine has been infected and that you can download a free antivirus from this website.
- Be cautious from phone calls claiming that your machine is infected.

Protect your social network account with passwords that cannot easily be guessed. If your password is compromised, someone else may be able to access your account and pretend to be you.

Additional Caution

Be cautious of using public computers. Don't use applications that require user authentication. You don't know what mischievous or malicious software is installed on these computers. Use **Private Browsing** should you be accessing the Internet in a public environment. See Chapter 4 for more details on Private Browsing.

5. Be Vigilant.

Be vigilant on what you click on.
Be vigilant in keeping your personal information confidential and secure.
Be vigilant in keeping your computer up to date.
Be vigilant in responding to requests from other people.
Be vigilant on the type of applications you access within your social networks.
Also, recognise that social networking is a medium where malware can cross the boundaries quite easily.

- Ensure that workstations are up-to-date with the latest antivirus definition file.
- Ensure that your operating system and applications are up-to-date with the latest patches.
- Regularly scan machines for viruses, trojans, and other malware.

If your machine has been infected, I would highly recommend rebuilding your system from scratch. Modern malware can leave undetectable backdoor entrances into your systems and may gather information such as bank account details passively, and in such a way that you don't even notice.

6. Be Guarded

The Social Network is the epicentre platform for entertainment, games, events, and various other forms of exciting media interactions.
Be guarded against

- Video lures claiming shocking or exhibitionist themes
- Requesting for donations or money for aid
- Requesting for your support for a good cause
- Requests for you to respond to questions and surveys
- Fake antivirus programs. Claims that your computer is infected. Seek proper advice from a recognised support organisation
- Free gifts such as an iPad, iPhone, MacBook will lure you into phishing attacks

The majority of threats today involve a web component for lures, redirects, malware delivery, and stealing data. Protection is about context protection awareness. Be on guard!

7. Be Sensitive

Remember, security technology is no silver bullet for all the threats that lurk on the Internet. Although organisations are implementing technological practices to ensure business integrity, availability, privacy, and confidentiality, most organisations are let down by the lack of education, training, and security awareness within the business.

- Educate and inform users of the correct processes and procedures to make them more security aware, while using social networking.
- Provide training so that the users are aware of their responsibilities. This leads to everyone being more vigilant and taking greater accountability.
- Develop a social network policy educating employees about the organisation values and about how to express themselves online in a way that is engaging and genuine.
- Help with the flow of information dissemination within the organisation. This encourages better understanding and ensures that the right messages are getting to the right people.

Secondly, users need to be sensitive in what they want to share. Sharing is deemed fine, if the information is not exposing corporate secrets, personal information, or intellectual property.

Sharing any kind of business information should be authorised prior to it being published online.
However, sharing information with haste or excitement, you threaten to put your business into trouble.

Example: An accidental email wiped $22 billion of market value (18th of October, 2012). Shares in Google were suspended after an accidental email to the US stock market authorities revealed that the company's latest quarterly results were far below Wall Street's demanding expectations.

For the more security-conscious user

- One of the best ways to ensure security practice adoption within the organisation is to appoint a 'security champion' within your organisation, in order to raise security awareness.
  - This should be a person with strong leadership and communication values, someone who is committed to being an agent of change within the organisation.

    - Someone who is committed to being a voice for security within your organisation.
    - Someone who can engage people's minds about security. This is the most important attribute of a security champion. It will ensure a sense of ownership regarding security and it will drive users to get behind organisational security practices.
- Recommend that once in every two months, you do a search on your name and see what comes up either on Google or Bing. This will at least provide you with an update of what information about you exists on the World Wide Web. Hopefully your name hasn't been hijacked or used inappropriately.
- Similarly, recommend that once a month, you do a search on your business name and see what comes up either on Google or Bing. Having the visibility is becoming increasingly important for two main reasons:

1. Understanding what people and business are saying about you.

2. Whether someone else has hijacked your brand for ill purposes.

7 THINGS YOU MUST NOT REVEAL ON THE SOCIAL WEB

There is a dark side to the Social Web, where Internet fraudsters and swindlers are determined to enrich themselves at your expense or to simply cause havoc. You and your organisation are susceptible to attacks from anyone and from anywhere in the world.

Although, you may think and wonder why you might be attacked and targeted, the simple truth to this is that you may have presented an opportunity for someone to take advantage without you realizing it.

Simply, it would be foolish to embrace these new social technologies tools without taking heed about the many risks associated with their use.

The following pages are taken from a white paper called "7 Things You Must NOT Reveal On The Social Web." It is a guide for helping you to understand some necessary actions in order to stay safe online. Remember, it only takes one sloppy oversight, misstep, or accidental mistake for you to find out how expensive breaches can be.

1. Pay attention to what you post

    Before you post anything online, think about what other people could do with that data. What would be the chance of you getting the job if your Facebook page is full of photos of you behaving in an irresponsible fashion?

    Most people do not realise the default configuration for most social media websites is that all information posted is viewable by anyone with access to the Internet and a search engine. Consider what would happen if you called in sick to work and then posted on Facebook that you were not sick. How embarrassing and fraudulent would you feel when your employer managed to find out your deception?

    Given the prevalence of digital cameras and videos, it is almost certain that photos of you will exist when you are under the weather with alcohol or being amorous with someone else than your partner. If these photos are published to Facebook, then your partner can find them.

    Employers in their due diligence employment process are now searching in Facebook for postings by potential new employees. Should they find photos of your inappropriate behavior, this may well reflect quite negatively in their employment decision process.

Suppose you are in a custody dispute with your ex-partner, the social networking sites are full of photos and posts indicating that you like to go out and party a lot.

Remember if you have not configured the privacy settings of the social media website correctly, all this information is available to your ex-partner who can use it in court to argue your negligence and irresponsible behavior and therefore award any custody rights to your ex-partner.

When posting to social networking websites, you should never post anything that you would not want to appear on the front page of the paper.

2. Be Discrete

Don't give away specifics. Don't post your address, date of birth, kids' names, pets' names, phone numbers, or any account numbers or financial information of any kind.

You really shouldn't even post children's photos online.

There are three dangers if you post this type of information:

a. **Identity Theft**—Identity theft is a form of fraud or cheating of another person's identity in which someone pretends to be someone else by assuming that person's identity. It results in the ability to defraud the person's capital, assets, and income What sort of information can a fraudster acquire? Your date of birth, phone number account numbers, your address, personal ID, etc. Of course posting your account number along with information that can be used to assume your identity could allow such theft to drain your accounts of all your money online.

b. **Pedophiles**—We all find pedophilia abhorrent. Unfortunately pedophiles are using automated techniques to mine social networking sites for people with children. Would you want a pedophile to know that you have children, and then where they live? How would you feel if a pedophile was looking at a picture of your children? You would be very upset if a stranger took photos of your children in public. Why would you post photos to a social media website where everyone can see them?

c. **Stalkers**—Do you really want a stalker knowing where you live, your likes, your dislikes? Do you really want the stalker knowing what hobbies you like; where you tend to spend time; what friends you visit; where you work?

3. Don't Reveal Your Location

Do not tell the world where you are going on vacation! And if you are just going to dinner or to the beach and won't be at your house for several hours, why would you let potential burglars know that you're away?

Turn off location-based services on your smartphone that automatically gives your location.

For example posting photos online will reveal your location unless you turn your location-based services off. Smartphones that contain GPS locator technology inside with a camera are already equipped with the specialised hardware to automatically add geo location information to the pictures at the time they are taken.

Secondly, don't use social media check-in features where you disclose you location.

Thirdly, don't post where you live!
Do you really want to advertise your place of residence to hundreds of people, strangers, charlatans, criminals, or offenders? Once you have posted your address online, it is there for any person who may want to take advantage.

A great little website about raising awareness about over-sharing called Please Rob Me—www.pi10m.com/b1/36

4. Think Before You Act!

Avoid clicking "**Agree**," "**OK**," or "**I accept**" in banner ads, in unexpected pop-up windows or warnings, on websites that may not seem legitimate, or in offers to remove spyware or viruses.

If you are running Windows, press **Ctrl + F4** on your keyboard to close the window.
If that doesn't close the window, press **Alt + F4** on your keyboard to close the browser.
If asked, close all tabs and don't save any tabs for the next time the browser starts.
Secondly, before posting pictures or videos, consider what any person might see? Could they be used against you in any way?

A further example: The former democratic congressmen of New York, Anthony Weiner, posted a lewd photo of himself (June 2011) to the social media website Twitter to a former college friend. Unfortunately for the congressman, the photo was published as viewable by the public and it was quickly passed on by his opponents to the news media. The result was the congressman was forced to resign and a long term political career came to a crashing end.

Remember the rule of thumb mentioned in Point 1: don't publish anything that you would not want seen on the front page of the paper or maybe they just didn't care!
Well with photos and videos, there is a 2nd rule to keep in mind. Would you want your Grandma to see this picture or video?

5. Trash Talk Is Best Left Internal

Using social networking as a tool for airing your organisation's dirty laundry will cause a lot of problems. Any dissatisfaction, frustrations, and unhappiness that you may feel are best dealt within your organisation rather than beyond.

The spreading of internal and private information becomes a relevant issue especially when it affects not only private life but also the working environment.

For example in 2008, Virgin Atlantic Airlines dismissed 13 staff members who had posted comments on Facebook which criticised the cleanliness of the company's fleet and of its passengers. Similarly, British Airlines' check-in staff at Gatwick posted messages on Facebook saying travelers were 'smelly' and criticised the chaotic operations at Heathrow.

Secondly, what do you do when you've just received a less-than-complimentary Facebook wall post?

Your next steps are key to retaining not only the business of the angry customer, but the business of other fans who like your page as well.

Responding with respect and understanding to customers' concerns will indicate your intention to rectify any problems. By addressing this upset fan, you are demonstrating that you value their fans' opinions, even the negative ones.

6. Keep Confidential Information Data To Yourself

Don't post confidential data!

By default everything you publish on social networking sites are publically viewable and searchable by Google. The data is not just viewable by your friends and their friends but the whole Internet.

If the information is confidential and you want it to remain confidential, you would not post it to the whole Internet so don't post it to social networking sites.

A very good example of what can happen if confidential information is posted to a social media website is the Israeli army raid that had to be called off. In March 2010, the Israeli army was planning to raid a village. A soldier posted on his Facebook page the details including the time of the raid. His superiors were alerted, the raid was called off, the soldier was court-martialed and sent to jail.

7. Don't Leave Clues Online

Don't post password clues online.

Fraudsters are looking for hints on your social networking sites, such as the name of your pet, your favourite car, mom's maiden name, pictures of what your house looks like, etc.

Fraudsters are looking for clues online for any information that can be used for logins, email addresses, authentication, etc. This information is then used as an attack vector for gaining access to your organisation network or possibly sending you an email that contains malware, that when activated by you clicking a link or attachment compromises your online bank account.

Unfortunately it is human nature to use common things like car names, mother's maiden name, wife name, or your family pet as a password. Computer hackers know this and always look for such information.

Based on the *Consumer Reports* magazine (June 2012—Facebook & Your Privacy), Americans during the past 12 months "liked," updated their profiles, and posted status updates to produce the following data:

- 39.3 million identified a family member in a profile
- 20.4 million included their birth date and year in their profile
- 7.7 million "liked" a Facebook page pertaining to a religious affiliation
- 4.6 million discussed their love life on their wall
- 2.6 million discussed their recreational use of alcohol on their wall
- 2.3 million "liked" a page regarding sexual orientation

For the report, *Consumer Report* surveyed 2,002 members of its interactive consumer online panel who were over the age of 18 and had a home Internet connection.

Consumer Report found that some people are sharing way too much, including an estimated 4.8 million who've potentially tipped off burglars where and when they're going on any given days and 4.7 million who've "liked" Facebook pages about health conditions that can be used against them by insurers.

7 STEPS TO DEVELOPING YOUR ONLINE REPUTATION

Who is looking at you right now?

Never before in history can any individual create a video, presentation, documents, or set of photographs and publish it instantly for the entire world to see.
No longer are we dependent on old media outlets (TV networks, radio, newspapers, magazines) to display our thoughts and our opinions.

The online social phenomena have opened the world for us to become global citizen journalists. We use social technology tools to locate and communicate to people easily, share our interests, and to broadcast our ideas. We also use social networks to sell services, to serve customers, resolve issues, and build relationships.

Do you know what your online presence is right now?

What happens when you put your name into Google, Facebook, or LinkedIn? If you don't know, perhaps you should. Chances are that someone soon will try and find out what sort of information they can learn about you. Perhaps it is a friend of yours or your partner. Maybe the bank, a client, a partner, or an employer. Worse still, it could be a spammer, a fraudster, or someone who may want to steal your identity.

Do you know what your social relevance is?

Your social relevance encompasses your online or your business reputation. Social relevance is making huge impacts in the way we interact with one another. In other words, organisations are starting to make online management practices and decisions based on the relevance of the information they can find about you, your business, or anything else online.

For example, the social relevance of your organisation will have an impact on whether or not another organisation wishes to develop new relationships, engage your services, or possibly pursue new opportunities. Similarly a professional social relevance will depend whether the person can make an appointment, land a new job, or close a sale.

We are moving to a phase where we will be evaluating people and organisation's relevance in the same way banks rate our credit-worthiness. Your online reputation and relevance are but the starting blocks of understanding the complexity and threats that this social online phenomenon provides us.

Do you know what the risks and challenges your social reputation is?

Social and Branding—If you have a business, then your brand is everything. You spend a great deal of time, money, and energy building your brand. Having employees carelessly share information, whether on Twitter, Facebook, LinkedIn, or some other social network platform can destroy goodwill in seconds, which took you years to build up.

We are sometimes all too familiar with social networks and can forget that what we post, goes out to the world. So whether it's trashing the competition or sharing a controversial political opinion, 140 characters and one mouse click can get you and your brand in a world of trouble.

Brand Leverage—If you have a well-recognised brand, it is highly likely that other scrupulous people will try and take advantage of your name.

The fraudster could be misrepresenting your brand, trademark, symbol of your image, your logo, your process, or other thereby causing serious harm.

Banks are often in the firing line where fraudsters setup phishing sites trying to lure the victim to their look-alike bank website, in the hope of capturing their authentication and identity information.

Using and leveraging a recognised brand can be easy for the fraudster to setup but hard for the viewer to discern the real purpose of the deception.

Free or unbelievable offers are a tell-tale sign of a possible and sinister fraud. Examples that I have regularly come across:

"How would you like to own an iPhone for $1?"

"Get a Free Pair of Ray-Bans! (limited time only)"

"Get a Free Pair of Toms Shoes!"

"Where do we send your free iPad?"

"Bill Gates Foundation Congratulates You"

"Congratulations! You have won today's MacBook Air"

People's excitement over the possibility of a free name brand product outweighs their common sense, it seems. Before you know it, you're being taken to web pages that ask you to hand over your personal information or take part in an online survey.

Brand Theft—For many people, brand theft rather than piracy is the biggest intellectual property risk. Brand theft occurs where one party establishes a brand but another party acquires rights to the brand (in bad faith).

A simple example of this can be the theft of your domain name. This could happen because:

1. You forgot to renew the registration of your domain and someone else took that advantage.
2. A fraudster managed to change the registration details of your domain.
3. Your website is directed to another similar look-alike domain.

The costs of fighting brand theft are high, so the best defence is to reduce the risk of it happening.

Brand Image—The dark side of this immediate flow of communication within social networks is that it becomes much more complicated for organisations to keep track of available information about themselves.

Organisations as well as people have lost control of their brand, image, or reputation as blogs, forums, videos, podcasts, and social networks have given access to the masses to start talking and spreading positive or negative news about them. This phenomenon is getting even worse with the rise of mobile connectivity.

Brand Trust—Online reputation is centred around word of mouth and trust. Word of mouth has always existed but what is new to our environment is the ease with which we can access various publishing tools to spread information.
Trust relies on sentiments shared by individuals, groups, communities, friends, or followers that we relate to and that we believe.
The danger of this overwhelming trust in other people's judgement is that perception tends to become reality.
The following section will provide a simple seven step guidance for creating an effective security mitigation strategy.

Seven essential steps

1. Manage Your Online Reputation—Yourself

A. Check your reputation on Google. This is the starting point, and it's what I call due diligence. See what others see about you. Do a search about the following:
- What has been written by you?
- What has been written about your corporation?
- Also suggest searching for similar words with different spelling or different abbreviations. This may suggest someone trying to use your brand.

B. Setup Google alerts (http://www.google.com/alerts) to continuously monitor what people are saying about you and your corporation. Why not make it easier for yourself. The web is huge. Why not use Google alerts to help you be informed.
- Google will email you every time someone mentions your name

C. Understand online networks. Understand what networks are important to you.
- Where are the conversations that take place regarding your industry?
- Where are your colleagues, peers, partners, competitors, or clients?
- What are the rules of this network?
- What are the expectations?

2. Manage Your Online Reputation—What and Where

Decide on what kind of information you should be tracking. Decide where this information could reside,

Enlarge your search to information related to

- Your industry segment. Where are the conversations that take place? (look for blogs, forums, message boards, Q&A sites related to your sector)
- Your competitors' websites
- Social networking sites (Facebook, Twitter, LinkedIn, Google+…)
- Video (YouTube, Daily Motion, Vimeo)
- Photo sharing (Flickr, Instagram, tumblr, Pinterest)
- Wikis related to your industry
- Social bookmarking sites (Delicious, Reddit, Digg)
- Customer reviews websites such as epinions.com or tripadvisor.com if you are in the travel industry
- Web analytics information using Google analytics.

3. Manage Your Online Reputation—Monitoring and Visibility

It's no secret that to be able to effectively manage your online reputation requires you to be vigilant and watchful of what others are saying about you in a positive and negative way.
There are plenty of tools available to help us with this process. There are some tools that are free and worth a mention.

- Google Alerts—www.google.com/alerts—Real-time alerts emailed whenever a pre-defined specific keyword is mentioned
- Social Mention—www.pi10m.com/b1/37 - Like Google Alerts, Social Mention search engine tracks user generated content in blogs, comments, bookmarks, events.

There are three key activities that we would recommend in managing your engagement strategy.

a. Listen—Keep track of what people are saying about you or your company online by implementing a well-defined listening process
b. Define & Respond—You must define a policy that will establish how you will respond to positive and negative things said about you, your brand, or your company.
c. Measure—You must adopt a measuring policy that will inform you what's been said about you or your company, how often people are talking about you, what kind of sentiments are coming out.

4. Manage Your Online Reputation—Web Site Protection

The popularity of websites has grown dramatically.
Your website and its applications are under attack 24 hours a day! More than 50% of visitors to your website are non-human visitors.

Web attacks are a serious challenge and threat facing organisations today. Typical firewall and antivirus solutions don't stop web attacks. They are not designed to stop such threats. They cannot differentiate between web crawlers and human users, so they cannot block business logic attacks like site scraping (data extraction) and comment spam.

To make matters worse, most of these attacks are automated. Cyber-criminals are increasingly using automation to carry out their attacks on website and applications. If you thought that you wouldn't be targeted as you pose little relevance, then think otherwise. Automated attacks don't discriminate!

What is your reputational risk?

The threat landscape for Internet and web applications is constantly changing. Key factors for this evolution are:

a. Huge motivation in successfully fleecing, stealing, and swindling the victim's personal and or corporate data.
b. Massive advancements made by attackers in developing even more crafty attack systems that are automated, persistent, and may be targeted as well.
c. New vulnerabilities are constantly discovered daily due to software flaws.

Key Security Threats:

- Website compromised with malicious code and links
- Website defaced

Websense 2013 Threat Report indicated that the number of malicious websites increased by 600%. Websense went on to say that 85% of these websites were found on legitimate web hosts that had been compromised.

What can you do?

Preventing your website being successfully breached requires you to do the following:

1. Ensure your web and associated applications have the latest patches and updates.

2. Run a comprehensive vulnerability assessment on your website and applications.
3. Run a comprehensive penetration assessment against your web-based applications.
4. Run a comprehensive database security assessment (since most websites have a database backend).
5. Develop a corrective strategy for those items discovered during the assessment.
6. Recommend using a web application firewall (WAF) to mitigate attacks. A more cost effective solution is using a Cloud WAF provider. Cloud WAF is provisioned as a service enabling organisations to jumpstart their web application security initiative in a matter of minutes.
7. Regularly assess the above process on a continual basis.

5. Manage Your Online Reputation—Domain Name Management

Domain hijacking or domain theft is the act of changing the registration of the domain name, without authority of its original registrant.
Domain sniping is the practice of an individual registering a domain name whose registration has lapsed in the immediate moments after expiry. More domain registrars will make multiple attempts to notify a registrant of a domain name's impending expiration.
Domain squatting is using a domain name with bad faith intent to profit from the goodwill of a trademark belonging to someone else.
In short, the reputation of your domain name data is no different from protecting other key business assets.

What can you do?

a. Your Domain Name Password. Each domain name in the registry database is password protected. Anyone who has access to your domain name password may be able to use it to access to your domain name, including your website and emails. Setting up a strong and secure authentication credentials is imperative.
b. Your Domain Name Registration Details. If you do not maintain accurate and up-to-date domain name registration details, including contact details, you may risk losing your domain name. You can check your domain name registration details at anytime, by doing a **WHOIS** search on your domain name registration.
c. Your Domain Name Expiry Date. All domain names have a fixed license period, meaning that you must renew your domain every period. Typically, it is around two years. You should keep a record of your domain name expiry date and make sure to renew it when the time comes. If you fail to renew your domain name, it will become available for registration on a first come, first served basis and you do not have any automatic rights to get it back.

For The More Security-Conscious Practitioner

One of the more technical areas through which websites are attacked is via Domain Name System (DNS). Think of it like a post box. For example, the domain name www.example.com hypothetically translates to the addresses 192.0.43.10 (IPv4) and 2620:0:2d0:200::10 (IPv6).

Tricking the principle provider of the DNS for your website name www.example.com to a rogue site provides a mechanism for leaking information about the internal structure and setup of your website infrastructure. This could be used to facilitate attacks of numerous kinds.

Similarly by tricking the DNS server to redirect requests from your website to a site set up by a hacker, inappropriate content could be displayed or attacks launched from the rogue website against your customers. Both of which could cause incalculable damage to your brand and its reputation.

The use of Domain Name System Security Extension (DNSSEC) by your DNS provider can greatly mitigate this risk. DNSSEC was designed to protect the public by ensuring that websites visited are the real deal and not imposters. Phony websites aim to steal users' login names, passwords, and money, and DNSSEC technology helps prevent such thefts by blocking bogus page elements and flagging pages whose DNS identity has been hijacked.

The use of DNSSEC is becoming more common with DNS providers. The US government has strongly invested with DNSSEC and many other government agencies will follow suit.
If you wish to make use of DNSEC, you need to ensure that your DNS provider makes use of it.

6. Manage Your Online Reputation—Acceptable Policies and Practices

Accessing the Internet is a privilege that creates risk and liabilities for the organisation as it allows users access beyond its network.

The most effective approach to ensuring an organisation security is a proactive one. Implementing security policies and acceptable practices must extend beyond your standard security governance that now includes online access to social networks and usage of mobile and smart device access such as smartphone or a tablet.

Policies should include the ability to enforce the type of applications users are able to access, have the ability to update settings, mandate passwords, or erase data remotely.

Policies should direct how users interact with an organisation systems and data.

Two very important points:

a. What are the ramifications if a user abuses the rules governing corporate use?
b. How will you know whether the user has abused the rules? For example, if a user decides to post on a social network that demeans the organisation, how would you know?

Measuring and auditing the effectiveness of mobile policy performance is therefore essential.

7. Manage Your Online Reputation—Raising User Awareness and Vigilance

One of the biggest threats within online reputation is social engineering attacks. Social engineering is all about the "art of deception." In fact it is the heart of most successful attacks.

One of the most important recommendations that we could put forward is use caution when you click links that you receive in messages from your friends on your social website.

Treat links in messages on social network sites as you would links in email messages.

Importantly, question yourself any time ANYONE is requesting you to do something, whether it is an email message or a phone call or a Twitter request. Why agree to that request! Verify whom this request came from.

Although organisations are implementing technological solutions to ensure security vigilance, most organisations still do not resolve the number one major factor that contributes to security breaches within a company, and that is the lack of security training and awareness. One of the best ways to ensure security awareness is to appoint a 'security champion'.

This should be a person with strong leadership and communication values, someone who is committed to being an agent of change within the organisation. A person who is committed in addressing security practices. A person who is committed to raising the security awareness within your organisation. Someone who is committed to being a voice for security within your organisation.

REMINDER! Don't forget to register at www.pi10m.com

By registering your details, we will be able to provide you with free updates to the book, critical security alerts, valuable security tools that you can start using right now for free, answer your questions and much much more.

SUMMARY OF POINTS

We live in a borderless world where users and businesses are constantly engaging, reflecting, attracting, selling, buying, cooperating on ideas, solutions, innovations, and establishing relationships. This is the social networking world.

Developing safe and secure online practices to social networks is not only vital but it needs to be in the forefront of every user and business.

Here are the seven key points:

1. **Be aware.** Be suspicious and cautious when online.
2. **Be skeptical.** Don't believe everything that you read online.
3. **Evaluate** your social network and privacy settings.
4. **Be cautious.** Be cautious of requests from people.
5. **Be vigilant.** Be vigilant in ensuring your personal information is protected.
6. **Be guarded.** Be guarded against promises and free offerings.
7. **Be sensitive.** Pay attention to better security practices.

FOR THE SECURITY-CONSCIOUS USER AND ORGANISATION

- Employ a security champion within your business.
- Manage your online reputation on an ongoing basis.
- Setup appropriate social networking business policies.

Further Resources

I have written a number of white papers that would add to your further understanding about the Social Web and the means of protection. These can be found a www.commsnet.com.au

- 7 Essential Steps to Social Networking Peace of Mind
- 7 Essential Steps to Securing Your Online Reputation
- 7 Things that you Must Not Reveal on the Social Web
- 7 Essential Steps to Securing Your Websites and Applications

8 Mobility Protection Guidelines

"Birds have wings; they're free; they can fly where they want when they want. They have the kind of mobility many people envy."

– ROGER TORY PATTERSON

Air, water, and food, are just three key elements of life. Smartphones and tablets are now an integral part of our lives and it's hard to imagine life without them.

More and more users are looking for greater working mobility, flexibility, and convenience. At the same time, business are looking to reduce their "footprint" and thereby decrease the overall costs.

In the United States, telecommuting grew by 73% between 2005 and 2011 compared to only 4.3% growth overall in the workforce (not including self employed)—American Survey Data 2011.

According to Gartner analysts, one in six people have access to a high tech mobile device as of the end of 2010.

The rapid upswing in sophistication in technology has resulted in a swift change in the way users want to be able to access and interact with either personal or corporate information, from anywhere and at any time.

More and more users and businesses use smartphones as communication tools, and also as a means of planning and organizing their work and private life. Within companies, these technologies are causing profound changes in the organisation of information systems and therefore they have become the source of new risks. Indeed, smartphones collect and compile an increasing amount of sensitive information to which access must be controlled to protect the privacy of the user and the intellectual property of the company.

For the first time, smartphones have become more popular than traditional computers. Research group Canalys estimates that 487.7 million smartphones were shipped in 2011, an increase of over 60 percent from 2010.

With this change, brings a wealth of new problems for security. In the new age of always being connected, maintaining integrity, privacy of networks, and ensuing personal and corporate data safety is increasingly being challenged.

In this chapter, we will review a number of security best practice guidelines, for protecting your computer, your wireless, and your smartphone.

WORKING REMOTELY

If you are using a work computer at home, the following steps will minimise risk to your computer and data stored on it:

a. If the computer is connected to the Internet, ensure that it has software-based antivirus and firewall solutions installed.
b. Minimise the use and installation of applications by family members.
c. Employ hard disk encryption to protect confidential data.
d. Do not allow USB storage devices from family members to be connected to the computer.
e. Disable autoplay

If you are working remotely in a public area such as an airport lounge, library, hotel, or a coffee shop, there are several important steps to take to minimise risks to the computer and data stored on it.

- Ensure that either or both the hardware and software-based firewall is installed before the computer is connected to the Internet.
- Ensure that antivirus software is installed and kept up-to-date.
- Ensure that your applications and systems are up to date.
- If you would like to access your corporate network, utilise either VPN (virtual private network) or SSL VPN (secure socket layer VPN) to access you corporate network.
    - A VPN is a virtual private network; it encrypts data in transit.
    - SSL VPN can be used as the preferred way to securely connect utilising a web browser.
- Utilise Two-Factor authentication. Two-Factor authentication seeks to decrease the probability that the authenticator is presenting false evidence of its identity. According to Verizon 2012 Data Breach Investigation Report, 98% of attacks stemmed from external agents. It is therefore important that your business enables two factor authentication for all remote access.
- Disable Bluetooth when not in use.

Want to know how to lock down your Windows laptop? Visit Chapter 2.

Want to know how to lock down your Apple Mac laptop? Visit Chapter 3.

SECURING YOUR WIRELESS DEVICE

Securing your wireless is critically important.

If your wireless network is not protected, a hacker could intercept any data you send, access your network and files, use your connection to connect to the Internet.

Process to ensure that your wireless is secure:

- Change the administrator password for your wireless router. It's easy for a hacker to find out the manufacturer's default password and use this to access your wireless network. Avoid using a password that can be guessed easily.
- Switch off SSID (Service Set Identifier) broadcasting, to prevent your wireless device announcing its presence to the world.
- Change the default SSID name of your device. Again, it's easy for a hacker to find out the manufacturer's default name and then use this to locate your wireless network. Avoid using a name that can be guessed easily.
- Enable encryption in your connection settings: WPA encryption is best, if your device supports it (if not, use WEP encryption).
- Ensure that your wireless device has the latest updates.

Turn off the wireless connection when you are not using the Internet!

If you are using an external Wi-Fi card, simply remove it.
For an internal card, look for a button on your laptop or a combination of keys that will cut the connection.

7 STEPS TO SECURING YOUR SMART MOBILE DEVICES

Mobile devices are on the move.

More and more people are now working remotely, demanding greater flexibility, greater functionality, and richer experience.

Most notable, it took Android less than three years to reach the volume of malware threats that took 14 years for the PC (Trend Micro—TrendLabs 2012 Annual Security Roundup—"Evolved Threats in a Post-PC World").

The greatest difference between smart mobile devices such as smartphones and tablets and desktops is that they are not just a smaller version of the traditional computer. These smart mobile devices are always on, always connected, portable, and have access to systems and data anywhere and anytime.

Alongside radical technology changes, business expectations have also changed. Now users of corporations want to use their personal devices (BYOD) to connect to corporate wireless, synchronise their emails, and access their data. Organisations want to be recognised as forward thinking and innovative and are therefore forced to change their culture.

In short, the risk presented by the mobile platform device is equal, if not more than, a desktop or notebook platform. It has fewer controls, fewer security measures, and these devices share and mix business and personal applications and information.

While we may worry about the traditional attacks such as phishing and malware on these devices, it is important to realise that they also open new opportunities that we are not really aware. Knowing your global positional, facial recognition, and integration into social media could leave users open for abuse.

It is inevitable that these smart mobile devices will grow more powerful and become even more integrated into personal and corporate life. Security is not the only challenge here; privacy will become even a more growing concern. We can expect our lives to come under greater scrutiny.

However, the biggest risk with these smart mobile devices is when they are accidentally misplaced, lost, or stolen. Such devices carry a trove of personal and corporate data and if not secured and land in the wrong hands, is a major source of data loss.

The following pages will therefore provide you with a suggested and accepted security baseline, which includes asset management, encryption, password policy, remote lock/wipe and email / Wi-Fi / VPN. Without these fundamentals, the mobile platform is not a viable technology and safe tool to use.

Practice 1: Password

Have you accidentally lost your smart mobile device?
Have you ever accidentally left it in a taxi, restaurant, or a hotel?
According to research done by a British insurance company LV=, the number of phones stolen annually has risen 25 percent in the last three years and is costing the UK £37 million a year. Apparently, only 1% of stolen phones are ever recovered by police.

Often when I do come across such instances, the person is extremely unnerved and goes into a frantic panic, not because they are afraid that someone might have access to their device, but are frustrated by the absence of their favourite mobile device.

How confident would you then feel that no one will be able to access your corporate data? Although you may think that you might not have any sensitive data, you may be holding people's email addresses, which is of high value. A fraudster could use your device to spam these users with requests for information, favours, or money.

According to researchers, 59% of adults do not have any form of password protection on their phone, and only a small number of people bother to log out of banking or social networking apps, making it too easy for criminals to steal information and exploit victims' identities.

First step is to ensure that your mobile device is locked and therefore requires a password to unlock it.

Secondly, I would highly recommend that you set your "auto-lock" to lock your mobile device within 15 minutes automatically when not in use.

Practice 2: Encryption

These devices are a very popular way to transport files between computers within your office and the outside world and can therefore be used as storage of information.
This clearly poses a potential threat to you and your business. For this reason, it is highly suggested that these smart mobile devices are encrypted.

In the event that these mobile devices land in the wrong hands of an unauthorised individual, the contents of that system needs to be unreadable and inaccessible. I highly suggest that you encrypt your device.

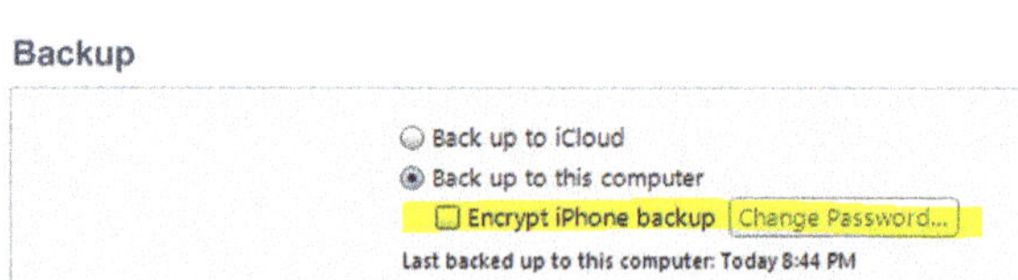

- **iPhone and iPad Encryption**—iPhone and iPad offer hardware-based encryption. Hardware encryption uses 256-bit AES to protect all data on the device. Encryption is always enabled, and cannot be disabled by users. It is enabled by default.
  - Additionally, data backed up in iTunes to a user's computer can be encrypted.

- **Android Encryption** support on Androids will come with Android 3.0 Honeycomb for tablets and Android 4.0 Ice Cream Sandwich for phones.

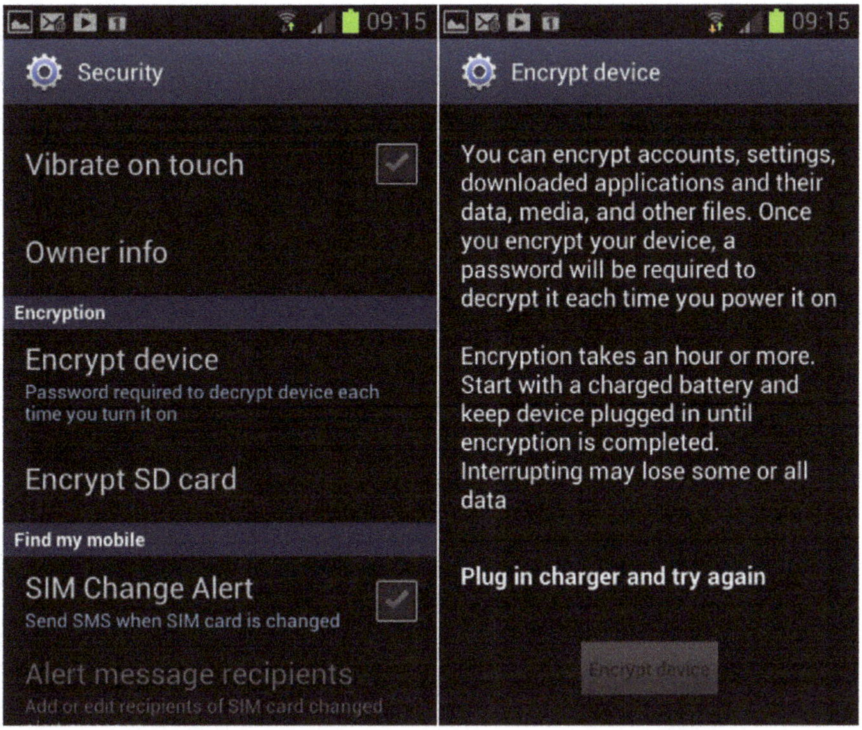

- **Windows 7 Mobile Encryption** has AES-128 file system encryption and comes with "On Device Encryption" and "Storage Card Encryption." The "On Device Encryption" encrypts User documents, Sync email, PIM data, Sync email stream properties, Sync email attachments, and Temporary Internet cache. On the other hand "storage card encryption" encrypts contents stored on removable card.

Users can enable Mobile Encryption through the Encryption Control Panel Application (CPA), which is available under

  - Settings > System > Encryption

- And on Windows Mobile Standard under Settings > Security > Encryption

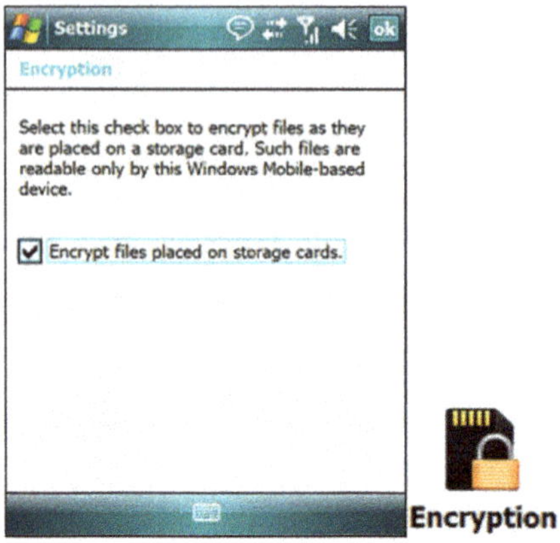

- **Windows 8 Mobile Encryption** has device encryption throughout the entire device including the OS and its applications. Designed along the same lines as Windows 7 PCs, encryption kicks in as soon as you power up the device.
- **Blackberry Encryption** can turn on content protection on a Blackberry device which then uses AES-256 encryption to encrypt stored data.
    1. On the Home screen of the BlackBerry smartphone, click Options.
    2. Click Security Options.
    3. Click General Settings.
    4. Change the Content Protection option to Enabled or Disabled.
    5. Click the track wheel/trackball and select Save.

For Blackberry 10

BlackBerry 10 devices are designed to protect work data by encrypting the files stored in the work space. Devices can also protect personal data by encrypting the files stored in the personal space if you or a user requires it. Devices can also encrypt the files stored on media cards that are inserted in devices. Only personal data can be saved to media cards.

Personal Space—You can use the Personal Space Data Encryption IT policy rule to turn on encryption for the personal space of devices. If the Personal Space Data Encryption rule is set to Yes, files stored in the personal space of the device are encrypted. If this rule is set to No, users can choose to encrypt files in the personal space using the Device Encryption option in the Security and Privacy settings on the device.

Practice 3: Remote Wipe

If a device is lost or stolen, the administrator or device owner can issue a remote wipe command that removes all data and deactivates the device.

- iOS Support—If the device is configured with Microsoft Exchange, the administrator can initiate a remote wipe command using the Exchange Management Console.
- Android—Same as above.
- Windows Mobile—Same as above.
- Blackberry—Blackberry Enterprise Server can remotely wipe the handheld device.

Remote wipe commands can also be initiated by Mobile Device Management (MDM) solutions, even if Microsoft Exchange corporate services are not in use..

Devices can also be configured to automatically initiate a local wipe after several failed passcode attempts. This protects against brute force attempts to gain access to the device.

Practice 4: Virtual Private Network (VPN)

When using your smart mobile device or smart tablet from a public wireless hot spot such as a hotel, McDonalds, public library, or a public area, you have no real control of who can view the information that is sent over the network.

One way to make this safer is to use a virtual private network (VPN) to encrypt the traffic all the way to your office. Many organisations these days have some form of virtual private network established. These secure network services typically require minimal setup and configuration for mobile devices.

Alternatively, Mobile Device Management solutions allow you to manage the accessibility of such devices but also enforce security policies which include integration of VPN.

Practice 5: Malware Protection

Let's be up front and frank, smart mobile devices will be the new vector for malware threats. With the huge uptake of such devices, this will result in malicious third parties seeking to focus their efforts in order to compromise and take advantage of this medium, for financial gain or identity information theft.

A compromised mobile device has the ability to open doors to your business without your knowledge or consent.

A secure smart mobile device needs to minimise malware infection by preventing it from being installed.

- Ensure that your smart mobile device has got the latest updates.
- Be wary to what websites you visit.
- Use third party anti-malware software for either the Android or Windows mobile platform. Use Cloud email and web solution to provide you with the first line of protection.
- Be vigilant and prevent the mobile from downloading unauthorised applications.
- Minimise services that are configures on the mobile device.
- Use Cloud web protection.

Practice 6: Enterprise Protection for Your Workforce

If you are responsible for protecting mobile phone devices used by your company's workers, then security will be an important issue for you. Potentially you have corporate secrets at risk if a user loses a phone.

Mobile device management (MDM) delivers management for business, enabling BYOD ("Bring Your Own Device") to work, managing what apps can be installed and ensuring policy compliance for all your mobile devices, whether they are iPhones, iPads, Androids, BlackBerrys, or Windows Mobile devices.

Here are the highlights of Mobile Device Manager:

- Enforces your security policies to ensure compliance.
- Lets you turn on the built-in security features of iOS (iPhone/iPad), Android, BlackBerry, and Windows Mobile devices, including password protection or any iOS encryption.
- Ensures that only registered devices that meet your policies (that is not rooted Android or jailbroken iOS) have full access to corporate data and that the users of non-compliant devices are blocked or face other consequences until the situation is rectified.
- Helps locate, lock, or wipe lost devices, from the admin web console or the self-service portal.
- The security dashboard gives you an immediate overview of your company's device status.
- Lets you prove your corporate compliance with easy inventory and reporting tools.

Practice 7: Develop Mobile Acceptable Usage Policy

Developing appropriate guidance for users to address what is and what is not allowed and what is required, if personal devices are permitted for work purposes, and are critical elements of organisation acceptance policy.

For more detailed overview of how to develop a mobile acceptable usage policy, visit Chapter 10 - Developing Security Policies Guidelines.

7 STEPS TO SECURING PORTABLE STORAGE DEVICES

Portable storage devices such as USB flash drives, memory cards, optical disks, external hard disk drives, and portable media players are very versatile tools that have come to serve us extremely well for different purposes. They have become pervasive in our busy lives. We take them for granted and we tend to use them within corporate and personal requirements.

Unfortunately, these devices lack security, controls and management tools. But most alarmingly, these devices can easily carry corporate, sensitive data, and malware in and out of your premise.

Here are three particular events that took place that clearly illustrate the points made in the paragraph above.

1. IBM hands out malware infected USB drives at AusCERT 2010 security conference at the Gold Coast in Australia in May 2010.
2. President Obama discussed the Department of Defence (DoD) malware infection, where malware got onto thousands of DoD computers from an infected USB flash drive—May 29, 2009.
3. A December survey conducted by the Ponemon Institute found that 4 out of 10 employees reported losing a laptop, mobile phone, PDA, or flash drive containing company data.

According to the Ponemon Institute in a sponsored study by secure USB flash drive developer IronKey in June 2009:5

- 69% of employees surveyed said that they copy confidential or sensitive business information onto USB devices.
- 61% admitted to copying confidential or sensitive business information onto USB devices, and then transferring the information to another computer that is not part of the corporate network.

When an employee stores organisational information on their non-secure portable storage device, they put their business at risk every time they step out of the door.

- What would happen if the device were lost?
- What would happen if the device were stolen?
- What would happen if someone managed to extract the data from the device?
- What would be the consequences should they be negligent in distributing malware?

The acceptance security requirement includes asset management, identify sensitive data, malware protection, and encryption. Without these fundamentals, these platforms are not a viable technology and safe tool to use, within your business environment.

Practise 1: Asset Management

The case for a strong asset management is one of the highest priority goals for any business that wishes to realise control and to monitor the assets that have a direct effect on their core business.

Understanding what you have, what you own, and what it has access to, is important.

- Audit all hardware and portable storage devices in your business, whether they are USB flash drives, memory cards, optical disks, external hard disk drives, portable media players, cameras, or otherwise.
- Tag all your assets. Tagging such devices will allow you greater control of the asset.
- Develop a media disposal procedure to ensure that devices that have been taken out of use, do not fall into the wrong hands.

Practice 2: Identify Sensitive Data

Sensitive data is constantly at risk of loss, theft, or exposure. Often the data simply walks right out the door without the business realizing this.

In order to protect sensitive data, you must know where data resides and which data types exist.

Once you understand how sensitive data is distributed across your business, you can better enforce security policies and apply more effective control.

Practice 3: Malware Protection

If you thought that malware only infects workstations and notebooks, than you are partially correct. Malware is even more easily found in portable storage devices since they have very little security protection or control. This arises because most USB sticks have an autorun feature that launches the malware before any antivirus software can access the USB stick.

A compromised portable device has the ability to open doors to the whole organisation network, thereby compromising the entire business. For this reason, such portable devices must be able to self protect against malware infection.

Some common best practice

- If someone hands you a USB or other form of portable storage, be wary. This may contain a malware.
- If you intend to use a USB, consider using a secure USB that has the ability to scan its own files against malware threats.

- It is highly desirable that your portable storage device is also encrypted. More about this in Practice 4.
- If you are running Windows, disable the autorun feature for windows.

Disabling autorun in Windows

In Windows 7 you navigate to Administrative Templates -> Windows components

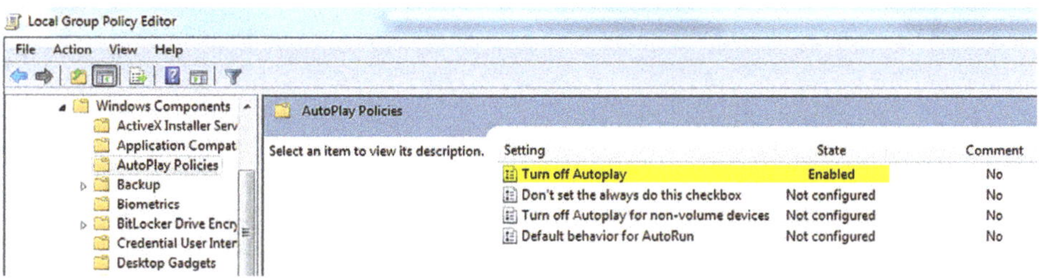

If your windows 7 system is fully patched, autorun will be turned off by default.

Alternatively if this is too technical, then holding down the **Control key** when you insert the USB key, will also disable the running of autorun and prevent malware from automatically installing itself.

In **Windows** 8, autoplay is disabled by default.

Practice 4: Encryption

Portability and flexibility of moving and carrying information has gained tremendous popularity. However, these traits that make these devices so convenient make them prone to theft and loss.

Sensitive data that is being stored on these devices must be just as secure as information stored behind organisation security systems. It is highly suggested to take the following steps:

- Ensure that your portable devices have a password to confirm validation of use.
- Ensure that the information on that portable device is encrypted.

In the event that these devices accidentally land in the hands of unauthorised individuals, these systems are reasonably secure from prying eyes.

Practice 5: Remote Wipe

If a device is lost or stolen, the administrator or device owner can issue a remote wipe command that removes all data and deactivates the device.

Practice 6: Leave it Alone

Have you found a thumb drive in a parking lot? Have you found some other media device lying around just outside your office? Leave it alone! Otherwise bring it to Lost & Found. But, don't connect it to your computer!

Practice 7: End User Device Control

We recognise that removable devices are valuable productivity tools that facilitate data access and movement for improved collaboration between employees and partners. But, the potential impact of data loss due to increased insider risk is a very real concern, be it accidental or malicious.

As more users depend on USB and portable devices to store and move data, the more tantalizing a target these devices are to cybercriminals looking for new paths into large networks.

To ensure that we have the visibility and control, a centralised solution is needed that automates the discovery of devices, defines and enforces device use and data encryption policies by user/group, and provides detailed forensic information to track data events.

Utilise **Device Control** solution that enforces flexible usage policies for removable devices, removable media, and data (such as read/write, encryption).

Many of the leading antivirus vendors have integrated device control management for greater visibility, control, and management.

REMINDER! Don't forget to register at www.pi10m.com

By registering your details, we will be able to provide you with free updates to the book, critical security alerts, valuable security tools that you can start using right now for free, answer your questions and much much more.

SUMMARY OF POINTS

Mobile security has become increasingly important in mobile computing. It is of particular concern as it relates to the security of personal and corporate information now stored on smartphones, tablets, and storage devices.

Smartphones, mobile computers, are becoming increasingly the preferred target of attack as well. These attacks exploit weaknesses related to the systems that can come from means of communication like Bluetooth, Wi-Fi networks, and GSM. There are also attacks that exploit software vulnerabilities from both the web browser and operating system and misconfiguration. Finally, there are forms of malicious software that rely on the weak knowledge of average user.

Here are the key summary points:

- Change your Internet facing device administrator passwords.This includes your router, firewall appliance, and Wi-Fi devices. Ensure devices have the latest system updates. When not in use, switch them off.
- When connecting remotely via a mobile computer, ensure that firewall is switched on,and your antivirus and operating system have the latest updates.
- Ensure that your mobile systems have been setup with encryption.
- When connecting remotely, ensure you use VPN or SSL-VPN.
- Consider using Two-Factor Authentication if possible.

FOR THE SECURITY-CONSCIOUS ORGANISATION

- Recommend implementing a Mobile Device Management (MDM) solution. There are many vendors in the market and some of the main antivirus vendors have also integrated MDM within their technology.

Further Resources

I have written a number of white papers that would add to your further understanding about remote mobile protection. These can be found at www.commsnet.com.au

- 7 Essential Steps to Securing Mobile Devices
- 7 Essential Steps to Securing Portable Storage Devices

9

Cloud Computing Protection Guidelines

What is a common trait between a Denial-of-Services Attack, a Hurricane, a Cyber Attack, and Data Stealing Hackers?

- A Complete Business Disaster!

– BOAZ FISCHER

INTRODUCTION

According to Gartner, US $58.6 billion was the amount the worldwide market for Cloud services was worth in 2009. It is predicted that by 2017, that the market will reach US $250 billion (Gartner Report, Forecast: Public Cloud Services, Worldwide and Regions, Industry Sector, 2011-2017) and Forrester Research estimated that it could reach US $241 billion by 2020 (based on their report called "Sizing the Cloud").

There is no question that Cloud computing is drawing strong interest and gathering considerable momentum. Certainly, organisations are looking for ways to raise their effectiveness, increase their agility to respond quickly in today's highly competitive environment, reduce capital and operational costs to become more competitive, and importantly empower users, partners, and suppliers with greater functionality, accessibility, collaboration, and resiliency.

If you ever had part of your business "outsourced" (outsourcing is often viewed as involving the contracting of a business function—commonly previously performed in-house to an external provider) then Cloud computing will hold some key similarities.

However, in this Cloud world, the delivery of information has dramatically changed the landscape. Organisation boundaries are disappearing as more of data is transmitted over the Internet. Employees, customers, suppliers, partners, and other stakeholders are able to access this data "wherever and whatever" they wish. In addition, the widespread adoption of smartphones and tablets is accelerating such connectivity, availability, and functionality.

The key theme here is the move from "physical" to "digital." The traditional bricks and mortar are being replaced by agile businesses that are based on software. Books have transformed to eBooks, CDs into MP3, and in-house physical and expensive servers to virtual systems sitting anywhere in the world that have full redundancy.

So what do we mean by Cloud computing? Simply put, Cloud gives your business the opportunity to expand your IT functionality without making significant IT capital expenditure. However, a key road block in driving businesses to Cloud computing has been security.
In traditional on-premise implementation of IT, organisations can define, implement, and monitor operational security practices and policies. The flow of information is controlled from end to end. In a Cloud environment, security information is more difficult to gain real control and visibility.

To make Cloud computing effective and safe, we need to weigh seriously the security requirements to ensure confidentiality, data integrity, and availability on the one hand against the improved economics of using Cloud computing on the other hand.

The debate bounces from side to side whether Cloud computing is safer than traditional in-house systems. There are undeniably risks associated with the use of Cloud service, just as there are risks associated with other delivery mechanisms.

Let's look at it this way, Cloud computing offers us new opportunities. Yet, this will also be accompanied by development of new security threats that represent the next generation of sophisticated targeted attacks which also include social engineering attacks, exploiting Cloud vulnerabilities, denial of service attacks, and data theft.

If your organisation is considering moving to the Cloud, this chapter will help you gain a better understanding of how you can ensure that your business data and its applications are better protected.

Considering moving to the Cloud?

In order to assess as to why you should consider moving to the Cloud, this can be best be answered by the following three key questions:

1. **Why do you want to move to the Cloud? Is it because it may offer…**
    a. Reduction in costs?
    b. Increase in revenues?
    c. Improve reliability?
    d. Improve agility?
    e. Increased marketability?
    f. Develop new services and products?
    g. Improve business process?
    h. All of the above?

2. **What primary business function are you considering moving to the Cloud?**
    a. Communications, such as email, messaging, team collaboration?
    b. Line of business applications?
    c. IT Infrastructure such as server infrastructure?
    d. Business process?

3. **What additional factors would you need to feel comfortable about moving to the Cloud?**
    a. Greater control?
    b. Tight security?
    c. Insight and visibility?
    d. Assuredness?
    e. Compliance?
    f. High-level SLA?

Traditional networks versus Cloud computing

Traditional networks are characterised by a single tenant, single physical premise, single physical infrastructure, single set of business controls, single storage of data, and single set of security measures.

With Cloud computing, multi-tenancy is a key domain, where services are shared amongst other organisations. Data is stored on shared platforms. Portions of data may reside anywhere in the world. Organisations are limited to the controls provided by the Cloud provider. Organisations subscribe to services on-demand while placing trust that these services meet data integrity, privacy, confidentiality, and availability.

Key risks facing Cloud computing

- Majority of Cloud computing services will be accessed via a web browser. However, web browsers are complex software applications that have continuously shown security flaws and may be compromised.

- It is assumed that Cloud providers are inherently more resilient. That should be the case; after all, they have much bigger pockets to spend on infrastructure resiliency. However, that is not always the case. A recent large Australian Cloud provider was hacked and their whole Cloud services came to a grinding hold, including 4800 businesses that depended on their hosting services (Distribute IT—June 21, 2012).

- It is assumed that Cloud providers are inherently available, but that is not the case. Amazon, Google, Facebook, Yahoo, and other Cloud providers do experience service downtime failures. They may not last long, but impact to businesses may be considerable.

- Where is my data? With Cloud providers, data may reside in various parts of the world. This makes it extremely challenging if you ever wanted to change to a different provider. To make things worse, different countries face different laws and jurisdictions.

Now being aware of the some of the key risks, the next set of questions will raise some key points that you to need address prior to moving to the Cloud.

- How would you be harmed if your corporate information became public and widely available?

- How would you be harmed if a Cloud provider accessed your corporate information?

- How would your business be harmed if your business processes or functions were disrupted or manipulated by an external party?
- How would you be harmed if the information were unexpectedly changed?
- How would you be harmed if your information wasn't available for a period of time?
- How would you be harmed if your Cloud services were used for cyber-criminal activities without your knowledge?
- How would you be harmed if your Cloud provider ceased to exist?

In the next seven principles outlined on the following pages, you will gain key insights and ability to gauge Cloud providers' ability to ensure that your online business is properly protected.

7 PRINCIPLES OF CLOUD SECURITY

Principle 1: Cloud Provider Resiliency

If you are new to Cloud computing and planning to stake your business on the reliability of the Cloud provider, then it is important that you don't blindly sign the contract without properly understanding your possible downside.

It is important to note that your Cloud systems are external to your organisation and you have no physical control.

Here are a number of key points:

- Determine whether Cloud provider has had an external audit assessed on their environment in the last twelve months?
- Determine whether they have a report of their outages over the last couple of years, which includes dates, times, and duration?
- Have they the necessary resources to respond to your request 365 x 24 x 7?
- Make sure that you understand the agreed service level agreement (SLA).
- Understand where your data is located. Is it located in a number of data centres in the same country or is it located in a number of different countries? Should you wish to discontinue the service, your key **exit plan** is to ensure that you can obtain all of your data from the Cloud provider. Equally important, that once your data has been retrieved, you need to have an understanding and assurance that the cloud provider has processes in place to be able to remove or deleting your data from their Cloud environment.

Principle 2: Cloud Provider Security Posture

As with so many different Cloud adoptions, Cloud computing depends on implementing the appropriate security, process, controls, and training.

Cloud providers are prone to ongoing threats, denial of services attacks, DNS attacks, and other intrusions. Their ability to manage risks and mitigate them as best as they can is a continuous process.

The Cloud provider needs to provide you with the necessary confidence that they have the resources, capability, and expertise to safeguard and protect your business to ensure privacy, confidentiality, and data integrity.

Three key questions that you can ask from your Cloud provider:

- How are you securing the infrastructure?
- How are you securing my applications?
- How are you securing my data?

Importantly, it is essential that all of your end user devices meet the proper security practices as described Chapters 2 and 3. The on uses are also on the end users to ensure that they have sufficient security awareness to follow business-designated policies and practices.

Practice 3: Cloud Provider Identity and Access

The Cloud introduces a new and yet familiar model for consumption and delivery of services. One thing that is central in consuming such Cloud services is understanding which users are accessing what application, what data has been retrieved, how it was accessed, and when.

A huge challenge when moving to the Cloud is the loss of control. As Cloud consumers, we hand our control to the Cloud provider and assume that they have the necessary processes and practices. We hand in our faith, trust, and expectations that they will do the right thing. How then do we verify and satisfy that Cloud providers are following and implementing effective security practice and controls?

Gaining visibility and some level of certainty will require the ability to manage identities and access information and applications to-the-Cloud, inside-the-Cloud, from-the-Cloud.

- Identity Control—The ability to provision and manage user credentials and authentication.
- Access Control—The ability to apply specific policies on specific services.
- Information Control—The ability to specify who can perform data-related operations (administration activities).

Importantly, the Cloud provider needs to provide you with the ability to audit and log access, which is most imperative

Practice 4: Cloud Provider Data Access

Where is my data? How is my Cloud provider guarding against data theft and data loss? When you subscribe to a Cloud provider, all the data that is generated and processed will reside in the premises, owned and operated by the Cloud provider.

The key question that you need to ask before you sign up with a Cloud provider is "What is my exit strategy? How will I leave with all my data?"

The key challenges for lifecycle Cloud data management are reflected in the following points:

- Gain assurance from the Cloud provider to know where your data is located at any point of time including backups and copies.
- Should you be required to delete the data, there is an effective method of locating the data and erasing it completely.
- Develop your own backup and recovery just in case your Cloud provider ceases to exist.
- Data encryption is the key to ensuring protection from prying eyes.

Engage with the Cloud provider or an external security expert to help you implement encryption practices when your data is:

- In transit;
- At rest;
- In memory;
- And importantly, your backups and other media are also encrypted.

Proper management of data encryption rests significantly in your being able to manage the keys. The keys must be:

- Properly protected.
- Access to keys must be limited to individual users (preferably within your organisation rather than the Cloud provider).

Principle 5: Cloud Provider Portability and Interoperability

It is without doubt that you will need to consider very carefully the possibility of moving to a different Cloud provider in the future.

Why is that?

- The Cloud provider ceases operations.
- The Cloud provider has a business operational failure.
- The Cloud provider ceases service offering.
- The Cloud provider has been compromised which could affect your business operations.
- The Cloud provider is under criminal investigations.
- You experience a business dispute.
- You have found a better, closer, or cheaper integrated Cloud provider.

There are a number of key questions that you need to ask as a result of any of the above points occurring:

- Will you have access to your data if the Cloud provider ceases business operations?
- Will you be able to move your business to another Cloud provider easily?
- How long will your business be able to cope being offline?

Portability and interoperability management are required to be part of your business continuity practice.

Principle 6: Cloud Provider Compliance

With the huge momentum push to the Cloud, organisations face new challenges as they migrate from traditional networks to Cloud providers. Delivering, measuring, and communicating compliance is vastly different in the Cloud.

Compliance, as defined by the Cloud Security Alliance, can be defined as the awareness and adherence to obligations including the assessment and prioritization of corrective actions, deemed necessary and appropriate.

Existing regulations were written to account for traditional networks. However as a Cloud consumer, you can be challenged to show auditors that your organisation is in compliance.
Understanding the interaction of Cloud computing and the regulatory environment is a key component of any Cloud strategy.

The key understanding you need to have:

- Consider what applications and data you wish to move to the Cloud.
- Consider whether you need to ensure compliance in the Cloud.
- Consider the division of responsibility for your Cloud business.
- Consider what implications could be for using a particular Cloud service or providers.
- Consider the Cloud provider capabilities for demonstrating compliance, including document generation, evidence production, and process compliance, in a timely manner.
- Consider the difficulty in gathering compliance evidence from your Cloud provider.
- Consider whether the auditor is at all Cloud aware.

Information technology in the Cloud is increasingly subject to overabundance of policies and regulations. It is expected therefore that you take a proactive approach to complying with regulatory guidelines should it require so, especially when you are considering moving to the Cloud.
Any information processed, transmitted, stored, or viewed that is deemed as Personal Identifiable Information or private information faces a number of compliance regulations worldwide that may vary from country or state.
The Cloud provider and you must therefore agree on how to collect, store, and share compliance evidence (e.g., audit logs, activity reports, system configurations).

Principle 7: Cloud Provider Legal Obligations

When engaging with a Cloud provider regarding an agreement that you intend to sign, it is important to note that the contract is somewhat different than on-the-premise system environment.

It is important to note that Cloud contracts may not have the same level of maturity as we would expect. As such, there has been little precedence of Cloud contract legal ruling.

Moving data into the Cloud means that your data will most likely be outside of the direct control and in some instances, the data may be processed and stored outside of your country of residence.

The physical location raises the question of legal governance over the data. Understanding data sovereignty is a consideration of what laws and regulations are in play when data from one country is stored in another country. For example, if data from a Belgian company is stored in systems in the United States—whose laws preside if there is a problem?

Should you consider offshoring your data, you need to answer the following questions:

- What are the local laws for offshoring?
- If you are required to have compliancy, are you able to enforce this regulation offshore?
- If the Cloud provider is hit with a disaster, are you aware of what the ramification and legal consequences are? The question is whether you are indemnified by the insurance company for loss of your business or not.

Clearly, the significant issue for any Cloud computing agreement where the provider holds or is able to access an agency's data is the security of that data. This issue is heightened from a risk perspective where the data is sensitive (including personal information) and/or it is held offshore.

- If a privacy breach occurs due to a fault of Cloud vendor, is there any liability coverage policy taken up by the vendor?
- If the Cloud provider gets hacked, can you move against the vendor for claiming lost of profits?
- Is your data protected under the intellectual property rights of that country? What would happen if your data is breached?
- Your data stored in the Cloud may have sensitive information; how secure will such information be in hands of the Cloud vendor?
- What would happen if the Cloud vendor granted some privileged third parties access to your stored data? Here, third party could be a legal authority, government, or even an internal employee.

To protect the interest of your business, you need to ensure that you read the Cloud vendor terms and conditions meticulously before signing up for Cloud-based services.

If the Cloud provider provides a standard form of contract, then you must be fully aware of all the terms and conditions during your buy cycle. It will save you from nasty surprises and you will be financially, mentally, and legally prepared to save your business from unfavorable consequences of Cloud computing.

SUMMARY

The meteoric rise of Cloud computing has been a highlight for the past few years. The notion that information technology can be delivered in a highly scalable, agile, reliable, and cost-effective model is generating great excitement for both customers and vendors alike. However as we have seen in this chapter, there are a number of important challenges regarding data protection.

The biggest fear in embracing Cloud computing is loss of control. There is some high degree of trust you have to place in the Cloud provider's hands.

The fundamental question that you need to ask when thinking of Cloud adoption is "What is my exit strategy?"

There are no guarantees that your Cloud provider of today will continue to operate in its current form over an extended timeframe. Furthermore, a Cloud provider may experience a form of disaster that may cause it to cease operation.

However, most likely you will reach the contract end and the risk therefore is whether you are able to extract your data and associated applications.

FOR THE SECURITY-CONSCIOUS ORGANISATION

- Gain insight in the governance, performance, availability, and security of your Cloud provider.
- Ensure that you read the terms and conditions meticulously before signing up for Cloud based services.
- Use multi-factor authentication.
- Track and monitor all access to the Cloud system.
- If your organisation deals with sensitive information, ensure your data is encrypted.
- Develop and define Cloud policies and accountabilities for your organisation.
- Develop a business continuity plan in the event that you need to exit your current provider and port it to another provider.

Further Resources

I have written a white paper that would add to your further understanding about Cloud protection guidelines. These can be found at www.commsnet.com.au

- 7 Essential Principles to Cloud Security

Also a very reputable organisation—The Cloud Security Alliance (CSA) is a not-for-profit organisation with a mission to promote the use of best practices for providing security assurance within Cloud Computing—www.pi10m.com/b1/38

10

Developing Security Policies Guidelines

"The ignorance of one user impairs the security for the whole organisation."

– BOAZ FISCHER

INTRODUCTION

It's not my responsibility! Well, then who's responsible?

What's the big deal? Isn't security the responsibility of the guys in the IT department? Shouldn't the firewall block the bad stuff form coming in? Shouldn't the antivirus programs block all the malware? Shouldn't we be able to stop hackers from defacing our website?

Besides, who reads those policy documents anyway? They're so long and wordy and hard to follow. I'm sure our corporation will not be harmed if I don't bother following business protocols.

Is security only the responsibility of the IT department? Is protecting the privacy of confidential business information only the responsibility of upper management?

Saying that security and privacy are solely the responsibility of IT and management and that as an employee, you have absolutely no responsibility in these matters is simply not true.

Saying that network and data security is solely the responsibility of your IT department is like saying that the maintenance of your car is solely the responsibility of your mechanic. But if you're driving along the highway and your oil light is flashing and you ignore it, you're going to have a problem.

Saying that confidentiality of business information is solely the responsibility of management is like saying that you can safely ignore the road signs and traffic lights when you drive your car. If you have an accident as a result of doing something like that, good luck trying to blame anyone other than yourself!

What is true is that all of your users are responsible for ensuring the security and privacy of your organisation.

Yes, you should, and must care about the security and privacy of your company's information system and resources. You do have a role in protecting your company against the theft, destruction, corruption, or accidental loss of sensitive business files and data.

Organisations today are investing a significant part of their information technology budget, protecting their network against various threats and vulnerabilities.

Although commendable, however, without placing these technologies within a framework of appropriate practices and policies, organisations will find themselves increasingly frustrated at not being able to achieve the desired outcomes.

Setting out the appropriate policies paves the way in which your organisation approaches security best practices. Such policies are the bedrock of a secure business environment. They can be perceived as a collection of guidelines that you can undertake to ensure business consistency, efficiency, effectiveness, confidentiality, and integrity.

Furthermore, having these policies in place helps you to enforce best practices and take appropriate action against employees who do not comply with your organisation's accepted practices.

The following section will provide you with Seven Essential Security Policies that you can adopt within your organisation for effective management.

There are two areas that we believe need emphasis for all policies:

1. All polices should be linked to your organisation's human resource policies. If a policy does not have direct and enforceable consequences when not complied with, the policy will never be followed.

2. All polices should be applied consistently irrespective of the value of the employee to your organisation.

IMPLEMENTING 7 ESSENTIAL SECURITY POLICIES

1. Email Usage Policy

Email is still the preferred business communication tool and will remain so for some time to come. The purpose of an email usage policy is to uphold the reputation and standing of your organisation and to use it in a responsible, effective, and in lawful manner.

When an email goes out from your organisation, the general public will tend to view that message as an official policy statement from your organisation. At a minimum the policy should specify the following:

- The email system shall not to be used for the creation or distribution of any disruptive or defamatory messages, including offensive comments about race, gender, hair colour, disabilities, age, sexual orientation, pornography, religious beliefs and practice, political beliefs, or national origin.

- Using a reasonable amount of company resources for personal emails is acceptable, but non-work related email shall be saved in a separate folder from work related email. Sending chain letters or joke emails from an organisation's email account should be prohibited. These restrictions also apply to the forwarding of mail received by a company employee.

- Employees shall have no expectation of privacy in anything they store, send, or receive on the company's email system. The company may monitor messages without prior notice but is not obliged to monitor email messages.

- It is suggested that all outbound emails should include a corporate signature. A corporate signature contains contact details, pertinent job titles, company names, and most important an email disclaimer. The reasons for adding such a disclaimer include confidentiality, copyright, contract formation, defamation, discrimination, harassment, privilege, and viruses. By adding disclaimers to emails, your organisation conveys a professional and trustworthy image. Disclaimers are typically attached to the end of emails.

By following the guidelines above, the email user can minimise the legal risks involved in the use of email. If any user disregards the rules set out in this email policy, not only is the email user liable but your organisation can be held liable and responsible.

You should therefore consider email as an important means of communication and recognise the importance of setting appropriate policy and training in place to all employees within your organisation.

2. Internet Usage Policy

The Internet Usage policy is a set of guidelines about the appropriate use of organisation Internet access.

The user needs to be made aware that browsing certain sites or downloading certain files is prohibited and that the policy must be adhered to. Otherwise, there could be serious repercussions for both the organisation and the employee.

While limited private use of the company's IT resources to access the web should be permitted, users are expected to exercise good judgement in using organisation IT facilities to access the web. However, organisations should reserves the right to monitor all web usage.

The Internet Usage Policy is an important document. All users should sign such an agreement upon commencement of work with an employer. The following guidelines should be included and mandatory in your documentation:

- Introduction of malicious programs into the network or server (e.g., viruses, worms, trojan horses, e-mail bombs, etc.).
- Using a company computing asset to actively engage in procuring or transmitting material that is in violation of sexual harassment or hostile workplace laws, in the user's local jurisdiction.
- Using company assets in conducting non-corporate but personal business activities.
- Making fraudulent offers of products, items, or services.
- Disrupting network communication via your web usage on company IT assets.
- Port scanning or security scanning is expressly prohibited.
- Executing any form of network monitoring which will intercept data not intended for the employee's host.
- Circumventing user authentication or security of any host, network, or account.
- Employees shall not engage in any web usage that may harm or tarnish the image, reputation, and/or goodwill of the company and/or any of its employees.
- Employees are also prohibited from making any discriminatory, disparaging, defamatory, or harassing comments when using the web or otherwise engaging in any conduct prohibited by the company's Non-Discrimination and Anti-Harassment policy.
- Employees may also not attribute personal statements, opinions, or beliefs to the company when engaged in web activity. If an employee is expressing his or her beliefs and/or opinions via the web, the employee may not, expressly or implicitly, represent themselves as an employee or representative of the company on the web.

3. Malware Protection Policy

Inherent in this responsibility is an obligation to provide appropriate protection against malware threats, such as viruses, trojans, spyware applications, data theft, and tarnishing the reputation of your organisation.

Effective implementation of this policy will limit the exposure and effect of common malware threats to the systems they cover. This policy should apply to all computer systems. At a minimum the policy should contain the following:

- All servers, desktops, and laptops MUST have an antivirus application installed that offers real-time scanning protection to files and applications running on the target system.
- The policy should specify the frequency of definition updates and who is responsible for ensuring the definition updates are applied in a timely fashion.
- If the target system is a mail server, it MUST have either an external or internal antivirus scanning application that scans all mail destined to and from the mail server. Local antivirus scanning applications MAY be disabled during backups if an external antivirus application still scans inbound emails while the backup is being performed.
- Define the procedure for safe handling of suspected malware infected devices.
- Unless specifically signed off by senior management, all connection to the Internet must be done using organisational IT assets with appropriate malware protection.

4. Mobile Policy

Today's portable devices aren't just used for entertainment purposes. The availability and accessibility to corporate data from anywhere and anytime is increasingly on the rise. This in turn, provides greater productivity and strategically positions the organisation to improve business interactions and agility.

To reap such rewards that users are now demanding, it is important that organisations secure and manage users' mobility by applying appropriate mobile policies that all users need to adhere to. The policies need to be simple, clear, and embracing.

The following Mobile Policy details how personal communication devices (PCD) whether it be smartphones, tablets, notebooks, or personal computers can interact with corporate networks. In short, PCDs are any mobile devices that can be used for communications either on voice or computer networks.

The reasons you need a policy for PCDs are as follows:

- These devices provide mechanisms for communication that bypasses your existing IT security controls. Inappropriate use of PCDs can lead to data leakage from your organisation and can compromise your internal network.

At a minimum, the following should be included in such a policy:

- Personal Communication Devices will be issued only to personnel with duties that require them to be in immediate and frequent contact when they are away from their normal work locations.
- Files containing confidential or sensitive data may not be stored in PCDs unless protected by approved encryption.
- Confidential or sensitive data shall never be stored on a PCD.
- Charges for repair due to misuse of equipment or misuse of services may be the responsibility of the employee, as determined on a case-by-case basis. The cost of any item beyond the standard authorised equipment is also the responsibility of the employee.
- Lost or stolen equipment must immediately be reported and remotely wiped.
- PCDs and voicemail are issued for organisational business. Personal use should be limited to minimal and incidental use.
- Conducting telephone calls or utilizing PCDs while driving can be a safety hazard. Drivers should use PCDs while parked or out of the vehicle. If employees must use a PCD while driving, the organisation requires the use of hands-free enabling devices.

What about "Bring Your Own Device" (BYOD)?

Before allowing people to bring their own mobile device into an organisation, a policy should be developed that specifies precisely what is and is not allowed with regard to privately owned mobile devices.

Compliance to this policy should be ensured by periodically auditing these devices or better still, if the size and budget of your organisation permit, use an enterprise-wide mobile device management technology. At a minimum your policy should contain the following:

- A statement that compliance to this policy is mandatory and users have no expectation of privacy when using their own mobile devices at work.
- That auditing of mobile devices will occur and the non-compliant devices will not be permitted to be used in the corporate environment.
- The list of permitted mobile device platforms it is willing to support.

- The list of permitted applications and what these applications are permitted to access and store.
- An open understanding of what fees the organisation is willing to pay.
- Encryption of file systems is mandatory and the policy should spell out what types of encryption keys are permitted and how these keys will be managed.
- Locking of device after a specific idle period.
- Devices will be configured so the devices can be wiped remotely.
- A procedure for reporting lost or stolen devices.

For The Security-Conscious Organisation

- A clear understanding of how this device is going to be managed. Will it be managed over the wire or synchronizing via a computer?
- What support will the organisation provide? Will it be first or second tier support?
- What are the privacy issues? Is the employee data private? How is the data going to be managed and stored?
- What are the legal concerns? What is the organisation responsibility if user is discovered being involved in illegal activities which aren't related to work?

5. Backup Policy

Organisation backup is the organisation lifeline. Taking care, attention, and ongoing management is critically important.

This policy is one of the most critical policies for an organisation to have in place. It is designed to protect data in the organisation and to be sure that it is not lost and can be recovered in the event of an equipment failure, intentional destruction of data, or disaster

Without a proper and adequate backup policy, your organisation's business continuity is put at risk. At a minimum the policy should contain the following:

- What data is to be backed up?
- How often is the data to be backed up?
- What technology is to be used to perform the backups?
- Who is responsible for ensuring the backups have been successful?
- How often will a test restoration take place to ensure that a successful backup can be restored?
- Where will the backups be stored?
- If you lose your backups, how will you restore your IT business function?

6. Remote Access Policy

The purpose of this policy is to define standards for connecting to your organisation network, from any external network.

These standards are designed to minimise the potential exposure to your organisation from damages, which may result from unauthorised use of organisational resources. Such damages include the loss of sensitive or company confidential data, intellectual property, damage to public image, damage to critical organisational internal systems, etc.

At a minimum the policy should specify the following:

- What types of remote access to your organisation's internal network are permitted?
- What type of devices will be permitted to connect to the corporate network?
- Who is permitted to use such remote access technology and when?
- What applications and data will users be allowed to access?
- What standards will the equipment be required to meet that is used to connect to the internal network?
- Who will engage in monitoring and auditing remote connection activities?
- How are remote access privileges granted and revoked?

7. Wireless Policy

The use of wireless technology has historically been a serious security risk to organisations. This is because it can be an easy access point to gain entry to an organisational network.

The purpose of this policy is to provide guidelines for wireless connectivity to an organisation's corporate network. It is designed to protect organisation resources against intrusions by those who would use wireless media to infiltrate the corporate network.

At a minimum such a policy should contain the following:

- This policy prohibits access to organisational networks via unsecured wireless communication mechanisms. Only wireless systems that meet the criteria of this policy or have been granted an exclusive waiver by the nominated delegate are approved for connectivity to an organisation's network.

- This policy covers all wireless data communication devices (e.g. personal computers, cellular phones, PDAs, etc.) connected to any organisation's internal networks. This includes any form of wireless communication device capable of transmitting packet data.

- All wireless Access Points / Base Stations connected to the corporate network must be registered and approved by corporate executive. These Access Points / Base Stations are subject to periodic security assessments and audits. All wireless Network Interface Cards (i.e., PC cards) used in corporate laptop or desktop computers must be registered with a nominated delegate.

- All wireless access devices must use corporate approved vendor products and security configurations.

- All computers with wireless devices must utilise a corporate approved encrypted protocol configured to drop all unauthenticated and unencrypted traffic. All implementations must support a hardware address that can be registered and tracked, i.e., a MAC address. All implementations must support and employ strong user authentication which checks against an internal database unless authorised by the corporate executive.

- The wireless network SSID shall be configured so that it does not contain any identifying information about the organisation, such as the company name, division title, employee name, or product identifier.

SUMMARY

Who's responsible? We all are!
Policies are a set of procedures or rules, which are required to set a path to a specific objective.

Security policies should balance access and security. Security policies should minimise risk while not imposing undue access restrictions on those who need access to resources. Yet, at the same time, security policies need to convey a strong corporate message in the way it identifies itself and the way it intends to interact with the outside world.

Just because a policy has been put in place, does not make your network more secure. It doesn't guarantee that you will not be breached. However, it minimises that possibility of happening if users adhere to corporate policies.

In short, policies need to define the following:

- Scope –To whom does this policy apply to?
- What actions are defined by the policy?
- Define when actions are to be done.
- Define where or on what equipment the policy applies to.
- Define the organisational level that the policy applies to, such as a division or the entire enterprise.
- Who enforces the policy?
- What are the consequences of failure to follow the policy?

For the security-conscious organisation

A key element with security policies is enforcement and auditing. Your organisation must determine how to enforce and audit security policies or they will be worthless.

Auditing is a process of determining whether the policies are being followed. Your organisation should create a complete Information Systems Security Plan and incorporate the security policies into it, along with the set auditing process. This means that there must be resources and personnel set aside to perform periodic audits and the management and executive must accept the Information Systems Security Plan.

WHAT DO I DO . . . ?

"The key to being security aware is to continually ask inquisitive questions.."

– BOAZ FISCHER

IF MY COMPUTER HAS MALWARE INFECTION?

The usual course of action to follow when your computer is infected is to take your computer offline from the Internet or your home or company network and rebuild it from scratch.

It is usually very difficult to remove a malware infection cleanly that has bypassed your antivirus software. You may have successfully removed the virus successfully, but are you aware of what possible trojans, other malicious programs, or back doors it may have installed on your machine?

I would highly recommend removing the computer from any network, formatting all media and reinstalling the operating system and associated applications from fresh. This may be quite tiresome and frustrating exercise, but at least it is the safest route.

Alternatively, you can re-image from a clean image/backup. However, if you are not sure if it is clean as your backup may be compromised too, then recommend reinstalling the operating system and associated applications from fresh. This is the safest way to ensure that no unscrupulous malware are lurking on your machine.

Having said that, if you would like to try to remove the infection, here are some broad guidelines:

- Microsoft has a "Malicious Software Removal Tool" that you can download. It will check you system and when it finds the malware, it will try to remove it and provide you with a report. For further information visit the following site: www.pi10m.com/b1/39
- If you can't connect to the Internet
- Microsoft Windows Defender Offline works with Windows 8, Windows 7, and Windows Vista.
- Use another computer to download Windows Defender Offline from www.pi10m.com/b1/75 and create a CD, DVD, or USB flash drive with the software on it. Then use the media to restart your infected computer and scan it for unwanted software

Post Diagnosis

Once you have successfully managed to remove the malware, continue to regularly scan your machine for malware on a daily basis.

Seek expert advice—If you want to be certain that your computer is completely cleaned or just want a second opinion, seek a security expert.

IF I SUSPECT I HAVE A BOT INFECTION ON MY COMPUTER?

Internet bots are known as "robots." These are software applications that run automated tasks over the Internet. Typically, these bots are used for malicious purpose and allow the remote attacker to control your computer.

Although antivirus software may miss bot incursions and infections, there are a few telltale signs to watch for that indicate your computer has been co-opted by a botnet.

- Your computer is unusually slow, crashes, or frequently stops responding to commands.
- Your network or Internet connection is unusually slow.
- There is unknown network activity when you're not using the Internet.
- Your computer cannot access some or any websites.
- The amount of spam you receive dramatically increases.
- Your antivirus may have been disabled.

If you still suspect that your computer is infected by a bot or some of malware, go to the previous page to assess whether your system is infected or not.

IF MY WINDOWS MACHINE WON'T START?

If Windows will not start or if the computer will not start in safe mode, it's possible that your system may be infected by malware.

First make sure that it is not a hardware issue.

If it not a hardware problem, I recommend using an antivirus rescue disk.

However, should you have not created a rescue disk, then you may have no option but to reformat your machine and reinstall the operating system and associated applications from fresh. This may be a quite tiresome and frustrating exercise, but at least this process is usually the best route to get your machine up and running.

An antivirus rescue disk allows you to scan an infected computer without having to start Windows. Many antivirus companies provide a free rescue disk. They are extremely effective at removing malware from a computer.

Antivirus vendors have the ability to create a rescue disk. This will need to be done while your machine is clean. Once created, keep it in a safe place.

If the rescue CD doesn't work, seek expert advice.

IF I SUSPECT A FILE MAY BE INFECTED ON MY COMPUTER?

If you suspect a file may contain an infection, here are a number of steps for you to follow:

1. The first thing to do is to contain the file so as to minimise possible infections. As such, quarantine the file.

2. The next step is to scan it with installed antivirus software.

3. Should your antivirus software not successfully detect the malware within the suspicious file, we highly recommend you to submit the file to other third party antivirus vendors. These vendors will scan the file through multiple antivirus scanners (such as the two websites listed below).

You can submit your file to see if it is malicious

- VirusTotal—www.pi10m.com/b1/76

- VirusTotal is a free service that analyzes suspicious files and URLs and facilitates the quick detection of viruses, worms, trojans, and all kinds of malware

- Metascan—www.pi10m.com/b1/77

- Metascan Online is a free online file scanning service powered by OPSWAT's Metascan technology, a multiple engine malware scanning solution

Be aware, if the test hasn't found anything, don't automatically assume that it is clean.

IF I SUSPECT THAT AN EMAIL ATTACHMENT MAY CONTAIN MALWARE?

If you received an email and you suspect that the email attachment may contain malware, here are a number of steps for you to follow:

- Do not open it!
- Do you know the sender? If so, contact the sender and establish whether they sent the email including the attachment and verify the content.
- If you do not know the sender then either quarantine the email or delete it. DO NOT respond to the sender in any manner.
- If you think the email comes from a reputable user then
- Confirm with user that they have sent you the attachment.
- Otherwise, submit file for malware inspection as mentioned in the previous page.

IF I GET AN EMAIL ASKING ME TO RESET MY BANK CREDENTIALS?

Ignore it!

Banks typically do not send emails asking you to reset or change your login credentials.

If you are still unsure, here are a number of steps for you to follow:

- Does the email address from the sender look as if it is coming from the bank? If not, delete email. Do not open any attachments.
- Contact the bank and verify whether they had sent the email. If not, delete email. Do not open any attachments.
- Do NOT click on any links within the email. It may direct you to a malicious website with the intention of infecting your computer.

IF I DON'T KNOW WHETHER THE EMAIL IS A HOAX OR NOT?

Some messages are a hoax. They often include fake announcements claimed to originate from reputable sources. Hoaxes are usually harmless and accomplish nothing more than annoying people who identify it as a hoax and waste the time of people who forward the message.

Some messages have malicious content within the email, such as attachments that contain malware which when opened will infect your computer.

Some messages are legitimate.

Essentially be on your guard. Be especially cautious if the message has any of the characteristics listed below, which most likely indicates it is a hoax. These characteristics are just guidelines.

- It suggests tragic consequences for not undertaking some action.
- It promises money or gift certificates for performing some action.
- It offers instructions or attachments claiming to protect you from a virus that is undetected by antivirus software.
- It claims it's not a hoax.
- There are multiple spelling or grammatical errors, or the logic is contradictory.
- There is a statement urging you to forward the message.
- It asks you to forward the email to all your friends.
- It has already been forwarded multiple times (evident from the trail of email headers in the body of the message).

IF MY SYSTEM IS TAKEN FOR HOSTAGE—RANSOMWARE?

Ransomware is a type of software which restricts access to a victim's computer system, and demands a ransom to be paid to the perpetrator in order for the restriction to be removed. Ransomware typically propagates like a conventional computer malware, entering a system through a downloaded file or vulnerability in a network service. The cyber- criminal then proceeds to download tools to encrypt user files, including PDFs, Microsoft Office files, and other directly attached storage devices, which are required for normal business operations.

Some ransomware do not use encryption. In this case, they are simply designed to effectively restrict interaction with the system, for example, by not allowing the operating system to start at all until it is repaired. Such ransomware utilises elements of scareware to coax users into paying for its removal. They may display notices supposedly issued by law enforcement agencies, which falsely claim that the user's system had been used for illegal activities, or contains illegal content such as pornography, and unlawfully obtained software. Some ransomware falsely claim that their computer's Windows installation is a counterfeit or requires re-activation.

In any case, the ransomware will attempt to extort money from the system's user by forcing them to purchase either a program to decrypt the files it had encrypted, or an unlock code which will remove the locks it had applied. These payments are often delivered using either a wire transfer or through an online payment system.

Recommendations

- Ensure that applications and operating systems are kept up-to-date with the latest software patches.
- Enforce strong password policies on user accounts.
- Make regular backups of important files and importantly store backups offline.
- Limit remote access connection attempts and log successful and failed connections.
- When remote access is required, use secure methods such as Virtual Private Networks (VPNs) with two factor authentication and/or certificate-based authentication for remote access.

What you can do, should you be ransomed?

Don't pay the cybercriminals. **IF** you are hit by a well-made encrypting ransomware and you have no backup, there is nothing you can do except pay the ransomware or face the loss of your data.

Note that if you do decide to pay the ransom fee the following may apply:

- There is NO GUARANTEE that it will decrypt your data
- If it does decrypt your data, there is NO GUARANTEE that your system will be left clean. You may be subjugated for further ransom.
- Go to another computer and start searching for a solution.
- Antivirus companies post free instructions and utilities to help users unblock their computers.

IF I GET A "POP UP" MESSAGE THAT MY COMPUTER IS INFECTED?

Watch out for fake virus alerts!

These tend to happen when visiting certain websites that may contain malicious malware. They will tend to instigate a "pop up" message that your machine is infected.

Such pop ups are also known as "scareware or rogue software." Such software appears to look beneficial from a security perspective but provides limited or no security, generates erroneous or misleading alerts, or attempts to lure you into participating in fraudulent transactions.

The "updates" or "alerts" in the pop up windows call for you to take some sort of action, such as clicking to install the software, accept recommended updates, or remove unwanted viruses or spyware.

What does rogue security software do?

Rogue software might report a virus, even though your computer is actually clean. The software might also fail to report viruses when your computer is infected. Inversely, when you download rogue security software, it will install a virus or other malicious software on your computer so that the software has something to detect.

Once it is on your system, it can disable your machine, slowly corrupt your computer files, disable Windows, disable your legitimate antivirus, lure you into a fraudulent transaction, use social engineering to steal your personal information, and much, much more.

What can you do?

1. Do NOT click on such messages!
2. Do NOT click on any "Action Buttons" in that Window!
3. Close your browser immediately.
4. Open your existing antivirus and run a scan on your computer.

Other recommendations:

- Make sure your firewall is on.
- Ensure your operating system and software are up-to-date.
- Ensure your legitimate antivirus software is up-to-date. Use your legitimate antivirus to scan your system regularly, especially if you get a "virus alert."
- Use caution when you click links in email or on social networking websites.
- Familiarise yourself with common phishing scams.
- Australian Federal Government Scam Watch site—www.pi10m.com/b1/46
- US Federal Consumer and Fraud site—www.pi10m.com/b1/47

IF I SUSPECT THE INTERNET LINK IS MALICIOUS?

Whether you received an email with an Internet link contained within the email or browsing a website that has a link to another website, before clicking on that link, ask yourself the following questions:

- "Is this a possible safe site?"
- "How do I know whether this site has malicious malware?"

Websites with malicious malware and content have grown by over 100% per year. Even well recognised websites around the world may contain some malware. It is therefore important to be highly suspicious and cautious before visiting such sites.

Some infected websites have what we call "Drive-by Download." This is a term which means that any download happens without a person's knowledge, often a computer virus, spyware, malware, or crime ware. Any such download is a serious cause for concern.

A drive-by download occurs when a user visits a legitimate website that has been temporarily compromised, enabling an adversary to install malicious software on the user's computer.

Here are some possible steps that you can do:

1. Ascertain whether the domain name looks suspicious. If you can't tell, copy the link and paste it in Google and do a search on it and see what it comes back.

2. Alternatively, use these free assessment tools to ascertain whether the site is malicious or not. Remember these two tools are useful to gain some further insight, but don't rely on them wholeheartedly.

   - Web Sense Ace Insight has the ability to check and report on the status of that website—www.pi10m.com/b1/28
   - Zscaler URL Risk Analyzer is a dynamic assessment engine that scores the safety of your website. It does take some time to asses, so be patient—www.pi10m.com/b1/29

3. Even after completing the above tasks, and the site has been reported with no malware, it is still better to err with caution.

For the more security-conscious organisation

4. Implement a robust web content filtering solution that inspects the content of all web traffic for potentially malicious downloads and blocks them based on that inspection.

IF SOMEONE IS OFFERING ME SOMETHING FOR FREE?

If it sounds too good to be true, it probably is—You have probably seen many emails promising fantastic rewards, money, and gifts. However, regardless of what the email claims to be, there are no wealthy strangers desperate to send you money. Beware of grand promises. They are most likely spam, hoaxes, or phishing schemes.

Also be wary of pop-up windows and advertisements for free downloadable software. They may be disguising spyware.

Remember the saying *"don't trust candy from strangers"*—Finding something on the Internet does not guarantee that it is true. Anyone can publish information online, so before accepting a statement as fact or taking action, verify that the source is reliable.

People can pretend to be someone else. So verify that an email is legitimate before opening an unexpected email attachment or responding to a request for personal information or divulging your personal information to a complete stranger.

IF I GET A PHONE CALL LETTING ME KNOW THAT MY COMPUTER IS INFECTED?

I have often received numerous phone calls letting me know that my computer is compromised. They seem to look beneficial from a security perspective but they attempt to lure you into participating in fraudulent download of software.

What can you do?

Ignore them! Put your phone down!

What do they do?

When you download their rogue security software, it will install malicious software on your computer.

Once it is on your system, it can disable your machine, slowdown or corrupt your computer files, disable Windows, disable your legitimate antivirus, lure you into a fraudulent transaction, use social engineering to steal your personal information, and much, much more.

Other recommendations

- Make sure your firewall is on.
- Ensure your operating system and software are up-to-date.
- Ensure your legitimate antivirus software is up-to-date. Use your legitimate antivirus software to scan your system regularly, especially if you get a "virus alert."
- Use caution when you click links in email or on social networking websites.
- Familiarise yourself with common phishing scams.
    - Australian Federal Government Scam Watch site —www.pi10m.com/b1/46
    - US Federal Consumer and Fraud site—www.pi10m.com/b1/47

IF I SUSPECT THAT I'M A VICTIM OF A SCAM?

If you suspect that you've responded to a phishing scam with personal or financial information, take these steps to minimise any damage and protect your identity.

- Change the passwords or PINs on all your online accounts that you think might be compromised.
- Place a fraud alert on your credit reports. Check with your bank or financial advisor if you're not sure how to do this.
- Contact the bank or the online merchant directly. Do not follow the link in the fraudulent email message.
- If you know of any accounts that were accessed or opened fraudulently, close those accounts.
- Routinely review your bank and credit card statements monthly for unexplained charges or inquiries that you didn't initiate.

How to report a scam with Microsoft tools?

- Visit the following Microsoft site about how to go about protecting yourself—www.pi10m.com/b1/68

Visit the Australian website called SCAM watch—www.pi10m.com/b1/46

- SCAM watch is a website run by the Australian Competition and Consumer Commission (ACCC). SCAM watch provides information to consumers and small businesses about how to recognise, avoid, and report scams.
- It has information about banking, monetary, and online account scams; health and medical scams; investment scams; lottery and competition scams; employment scams; mobile phone scams; identity theft scams; online scams; Nigerian scams; small business scams.
- Gain better understanding of how scams work and importantly ways to protect yourself.

Visit the US government website called Consumer Fraud and Scams —www.pi10m.com/b1/47

- A site wanting to raise awareness against consumer fraud and scams
- It has information about banking and ATM fraud; credit card scams; education scams; Internet fraud; investment fraud; phone scams; nutrition scams; car scams; and many others.
- You can also report consumer frauds.
- Gain understanding of how to stop fraud.

IF I HAVE ENTERED MY PERSONAL OR FINANCIAL INFORMATION INTO A PHISHING WEBSITE?

If you think you have accidentally entered your details to a probable Phishing website, immediately go through the following steps.

- Change the passwords or PINs on all your online accounts.
- Place a fraud alert on your credit reports. Check with your bank or financial advisor if you're not sure how to do this.
- Contact the bank or the online merchant directly. Do not follow the link in the fraudulent email.
- If you know of any accounts that were accessed or opened fraudulently, close those accounts.
- Routinely review your bank and credit card statements monthly for unexplained charges or inquiries that you didn't initiate.

IF I DISCOVERED THAT I HAVE BEEN A VICTIM OF FRAUD?

Immediately doing the following might help:

- File a report with the local police.
- Place a fraud alert on your credit reports. Check with your bank or financial advisor if you're not sure how to do this.
- Change the passwords or PINs on all your online accounts.
- Contact the bank or the online merchant directly. Do not follow the link in the fraudulent email.
- If you know of any accounts that were accessed or opened fraudulently, close those accounts.
- Routinely review your bank and credit card statements monthly for unexplained charges or inquiries that you didn't initiate.
- Quarantine your computer from the Internet. Check for malware.

IF I WANT TO REPORT A CYBER INCIDENT?

- If you wish to report a cyber incident with a well recognised governing body, I would recommend using the Computer Emergency Response Team (CERT).

- CERT focuses on security breach and denial-of-service incidents, providing alerts and incident-handling and avoidance guidelines. CERT also conducts an ongoing public awareness campaign and engages in research aimed at improving security systems.

- Most countries have setup a CERT body. Here are the following links:

- Australia—www.pi10m.com/b1/78

- Asia Pacific—www.pi10m.com/b1/79

This website provides you with a list of Asian Pacific countries with their respective CERT body

- Europe—www.pi10m.com/b1/80

- This website provides you with a list of European countries with their respective CERT body.

- US—www.pi10m.com/b1/81

IF I WANT TO MANAGE ALL MY ONLINE PASSWORDS SECURELY?

If you are like many online users around the world, you probably have around a dozen passwords if not more which you need to remember for various different accounts, such as your online banks, Facebook, LinkedIn, Hotmail, Gmail, Twitter, Work, etc.

The challenge with any user is to ensure a unique and strong password for every online access is quite difficult.

Typically, users solve this problem by either of the following:

- By writing it down on a posted note and stick on their side of their screen.
- By having their machine (Windows) remember their user credentials login.
- By using the same user credential authentication for every account login.
- By using a recognised third party authentication provider to access other online accounts. For example, you might use your Google or Facebook credentials to log into your other online accounts.

All of the above present considerable security risk, especially the first three points. I would highly recommend that you do not use these methods!

So how do you manage all these passwords effectively, securely, and safely?

Use a third party software that specialises in password management. One that I would highly recommend is LastPass—www.pi10m.com/b1/3

- Generate a unique password for each online access.
- All of your passwords are encrypted.
- You can access your account from anywhere and anytime.
- All you need to remember is just one password.
- Predominantly it's free on all your computers.

Having said that, antivirus vendors are now including password management functionality as part of their offering.

IF I NEED TO SEND A LARGE AND SECURE DOCUMENT VIA EMAIL?

Questions:

1. Are you having a problem sending large documents via email?

2. Is your Internet service provider throttling the size of attachments that you can send?

3. Is there a sensitive document that you need to send to someone but afraid that someone else might access it?

The above three questions are typical scenarios that I see regularly.

The first two questions usually relate to the bandwidth limits that you have with your Internet service provider. Often when users try to send attachments that are larger than 10 MB, they fail.

Two possible solutions.

A. You can negotiate with your Internet service provider for the ability to send larger document attachments. OR

B. Utilise a third party Cloud software provider where typically you upload the attachment to the Cloud service provider. Then a communication is sent to the recipient where to find this Cloud document. There are many such organisations that can provide you with this service. Some of the more popular are ShareFile, WatchDox, Dropbox, YouSendit, Microsoft SkyDrive, and Send this file.

Some of these third party Cloud providers also provide password management functionality for mobile smart phones and tablets.

Regarding question 3, sending a sensitive document to a colleague via traditional email has definitely an element of security risk. Emails are not encrypted and anyone who has some way to intercept your email, will be able to read its contents. Solutions such as Share file, WatchDox, YouSendit and Send this file solve this problem very well by ensuring that any message that gets sent is encrypted all the way through.

IF I NEED TO DISPOSE OF MY COMPUTER SAFELY?

There comes a time when your computer is old, slow, or non-functioning. There may be a time that you need to invest in a new system and wish to discard your old system in a safe manner. You may also decide to donate or sell your computer that is no longer needed.

What is then the best process for discarding an old computer?

Before disposing of your machine, you should take the following steps to ensure that no confidential information is passed on with the computer.

1. Save all important documents onto a secure removable storage device. Then delete all sensitive data from that machine.
2. Extract any software license keys for reusable software using utilities such as Belarc Advisor—www.pi10m.com/b1/49
3. Erase data from your hard disk drive. Cleaning your hard disk with disk wiping or using data destruction program.

Note, when you format a hard drive you don't actually erase the hard drive of data, you only erase the location information for the data, making it "lost" to the operating system.

However, the data is still there, unless you truly erase the hard drive

Here is a list of some common utilities:

a. Eraser. Works for Microsoft Windows —www.pi10m.com/b1/50
b. C Cleaner by Piriform. Works either for Mac or Windows —www.pi10m.com/b1/51
c. Wipe Drive by WhiteCanyon. An excellent solution for deleting data on your machine—www.pi10m.com/b1/52

4. Remove any reusable cables or parts such as a network card. (A backup NIC is always handy)

5. Remove any batteries and recycle them properly.

For the security-conscious organisation

- Low level: Format your disk drive. This will minimise the possibility of someone finding sensitive data on your machine. This process may take some time, but the essential task is preparing the disk drive for new use. General rule, format is a "destructive" process in that any existing data and systems are lost during this operation.
- Consider destroying your hard disk drive either by smashing it with a hammer; drilling through the disk drive; crushing the disk drive. This should prevent anyone from trying to read it.

IF I RECEIVED A COMPUTER, BUT IS IT LEGITIMATE?

If you received a computer, notebook, laptop, tablet, or another computer device irrespective of where it came from, you should take some precautions before using it. These old devices may still harbor dormant malware! The following steps detail how to clean a machine in order to be used in a safe operation.

1. Cleaning the hard drive. This is the minimum recommended step.

    - Check the system for malware. Most antivirus vendors have the ability to scan your machine.
    - Use third party software to assess workstation files, registry and Internet browsers.
    - C Cleaner by Piriform. Works either for Mac or Windows —www.pi10m.com/b1/51
    - Wipe Drive by WhiteCanyon. An excellent solution for deleting data on your machine—www.pi10m.com/b1/52

2. Software Licensing. Please make sure that all relevant software that has come with the respective computer has also come with the appropriate software licensing.

For Microsoft software, check the following websites

- www.microsoft.com/b1/53 —You can validate your Windows operating system and Office productivity genuine software

- www.microsoft.com/b1/54 – How to identify counterfeit or other misuse of software

- www.microsoft.com/b1/55 – How to tell whether your Microsoft software media is genuine

For The Security-Conscious Organisation

I highly recommend you format the disk drive completely. Start from fresh.
This process may take some time, but the essential task is preparing the disk drive for new use. General rule, format is a "destructive" process in that any existing data and systems are lost during this operation.

The following tools can be used for wiping drives on a Windows computer:

- Wipe Drive by WhiteCanyon. An excellent tool for completely wiping out your entire system —www.pi10m.com/b1/52
- Kill Disk. A free solution for wiping out your old Windows machines—www.pi10m.com/b1/56

Once you have formatted your disk drive, install operating system and applications from trustworthy media.

If you have an Apple OS X device, you need an Apple USB SuperDrive or USB Software Reinstall Drive to complete this procedure. This procedure has four parts:

1. Erase the hard drive.
2. Reinstall the operating system.
3. Complete the Mac OS X Setup Assistant.
4. Install bundled applications.

RESOURCES

"Only those means of security are good, are certain, are lasting, that depend on yourself and your own vigour."

– NICCOLO MACHIAVELLI

COMMON MYTH ABOUT SECURITY AND WHAT THE TRUTH IS BEHIND THEM

*{**Myth:** Antivirus software and firewalls are 100% effective.}*

Truth: Antivirus software and firewalls are important elements for protecting your information. However, neither of these elements is guaranteed to protect you from an attack. Combining these technologies with good security habits is the best way to reduce your risk.
See Chapters 2 & 3 for Endpoint protection.

*{**Myth:** Attackers only target people with money.}*

Truth: Anyone can become a victim of identity theft. Attackers look for the biggest reward for the least amount of effort, so they typically target databases that store information about many people. If your information happens to be in the database, it could be collected and used for malicious purposes. It is important to pay attention to your credit information so that you can minimise any potential damage. **See Chapter 6—Internet Fraud Guideline.**

*{**Myth:** There is nothing important on my machine,
so I do not need to protect it.}*

Truth: Your opinion about what is important may differ from an attacker's opinion. If you have personal or financial data on your computer, attackers may be able to collect it and use it for their own financial gain. Even if you do not store that kind of information on your computer, an attacker who can gain control of your computer may be able to use it in attacks against other people. **See Chapters 2 & 3 for Endpoint protection.**

*{**Myth:** Once software is installed on your computer,
you do not have to worry about it anymore.}*

Truth: Vendors may release updated versions of software to address problems or fix vulnerabilities. You should ensure that your machine is continuously updated. Some software even offers the option to obtain updates automatically. Making sure that you have the latest virus definitions for your antivirus software is especially important. **See Chapters 2 & 3 for Endpoint protection.**

*{**Myth:** I have an Apple machine,so I'm totally safe from malware}*

Truth: Apple systems are vulnerable to malware. Over the past couple of years, there have been increasing reports of new malware affecting Apple machines, and this is only going to get worse. Take the steps in protecting your machine by implementing antivirus and ensuring that your firewall is turned on.

*{**Myth:** I can only get infected if I download files.}*

Truth: Much of malware infections now occur through a "drive-by" download. Hackers inject the malicious code into the actual web page content, then it downloads and executes automatically within the browser as a by-product of simply viewing the web page. Take steps to ensure that you visit credible websites and ensure that your machine has the latest updates including operating system, applications, and antivirus.
See Chapter 4 for Web Browser Protection Guidelines.

*{**Myth:** When the lock icon appears in the browser, it means my connection is secure.}*

Truth: The lock icon indicates there is an SSL encrypted connection between the browser and the server to protect the interception of personal sensitive information. It does not provide any security from malware. In fact, it's the opposite because most web security products are completely blind to encrypted connections: it's the perfect vehicle for malware to infiltrate a machine. Take steps to ensure that you visit credible websites and ensure that your machine has got the latest updates including operating system, applications, and antivirus. **See Chapter 5 for Internet Usage Guidelines.**

*{**Myth:** Google Chrome or Firefox are more secure than Microsoft Internet Explorer}*

Truth: All browsers are equally at risk because all browsers have some form of vulnerabilities, and more importantly, browsers also allow programs such as Java and JavaScript to execute. These programs have been well-targeted by malware authors to initiate an attack. Furthermore, all browsers allow plug-ins such as Adobe Flash and Java which pose a point of vulnerability.
See Chapter 4 for Web Browser Protection Guidelines.

MICROSOFT AND SECURITY

Microsoft offers a number of tools that support users in planning, deploying, and monitoring security of their Windows systems and associated Microsoft applications.

- Microsoft Safety & Security Centre website—www.pi10m.com/b1/57
- Microsoft Safety Scanner is a free downloadable security tool that provides on-demand scanning helping to remove viruses, spyware, and other malicious software—www.pi10m.com/b1/12
- Malicious Software Removal Tool checks systems running Windows systems for infections by specific prevalent malicious software and helps remove any infection found—www.pi10m.com/b1/39
- Microsoft Malware Protection Centre (MMPC) provides a list of the latest threats—www.pi10m.com/b1/58
- Microsoft Security Response Centre responds to Microsoft software security vulnerabilities—www.pi10m.com/b1/59
- Microsoft Windows update is a useful tool to ensure that your Windows system is up to date—www.pi10m.com/b1/60
- Microsoft Trustworthy Computing. Based on the following: security, reliability, privacy, business practices, and policymakers—www.pi10m.com/b1/61

For The More Security-Conscious Organisation

- Microsoft Enhanced Mitigation Experience Toolkit (EMET) is a security tool that provides mitigation protection against application vulnerabilities. Microsoft does not guarantee that vulnerabilities cannot be exploited. However, they work to make exploitation as difficult to perform as possible—www.pi10m.com/b1/62
- Microsoft Baseline Security Analyser (MBSA) has been in operation for a number of years now. It is a free and easy-to-use tool designed for use by IT professionals in determining their security state— www.pi10m.com/b1/63
- Security TechCentre. The Microsoft Security Bulletin site will allow you to subscribe to their notifications and advisories—www.pi10m.com/b1/64
- Microsoft Privacy. Providing advice and resources to help you protect yourself online—www.pi10m.com/b1/65
- Microsoft Cybersecurity provides an overview of frameworks, guides and vision—www.pi10m.com/b1/66
- Cyber Trust Blogs. Read about Microsoft Cyber approach to Cloud, Privacy, Tips and other topics—www.pi10m.com/b1/67

COMMON ACRONYMS

- **Adware**—Is the general term applied to programs that either launch advertisements (often pop-up banners) or re-direct search results to promotional websites.
- **APT**—Advancement Persistent Threat, short for "highly targeted attacks."
- **Blended Threat**—Use a combination of different malware techniques in an attack.
- **Botnet**—The term used for a network of computers controlled by cybercriminals using a trojan or other malicious program.
- **Brute Force Attacks**—This occurs when a hacker tries to gain unauthorised access to a system using a large number of possible keys or passwords.
- **Cookie** –This is usually a bit of data sent from a website and stored on a web browser. When the user browses the same website in the future, the data stored in the cookie can be retrieved by the website to notify the website of the user's previous activity.
- **DoS Attacks**—Denial of Service Attack. Designed to hinder or stop the normal functioning of a website, server, or other network resource.
- **DDos Attacks**—Distributed Denial of Service attacks occur when multiple systems flood the bandwidth or resources of a targeted system.
- **Drive by Download**—Computer becomes infected just by visiting a website containing malicious content.
- **Click jaking**—is a malicious technique of tricking a web user into clicking on something different to what the user perceives they are clicking.
- **Command and Control Centre(C&C)** –Is a system that controls and manages a botnet (a network of compromised computers often referred as Zombies).
- **Crimeware**—Is malicious software that is covertly installed on computers. Most crime ware programs are in fact trojans.
- **Cyber Theft**—Describes financial loss or identity fraud that could happen to you as a direct result of entering personal information while on the Internet usually for the purposes of banking, shopping, or gaming
- **Data Leakage**—Is the unauthorised movement of data outside of an organisation. It can be deliberate (data theft) or accidental (data loss).
- **Email Spoofing**—Is an email message that claims to be from someone else. For example, it could be an email from the administrator or authority requesting you to send them sensitive information.
- **Keylogger**—These are programs which record key presses (i.e. what a user types on the keyboard) and can be used by a hacker to obtain confidential data (login details, passwords, credit card numbers, PINs, etc.).
- **Malware**—Short for malicious software—is an umbrella term that refers to any software program deliberately created to perform an unauthorised and often harmful action.
- **Phishing**—Is a very specific type of cyber crime designed to trick you into disclosing personal and financial details by masquerading as a trustworthy entity.

- **Ransomware**—Is a software that denies you access to your files until you pay a ransom.
- **Root kit**—A collection of programs used by a hacker to evade detection while trying to gain unauthorised access to a computer.
- **Scareware**—A type of malware designed to trick users into purchasing or downloading useless or potentially dangerous software, usually phony antivirus software. It's called scareware because users are scared into thinking something is wrong with their machine to get them to download the software.
- **Social Engineering**—The act of manipulating a user into performing certain actions or divulging personal information, rather than simply using technical means to get what the cybercrook wants.
- **Spam**–Unsolicited form of communication (email, fax, voice) that comes into your inbox.
- **Spear Phishing**—Like Phishing, but this time it is targeted at a specific individual or a business.
- **Spyware**—Software that is designed to harvest your data and forward it to a third party without your consent or knowledge.
- **trojan**—Is a program that poses as legitimate software but when launched will do something harmful. trojans are typically installed secretly and deliver their malicious payload without your knowledge.
- **Virus**—Is a program that replicates, i.e. it spreads from file to file on your system and from PC to PC. In addition, it may be programmed to erase or damage data.
- **Whaling**—Is highly targeted phish attack directed at high profile individuals such as CEOs, celebrities, and other well recognised luminaries.
- **Worm**—Is a computer program that replicates, but does not infect other files.

COMMON SECURITY TECHNOLOGIES—EXPLANATION

Antivirus

A software program that defends machines against viruses and other malware threats including—trojans, worms, and spyware.

Antivirus scanners use scanners to identify programs that are or may be malicious. It tries to detect for the following:

Known viruses. The scanner compares files on a system against a library of known viruses. If it finds a match, it issues an alert and blocks access to the file. Detection of known viruses depends on frequent updates.

Unknown or suspicious viruses. The scanner analyzes the likely behavior of a program. If it has characteristics of a virus, it either blocks access to the program or warns that it may be a virus.

Anti Spam

A software program that detects unwanted emails and prevents it reaching the user's inbox. These programs use a combination of methods to decide whether an email is likely to be a spam. For example, they will check where the email comes from: Is it a legitimate domain? What phrases or words it might contain? Whether it contains any web addresses? Whether it contains any HTML code? And many other assessments.

The program using all these different assessments will then decide the probability that the email is likely to be a spam.

Application Control

Application Control builds on the foundation of white listing (see below) by providing an effective way to block unauthorised applications and code on servers, corporate desktops, and fixed-function devices.

Some of the Application Control solutions are built on the following key categories:

- Visibility of knowing what is running on each machine.
- Detection of unauthorised applications.
- Protection. Stopping unauthorised programs in executing their code.
- Management. Policy based control.
- Reputation assessment of software.
- Analysis. The ability to assess and understand what is happening in your environment right now.

Application White Listing

Application White listing defines what applications are allowed to be used within your environment. It aims to ensure that only specifically selected programs and software libraries can be executed, while all others are prevented from executing.

Application white listing comprises the following steps:

1. Identifying specific executable and software libraries which should be permitted to execute on a given system.
2. Preventing any other executable and software libraries from functioning on that system.
3. Preventing users from being able to change which files can be executed.

Data Loss Protection

Data Loss Protection (DLP) is also known as Data Loss/Leak Prevention. It is often used interchangeably. DLP in short is a strategy for making sure that end users do not send sensitive or critical information outside of the corporate network whether it is accidentally or on purpose.

The term is also used to describe a security solution that is designed to monitor, detect, and block potential sensitive data breach whether it is in-use, in-motion, or at-rest.
Data Loss occurs when data is accidentally lost. However, it may turn into data leakage if an unauthorised party acquires the sensitive information.
Data Leakage occurs when the data has been intentionally leaked out.

Device Control

Device control helps you control the use of removal storage such as such as USB drives, MP3 players, CDs, and DVDs.

It is a central element in the ability to prevent data leakage and also preventing malware infection, in the first place.

It enables you to specify and categorise which devices may or may not be used and enforce which data can and cannot be transferred to these devices whether it is in the office, at home, or on the move.

Endpoint Protection

Endpoint security is an approach to network protection that requires each computing device to be protected against a wide range of security, productivity, and compliance threats, and more importantly, that they are centrally managed.

Endpoint protection is typically a software-integrated solution bringing together individual products to protect against modern threats in one solution. They can include the following:

- Antivirus/anti-malware
- Firewall
- Device control
- Application control
- Encryption
- Central management

Firewall

A Firewall is a security tool (either a software or a hardware device) to permit or deny traffic, based upon a set of rules and is frequently used to protect networks from unauthorised access, while permitting legitimate communications to pass.

Here is a simple diagram that explains how the firewall works.

In short, a Firewall device is a piece of software which controls what traffic can travel from your computer to the Internet and from the Internet to your computer.

A Firewall is one of the key elements in protecting your computer system. Typically most antivirus software solutions have the ability to enable the firewall component on the computer. Windows, Mac OSX, Linux, and UNIX systems have also the ability to have a firewall enabled.

The challenge with having a software firewall is that it only protects your machine. Secondly and more importantly, the machine with the installed firewall then contends its resources to protect it from unwanted traffic.

Alternatively, you can use a hardware appliance firewall, which is a suggested approach (as can be seen from the above diagram). The physical firewall appliance has dedicated processing resources, to carefully check and handle greater amounts of network traffic as well as other characteristics, such as packets nature and actual origin (i.e. did it come from the Internet or from the local network?) and whether incoming traffic is a response to existing outgoing connections, such as a request for a web page.
Let us look at the difference between the two this way: Think of a bank. The security guard

and the scanners are like the hardware firewall. They will ascertain whether you look safe and whether or not you are carrying any weapons.

Once you are in, you need to exchange your credentials with the bank teller. That's the same way a software firewall works.

Question: Can you use your NAT (Network Address Translation) router device as your "firewall?"
Answer: One of the key benefits of NAT routers (and the main reason for their purchase by residential and small office users) is that the router appears to the Internet as a single machine with a single IP address. This effectively hides the fact that many computers on the inside of the router may be simultaneously sharing that single IP.

However NAT devices are not designed to provide the necessary security features and benefits from protecting you against unwanted traffic. As such, firewalls are designed to block network traffic and applications based on designated corporate security policies.

Caution

- Never connect your computer directly to the Internet. Always connect behind a firewall (software or hardware) before connecting to the Internet.
- Should you choose a firewall appliance, ensure that you change its default password.

Unified Threat Management (UTM)

UTM is the evolution of the traditional firewall into an all-inclusive security product able to perform multiple security functions within one single appliance: network firewalling, network intrusion prevention, and gateway antivirus, gateway anti-spam, VPN, content filtering, load balancing, data leak prevention, caching, application control, and on-appliance reporting.

These days UTM tends to be specific proprietary hardware appliances that have sufficient horsepower and resources to successfully run many of these security features in one system. UTMs have also been very popular because organisations have been able to consolidate their security solutions into a single system, thereby simplifying management and reducing costs.

The Next Generation Firewall

There has been a new evolution and advancement to the security firewall environment in the past few years.

The Next Generation Firewall is the security solution to the ever-evolving more sophisticated level of threats. It's the evolution of a firewall to deal with changes in both the way business processes use IT and the ways attacks try to compromise business systems.
As such, the Next Generation Firewall has the ability to gain visibility and control of network traffic based on applications, users, and content.

With Next Generation Firewall, you can block a wide range of unwanted applications and then inspecting the allowed applications for threats—both known and unknown, thereby enabling businesses to reap the benefits of being online while mitigating the associated security risks.

Intrusion Detection System / Intrusion Protection System

Intrusion detection system (IDS) is a type of security management system for computers and networks. An IDS system gathers and analyzes information from various areas within a computer or a network to identify possible security breaches, which include both intrusions (attacks from outside the organisation) and misuse (attacks from within the organisation).

Intrusion prevention system (IPS) is a pre-emptive approach to network security used to identify potential threats and respond to them swiftly. Like intrusion detection system (IDS), an intrusion prevention system monitors network traffic. However, because an exploit may be carried out very quickly after the attacker gains access, intrusion prevention systems also have the ability to take immediate action, based on a set of rules established by the network administrator. For example, an IPS might drop a packet that it determines to be malicious and block all further traffic from that IP address.

Mobile Device Management

Mobile Device management (MDM) is a software that monitors, manages and supports mobile devices deployed across mobile operators and the enterprise. Typical MDM functionality allows the organisation to distribute applications, data, configurations settings as well as security policies.

Consumer and employee demand for "Bring Your Own Device" (BYOD) has created strong need for MDM technologies to allow for greater risk management and visibility of such devices.

Network Access Control

Network access control (NAC), also called network admission control, is a method of bolstering the security of your network by restricting the availability of network resources to endpoint devices that may not comply with a defined security policy.

There are three main aspects of a NAC:

1. Authentication—To check whether they are who they say they are.
2. Assessment—To make sure that they are virus free and they meet a set of security criteria.
3. Enforcement—Each user can access information appropriate to his or her role.

Secure Email Gateway

Secure email gateway solution provides email transfer capabilities, offering protection against inbound and outbound threats (such as spam, phishing attacks, and malware) and satisfy outbound corporate and regulatory policy requirements.

These solutions can be offered in the form of software or appliances that go on customer premises, hosted solutions that reside in solution providers' data centers, or in the Cloud.

Secure Web Gateway

Secure web gateway solutions protects web surfing PCs from infection and enforces company policies.

A secure Web gateway is a solution that filters unwanted software/malware from user initiated Internet traffic and enforces corporate and regulatory policy compliance.

These gateways tend to include URL filtering, malicious code detection, filtering, and application controls for popular web based applications.

Two Factor Authentication

When accessing information is particularly sensitive, using a "user name" and a "password" alone does not guarantee sufficient protection.

Two Factor Authentication is a stronger process of ensuring that the user is who they claim to be. Two Factor Authentication is a security process in which the user provides two means of identification.

- Something you know—password or pin.
- Something you have—token or smart card.
- Something you are—biometrics such as fingerprint, iris.

If you combine any of the two, it is called Two Factor Authentication. If you combine all three, it becomes Three-Factor Authentication.

Web Application Firewall

A Web Application Firewall (WAF) protects applications from threats. As such, a web application firewall must understand application structure, elements and expected user behavior in order to accurately detect attacks.

A web application firewall is not a Network Firewall as described in the above pages. A WAF is an operational security control which monitors HTTP traffic in order to protect web applications from attacks which a Network Firewall is not able to perform.

The key elements are:

Operational control—a WAF protects applications in real time, rather than hardening them or fixing them in advance.

HTTP traffic—a WAF analyzes the traffic between the untrusted client and the web server.

Protect web applications—WAFs protect web applications. Mostly custom written and very dynamic.

SPONSORS

Most people want security in this world, not liberty.

– NICCOLO MACHIAVELLI

Imperva

Imperva is a pioneer and leader in providing security solutions that protect critical applications and sensitive data from theft, insider abuse, and fraud, while at the same time streamlining regulatory compliance. Imperva provides a comprehensive solution for monitoring and controlling all data usage and business transaction across the data centre, from storage in a database, or on a file server to consumption through applications.

What Problems does Imperva solve?

A new category of business security solution has arisen to help organisations address data theft, insider abuse, fraud and streamline regulatory compliance. Attacks, whether perpetrated by sophisticated hackers or malicious insiders, targeting high-value data and business applications has increased in sophistication, scale, and frequency. Imperva solves by providing a comprehensive business security suite designed to secure business data and application by monitoring and controlling data usage and business transactions across these systems.

What is unique about Imperva?

According to the Gartner, Inc. report "Hype Cycle for Application Security" in July 2012: "Applications and data are the main target for modern attacks. Adoption of dedicated application and data security concepts, technologies, and methodologies is a must for all enterprises."

The solution to today's security threats is a new protection layer positioned closely around business data and application systems in the data centre. Imperva Application Security and Database Security solutions address the key requirements in the data centre.

- Application Security Solution—To protect your Web applications, Imperva provides a dedicated application security solution that can protect against Web attacks, including attacks that exploit custom application vulnerabilities. From its Web application firewall to advanced reputation and fraud prevention services, to easy, flexible cloud-based security services, Imperva provides a comprehensive set of application security solutions that protect against dangerous application threats.
- Database Security Solutions—Imperva offers a comprehensive data audit and protection suite that protects against data theft, audits sensitive data, and privileged users, strengthens data privacy, and manages user access rights. The Imperva suite provides automated monitoring and controls for database and file usage, and integrates with a range of related data security products to protect high value data and streamline regulatory compliance.

Contacting Imperva

Inquiries can be made to any of their global offices or through their website (www.imperva.com).

Know Ur Risk

The Online Parenting Safety Survival Guide

It's very hard to ignore the fact that our children and families are part of the fastest growing community in the world, the Internet—with well over 1.5 billion people online.
Our children seemingly join and participate in this online community from the youngest of ages, whilst on a daily basis we hear of the dangers and concerns.

So how do you perform your role as a parent in this online community to keep your children safe?

The *Online Parenting Safety Survival Guide* written by **Scott Deacon** is aimed at helping parents navigate the online world and providing children with the best chance of staying safe and growing up as a respectable member of the online community.

The book is an invaluable tool and reference for parents being parents in the online world, and the author Scott Deacon provides a truly valuable insight into the most effective methods you can use to keep you and your children safe online.

For more information visit www.knowurrisk.org

I'm currently taking requests for presentations to Australian and New Zealand community and school groups. Please contact me at scott@knowurrisk.org if you would like to discuss the possibility of a presentation.

MYOB

A guide to online accounting (aka accounting in the cloud) Knowledge is power when it comes to making important business decisions. Accounting software provides reporting and insights that can help you manage your finances, uncover trends and comply with taxation and other business legislation.

Businesses are increasingly shifting to online accounting. The time, cost and productivity gains are among the big benefits. Increased business productivity means you have more time and resource to concentrate on growth building activities and staying competitive.
MYOB's tips to choosing a cloud accounting solution:

1. **Research trustworthy providers**
Look for cloud accounting providers that offer credibility, technology expertise and reputation. Going with an established, profitable and trusted provider is a good idea—you don't want them going out of business and your financial data going out the door with them!

2. Review different cloud models
Cloud accounting solutions can take many forms; some require time to get to know your way around. Research the training involved with getting set up and make sure you have time to allocate. Often the more feature-rich solutions take a bit of training, which should be offered by the provider or perhaps an accredited local consultant.

3. Secure your bank transaction feeds
A reputable provider will empower you to securely and directly link your business bank transactions to your online accounting solution (e.g. MYOB cloud accounting solutions use BankLink). This saves you plenty of time in manually entering all your business bank transactions. Avoid companies who use a risky practice called 'screen scraping'. Here, you provide your banking login and password to the provider, who passes them to a third party to 'screen scrape' your transactions. They then feed that data back through your accounting solution. It leaves business owners at risk of breaching bank T&Cs (different banks have different policies), plus it increases the risk of data errors and potential fraud.

4. Read the fine print

Importantly, read the cloud provider's T&Cs closely. Map out a transition plan to make the move to cloud as seamless as possible. You want little to no disruption to your business. Always check service level agreements and hidden costs, add-ons and other features that will take up extra time and money while you set up your full solution. For more information, please visit http://myob.com

ObserveIT

ObserveIT is recognised as the world-wide leader in User Session Activity Recording Software. The company has nearly 1000 enterprise customers worldwide, including 1 in 5 Fortune Global 500 companies, and more than 100 channel partners covering five continents.

ObserveIT's session recording and analysis system captures video of all on-screen activity while users work on Windows and Unix/Linux servers and desktops, along with searchable user activity logs. ObserveIT records and analyzes all user behaviour in every application, Web page and system area, over any connection protocol (RDP, SSH, Telnet, ICA, Citrix, direct console login, etc.).

What problems does ObserveIT solve?

- IT security by monitoring and auditing privileged users, third-party vendors and regular employees
- Compliance and security accountability
- Monitoring of access to cloud-hosted servers, applications and data
- IT forensics and root cause analysis
- IT configuration change documentation
- Help desk efficiency

What is unique about ObserveIT?

- Beyond recording on-screen activity to video, the software transcribes every session into an easy-to-read summary so that watching the video isn't necessary to know what the user did. Clicking on any particular event in the summary launches the video playback from that exact moment.
- Detailed session data is immediately available for free-text keyword searching. Resulting search hits are linked directly to the specific portion of the video where that action occurred.
- Realtime alert triggers based on complex combinations of user action, environment and context, provide early warning of both human error and malicious actions.

Contacting ObserveIT

- www.observeit.com

WatchGuard

Who is WatchGuard?

Since 1996, WatchGuard® Technologies, Inc. has been a global leader of business security solutions. The WatchGuard family of Smart Firewalls provides smart and affordable security by combining many security functions in a single device including web content security, data loss prevention, and email encryption to an already strong product range. WatchGuard is headquartered in Seattle, Washington with offices throughout North America, Europe, Asia Pacific, and Latin America. To learn more, visit www.watchguard.com.

What problems does WatchGuard solve?

For many people, even industry experts, security has become all too difficult and problematic. Is it too hard or just too hard to MANAGE? Verizon's Risk Team studied over 1700 network breaches, and 96% of breaches were avoidable through simple or intermediate controls. In 2011 Gartner research showed that more than 95% of firewall breaches are caused by firewall misconfigurations, not firewall flaws. WatchGuard removes this risk by combining AntiVirus, Web Browsing Filtering, Anti-Spam, Intrusion Prevention and Application control into a single, simple to manage appliance. We call this concept Unified Threat Management (UTM). In almost every instance, combining security platforms will give your network better coverage and make significant cost savings. In addition, WatchGuard provides multi-layer security protection at network speeds and has the strongest UTM performance in the market.
http://www.watchguard.com/performance/what-smart-performance-means.asp.
WatchGuard Unified Threat Management (UTM) expands upon Next Generation firewall (NGFW) security with capabilities including: Web Blocking; Application Control; Reputation Enabled Defence; Spam Blocking; Gateway Antivirus; Intrusion Prevention. WatchGuard also incorporates powerful data loss prevention (DLP) capabilities to ensure that content leaving your network is in strict accord with your organisation's confidentiality and regulatory compliance policies.

What makes WatchGuard unique?

WatchGuard pioneered the UTM industry. Rather than try to invent a new offer in every space, WatchGuard picks the BEST possible solution in each category and partners with those products. This allows us to be the best in ALL categories with no compromise. We call this best in class. It means our customers get the best of both worlds and we focus on what we are really, really good at, which is making rock solid, incredibly fast, UTM firewalls and content filters.

Contact WatchGuard

- Office: +61 2 8413 3905 (Australia)
- E: Inquiry.ANZ@watchguard.com - W: www.watchgaurd.com

CommsNet Group

CommsNet Group is an Australian-owned company, helping organisations protect their key most valuable information assets, every day. That is their "crown digital jewels".

We do this by focusing on three key principles:

1. We help organisations strive for system resiliency
2. We help organisations gain visibility and understanding of how their systems are performing
3. We help organisations implement security best practices.

We have been in the forefront helping businesses worldwide raising security awareness. This consists of:

- White papers
- Videos
- Books
- Articles

To find out more, visit our website—www.commsnet.com.au/resources

For further highly informative and practical step-by-step guide in gaining Security Peace of Mind, invest in my first book *The Essential Guide to Information Technology Security Best Practice.*

In this guide, you will learn the following:

- The 7 key facts about security
- The 5 minutes questionnaire that will reveal all your business security weakness and what you can do about it.
- Simple step-by-step processes to help you solve identified security concerns
- How to manage risk for each security concern
- A quick self security assessment that you can do in 5 minutes that will reveal your organisation's security health status
- How to embed security culture within your organisation
- How to build an investment case for adopting new security programs
- This book can be found at www.commsnet.com.au/resources/books

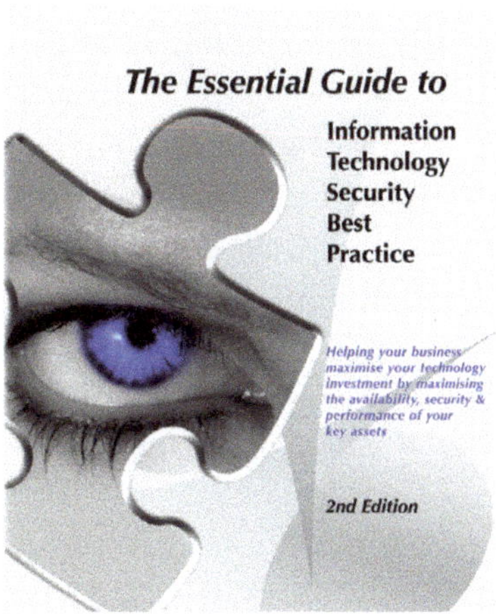

Up Coming Books

Protecting Your e-Health From Cyber Attacks In Only 10 Minutes A Day

The book is designed to help health institutions and organisations develop resilient practices with only 10 minutes a day. With the likely move of most medical practices to some form of "digital health" or "e-health" systems, the resilience of a medical institution to be able to cope against cyber security incidents, data theft, or inadvertent data loss, safeguarding confidential and privacy of medical records, and maintaining the integrity of data is critically important. *Protecting Your e-Health In Only 10 Minutes A Day* helps organisations develop best security practices based by following a very simple 10 minutes process.

Protecting Your Social Reputation From Cyber Attacks In Only 10 Minutes A Day

This book is designed for anyone who needs to develop social web security best practices either for themselves or for their organisation in only 10 minutes a day. Protecting your social reputation is subdivided into seven key security practices. This book helps users gain security awareness, confidence, and understanding in dealing with day-to-day business operation safely, easily, and practically on the social web.

Other CommsNet Group Services

Cloud and Web Protection Services **O2SEC**—www.02sec.com

O2SEC is specifically designed to help and secure organisations websites and associated application from threats and attacks. All services are provided "as a service". Services such as

- Web Application Firewall
- Denial of Service (DoS) Protection
- Web Failover
- Website Security Assessment
- Secure File Transfer
- Secure Data Backup
- Web Fraud Protection

Cloud Performance Monitoring **MyndIT**—www.myndit.com.au

MyndIT is specifically designed to help organisations optimise their web and mobile applications. All services are provided "as a service". Services such as:

- Web Performance Monitoring
- Mobile Performance Monitoring
- Web Load Testing
- End User Experience Monitoring
- Real User Monitoring for Mobile and Web Applications
- Infrastructure Performance Monitoring

www.ingramcontent.com/pod-product-compliance
Lightning Source LLC
LaVergne TN
LVHW070907210926
848482LV00017B/1017
* 9 7 8 0 9 9 2 5 8 0 9 0 2 *